MW01707927

Who he?

To Vicky Lok
with best wishes.
If you're interested in
writing I hope it gives
you as much pleasure
as it has given me.
Robert Collins
(by way of Stuart Slayen)

OTHER BOOKS BY ROBERT COLLINS

Legend of the Devil's Lode
Rory's Wildcat (in paperback as *The Mystery at the Wildcat Well*)
East to Cathay
A Great Way to Go
The Medes and the Persians
The Age of Innocence: 1870–1880
A Voice from Afar
Butter Down the Well
One Thing for Tomorrow (with Joyce Brack)
The Holy War of Sally Ann
The Long and The Short and The Tall
The Kitchen Table Money Plan (with Barbara McNeill)

Who he?

reflections on a writing life

•

ROBERT COLLINS

GREYSTONE BOOKS
Douglas & McIntyre
Vancouver/Toronto

93 94 95 96 97 5 4 3 2 1

Greystone Books
A division of Douglas & McIntyre Ltd.
1615 Venables Street
Vancouver, British Columbia V5L 2H1

Canadian Cataloguing in Publication Data

Collins, Robert, 1924-
Who he?

ISBN 1-55054-132-3

1. Collins, Robert, 1924- 2. Journalists—Canada—Biography. 3. Authors, Canadian (English)—Biography.* I. Title
PN4913.C64A3 1993 070.92 C93-091625-5

Editing by Jane McHughen
Cover and text design by Tom Brown
Cover photo by Randall Cosco
Typeset by Vancouver Desktop Publishing Centre
Printed and bound in Canada by Best Gagné Book Manufacturers Inc.
Printed on acid-free paper ∞

For the late George Ronald
who was everything an editor should be

CONTENTS

ACKNOWLEDGEMENTS

This memoir was assembled from my pack-rat files (which have been the despair of all the tidy people in my life) and from an avalanche of scribbled notes on used envelopes, backs of old manuscripts, the pull-out cards from magazines and the cardboard stiffeners that cleaners used to put in laundered shirts.

Thanks to these strangers and friends who helped verify facts or reinforce recollections: Tom Alderman, Gerald Anglin, Archie Barr, Ian Bickle, Silver Donald Cameron, Chick Childerhose, Nancy Colbert, Ron Cole, Roy Cottier, Jean Danard, Sir William Deakin, Moira Farr, Pat and Stan Fillmore, Tomasina Fountain, Douglas Gibson, Glen Hancock, Douglas How, Michael Jacot, Brian Lam, James B. Lamb, Max Macdonald, David MacDonald, Anne Marshall, Heather McCallum, Pauline McGibbon, David Moller, Barbara Moon, Steve Osborne, Bruce A. Powe, Robert J. Riddell, Richard Rohmer, Jane Rule, Gordon Sanderson, Linda Scott, Carol Sprachman, Christine Strauss, Edythe Stockton, Patricia Tennant and Janice Tyrwhitt.

An earlier version of "First Break" appeared in Imperial Oil *Review,* #2, 1985. My sequence on Indian treaty payments is adapted from "When the Dogribs Get Their Treaty Money," *Maclean's* magazine, November 26, 1955. The segment "Dreaming of a Better Me" is excerpted from *FP* magazine, December 1972. "Broadloom" originally appeared in a 1960's edition of *Gambit.* Remembrances of Sophie Simkin are adapted from my article "Sophie" in *Toronto Life,* December 1971. Notes on the

Hercules cargo drop over the Northwest Territories are from "Kosmos 954: The Spy That Fell from the Sky," *Reader's Digest,* August 1978.

Some background for the chapter on Sir William Stephenson came from *The Quiet Canadian,* H. Montgomery Hyde, Constable and Company, London, 1962; *"C" The Secret Life of Sir Stewart Graham Menzies,* Anthony Cave Brown, Macmillan, New York, 1987; *A Man Called Intrepid,* William Stevenson, Harcourt Brace Jovanovich, New York, 1976; *Camp X,* David Stafford, Lester & Orpen Dennys, Toronto, 1986; and *Wild Bill Donovan: The Last Hero,* Anthony Cave Brown, Fitzhenry & Whiteside, Toronto, 1982. I'm also grateful for the assistance of Lt. Col. Anthony Mather, Secretary, Central Chancery of the Orders of Knighthood; the Secretary, The Imperial Society of Knights Bachelor; and the Principal Private Secretary to the Prime Minister–all in London, England.

I'm indebted to Lesley Collins for her many hours of library research and computer-inputting, and to Catherine Collins, my first reader, for her invaluable editorial comments and suggestions. In these and a thousand other ways, my daughters helped make all this possible.

Last but far from least, thanks to my editor, Jane McHughen, whose perceptive questions and gentle editorial nudges frequently saved me from myself.

INTRODUCTION

It was one of those stereotypical parties where strangers, hugging tumblers of gin or white wine, accost other strangers with the obligatory challenge: "And what do you do?"

I was the token writer, a species that baffles the average civilian. Unaware that most writers are egocentric bores, they circle us warily, hopefully, looking for signs of the exotic. They fumble for openings with, "That must be really interesting," or "So what are you working on now?" They ask, "Where would I see your write-ups?" or "What have you done lately?" and you mumble, "Nothing you'd have heard of," to ease the mutual embarrassment when that turns out to be true.

But this night one woman fixed herself forever in my memory, not for tact or adulation but for getting straight to the point.

"So you're a writer," she said briskly. "Should I know you?"

Well, no.

I am neither famous nor infamous. I have never won a Governor General's Medal nor (proud to say) received a Canada Council grant. Nor have I ever received the key to a city, although I have a splendid collection of lapel pins, including one of the water tower at Weyburn, Saskatchewan, which was and perhaps still is a leading water tower of its kind.

I have never called Margaret Atwood "Peggy." My life was not changed for the better by Barbara Frum. Nobody has invited me to a Great Literary Dinner Party. I have never been attacked by the Bloc Quebeçois. I have shaken hands with Queen Elizabeth II but never with Madonna. I once met Gainer the Gopher, official mascot of the Saskatchewan Roughriders football team (actually, half of him: the full-Gainer was two people in a gopher suit), but never Arnold Schwarzenegger.

I have written thirteen books (mostly nonfiction) and hundreds of articles for some thirty-two periodicals, including *Maclean's, Reader's Digest,* Imperial Oil *Review, Toronto Life* and the now-defunct Toronto *Star Weekly*. But although four of my books have exceeded sales of eleven thousand, I have never been on a best-sellers' list. Occasionally school children say they are "doing a project" on me, but the highest mark ever attained by these chroniclers of my career was fifteen out of twenty.

Yet do not think that mine has been a wasted life. I have lurked at the fringe of great events. One such was the night I met Joe Clark, then Leader of the Progressive Conservative Party, preparing for his fleeting moment as prime minister. He was inspecting the Tory faithful in Toronto Rosedale. Two Tories had dragged me there for indoctrination (having vacillated between Liberals and Conservatives most of my voting life, I was just recovering from a nasty case of Trudeaumania).

Clark began working the room, grave and dignified, grasping hands, greeting supporters in his deep mellifluous voice.

Suddenly an elderly Tory in a wheelchair beside me lost control of his bladder. A pool formed under his chair. Others noticed but none of us knew what to do. Wheel him away? Certainly not. The fellow was here to shake the Leader's hand and should not be denied the pleasure. We watched and waited with fascination as the official party drew closer and the pool crept outward. Would it lap against the Leader's polished shoes?

No. Clark, moving faster than urine, pressed the man's hand, then mine, and marched onward safe and dry.

But the solemnity of the moment was lost. In retrospect it seemed to me a metaphor for life: Joe Clark–that basically decent politician with his seemingly infinite capacity for humiliation, soon to be bushwhacked by Mulroney, rejected by the electorate and badgered almost to his political death by the media–was being pissed on yet again.

For most of us writers, as for Mr. Clark, rejection is commonplace and fame is elusive. Of the 2,200 members of The Writers' Union of Canada, the Canadian Authors' Association, the Canadian Science Writers' Association and the Periodical Writers Association of Canada, only a dozen or so can claim true celebrity, in the sense that their faces or names are familiar to most of their countrymen. Several of those have achieved their notoriety on television.

Despite this near-guarantee of obscurity, the urge to put words to paper infects thousands of hopefuls. Once in the early 1980s I drove into a United States Customs kiosk at Ogdensburg, New York. It was a slow weekday and two young officers awaited me.

"Purpose of your visit?"

"Business."

Their eyes narrowed. I wore a sports shirt. Had they nabbed a Canadian wetback, sneaking in to work without a green card? I explained I was going to the Adirondacks to talk to ecologists and examine lakes ravaged by acid rain. I produced a business card identifying me as a "roving editor" of *Reader's Digest*.

Their eyes rounded into something close to respect. For one thing, the *Digest* is Mom-and-apple-pie in America. They plied me with questions. Was this what I actually did for a living: drove around, looked at things, wrote about them? As I pulled away one exclaimed to the other, "I've always wanted a job like that!"

Of course. Nearly everyone does, and thinks it attainable. An article on creativity in the magazine *Utne Reader* remarked: "At an early age, we come to believe that artistic talent is a finite substance randomly doled out at birth to a blessed few." Maybe we believe that of sculpting, glass blowing or basket-weaving, but not of writing.

"I know I could write if only I had the time," say the wannabe writers. Any who once get into print feel qualified to label themselves "freelance writer" ever after. They have written; ergo they could write again, time permitting. Every day we read newspaper columns or essays by a "freelance writer" who is actually a lawyer, teacher, doctor or business person. My favourite is one who identified himself as "freelance writer and part-time priest." Very few actual writers are freelance doctors, lawyers or priests.

The members of the aforementioned writers' organizations (not all of whom are professional, by a long shot) are only the tip of Canada's literary iceberg. There are leagues of poets, leagues of playwrights, provincial writers' guilds. Journalism schools, extension courses and CanLit classes across the land are crammed with people who have always wanted to write and are certain that finding the necessary few minutes is all that stands in the way of success.

The hobbyists soon discover that writing for a living requires more discipline, hard work and talent than they will ever muster. (Even with those qualities, fiction writers in particular may search in vain for a market.) They continue to dabble, go to conferences and read their work aloud to one another. More power to them, if it provides a modicum of fulfilment. A while ago the Toronto *Globe and Mail* ran a classified ad that would make strong men or women weep:

> FRUSTRATED UNPUBLISHED WRITER AND FULL TIME TRAVEL AGENT ORGANIZING A SUMMER GROUP PILGRIMAGE TO FRENCH RIVIERA FOR CAFE STYLE IDEA BASHING, SHARED EXPERIENCE AND INTER-GROUP WRITING CRITIQUES.

I empathize with his frustration and salute his ingenuity. Someday, maybe, his stint as travel agent will shine out from the biography on his book jacket.

But what of the published writers? Why their fascination with the writing life? Why condemn oneself to a median income of fourteen thousand a year, which in many parts of the land is below the official poverty level? Hobby writers earn even less but professionals rarely earn proportionately more. Most are scandalously underpaid. My own accumulated income over the past twenty years of steady and productive labour, at top rates, was a little less than half of what Mark Messier recently earned for a single year of scowling, scoring and bashing bodies for the New York Rangers.

Why stake your reputation on a profession in which your every error or boneheaded lapse is on public display? At best you are an easy target for the habitual letter-page correspondents whose raison d'être is catching writers in blunders. At worst you are liable to be bankrupted by some litigious corporate prince. There isn't a writer among us who hasn't suffered from postpartum paranoia: *Did I do right by my sources? Is anybody gonna sue?*

Why slave in solitude for weeks or months on end, honing phrases, rewriting drafts, only to receive a form-letter rejection, or have a junior editor with a tin ear for dialogue whittle it to bits, or have some failed academic trash you in a review laced with malicious wit?

Writing has preyed upon my two failed marriages. It has given me the compulsive habit of "interviewing" everyone, causing skittish friends to fear they will appear in my next write-up. It has given me a permanent hunch, bloodshot eyes and a chin that flows directly into my neckline from a lifetime of crouching over manuscripts, keyboards and interviews across a thousand coffee tables.

No matter the hundreds of times I have written, each time is new. There is a little fillip of apprehension: I must prove myself all over again. Until the mass of research takes shape—that euphoric moment when it turns into something coherent, maybe even enlightening or witty or poignant—I trudge on like a foot soldier in mud, one step after another, knowing the end must be in sight but half-doubting I'll ever see it.

Yet I cannot recall a single moment—even in times of outrage, discouragement or despair—when I wanted to do or be anything else. Writing is my calling and my solace. A few days without it and I am restless for the comfort of paper and pen or keyboard.

My passion is not easily explained, although this book will try. I feel about writing the way some people feel about getting to Heaven: the alternatives are simply unacceptable.

The title of this memoir is in part a reminder, for others of my kind, of those bad old days when editors habitually trampled on our human rights. A time when such editors would have laughed hysterically at the thought of showing to a writer, before publication, the mayhem they had wreaked on our manuscripts. A bleak and painful time when editors filled our snow-white margins with jeering comments scrawled with Eagle Alphabet No. 1 pencils: "Not really!?" "Who says?" and, above all, "Who He?"

It happened always when the writer, temporarily brain-dead, failed to fully identify a subject: referring vaguely to, let us say, a "Mr. Wells" instead of "J. Quincy Wells," or mentioning "J. Q. Wells" without explaining that the wretched Wells was chairman and C.E.O. of Infinite Plastics Inc., Akron, Ohio, father of five and a sidesman in the Episcopal church.

Instantly, the crouching editors pounced.

"WHO HE?" they shouted blackly in the margins, leaving dents four pages deep. It was meant to heckle and humble the writer and it worked. It was immensely satisfying for the editors. I know. I have etched it into margins myself.

My title may also give comfort to certain reviewers (and if this be true, my life's work is complete). I hear them now:

> A light, sometimes pleasant, little read but the author has ventured onto a metaphorical limb. Did he not realize how deliciously apropos is his title? Who He, indeed! Collins, no literary heavy-hitter, is at best a utility outfielder . . .

Most importantly, *Who He?* is addressed to myself. This book–last of a personal odyssey after *Butter Down the Well* and *The Long and The Short and The Tall*–is an effort to make sense out of a writing life; to reflect on what I have learned in forty-three years of journalism; to examine what I have taken for granted all these years: why I, or anyone, would want to be a writer. I hope it contributes a little to Canada's journalistic lore, while saluting some memorable persons, publications and times in what for me continues to be the most fascinating job on earth.

1

FIRST BREAK

One summer day in 1983, while on a cross-country trek researching a book about the Salvation Army, I sat down with a roomful of thoughtful and articulate Gitksan Indian people in Hazelton, British Columbia. Many of the area's Gitksan (pronounced KUH-SAN) are devout Salvationists, and I wanted to know how their traditional ways and views about life, death and doing right by your neighbour meshed with the Army religion.

To break the ice (and establish that I was not your average dumb cluck from Toronto), I mentioned that I'd grown up in rural Saskatchewan. The handsome, sophisticated wife of a Gitksan elder looked at me so fixedly that I began to twitch. Finally she asked if I'd ever written in *Reader's Digest* about the Royal Visit to Canada of 1939. She meant "The Night the King Came to Moose Jaw," my reminiscence of a time when royal tours really meant something.

The piece had originally appeared in an early seventies *Digest,* then as a chapter in my book *Butter Down the Well,* then again in the *Digest* by reader request. Even so, I was mildly amazed that it and I were known in this remote northeastern town.

A year or two later another total stranger, a Sault Ste. Marie doctor, wrote to me: "You are the only Canadian author who expresses the true memories of the life we lived in western Canada during the pioneer and Depression years. . . . Congratulations for your contributions to Canadian literature and for your unique and compassionate insights and skillful expression."

Even after forty-three years, incidents like these continue to be as surprising as they are gratifying. How on earth did a one-time prairie farm boy who has generally kept a low profile (by nature, but also on the premise that journalists *should*) come to be "known" even on this modest scale? Who he, and how did he get there?

The itch to write had been in me as long as I could remember, the product of genetics and gentle example. So many sins are laid at the feet of parents these days by muggers, rapists, addicts, dropouts and Young Offenders that I feel rather left out. I cannot blame my mother or father for anything. True, they made me well behaved and obedient: "Little boys should be seen and not heard," my father said–the worst possible training for journalism, where good manners and obeying rules are definitely not requisite.

But I do not fault my parents for that. They gave me words, for which I am eternally grateful. Words ebbed and flowed all around my brother and me throughout our growing up. Our mother, a former teacher and frustrated writer (in her seventies she self-published a book about a brother who'd been a missionary in South America), taught us to read before we were five. She composed stories for us. She assembled homemade books of Thornton W. Burgess animal tales, clipped from the Regina *Leader-Post* and pasted on multi-coloured pages made of scraps from her ragbag.

Our father was a farmer by chance: "Get out in the fresh air," a doctor told him after he was gassed in World War I. A literate man, he chose a book or newspaper over a pitchfork any day if he had the option. He loved to keep accounts, write minutes of community meetings and compose letters in a bold script full of flourishes and curlicues. (Once he wrote a witty letter to the municipal secretary on the unlikeliest of subjects: why he was going to be late paying his taxes that year.)

Somehow, the two of them raised us well on the farm's meagre output plus fifteen dollars a month from his World War I disability pension. They also scratched together a small eclectic library, mostly secondhand. A great ugly black-bound set of Alexandre Dumas. The poems of Service and Tennyson. *The*

Moonstone and *The Woman in White* by Wilkie Collins. Louisa May Alcott's *Little Women* and Margaret Sidney's *Five Little Peppers and How They Grew.*

I read them all (not admitting *Little Women* or *Five Little Peppers* to the toughs at school), plus the *Boys Own Annual, Chatterbox, Uncle Wiggily, Billy Whiskers* (a goat), *King of the Royal Mounted, Slim Evans and His Horse Lightning* and a couple of Horatio Alger potboilers. I especially liked Alger's *The Adventures of a Boy Reporter,* in which a poor but honest lad achieves instant and glittering fame in journalism.

My parents did not deem *The Three Musketeers* or *The Count of Monte Cristo* too old for small boys but thought Hemingway's *For Whom the Bell Tolls* was dirty. Naturally this was the best possible recommendation, and I read it as fast as I could smuggle it inside a copy of *The Saturday Evening Post.* I was disappointed. There was no explicit sex, and the celebrated scene where Robert Jordan and the girl Maria got into a sleeping bag, and felt "the earth move," seemed to defy the laws of nature and geophysics as I understood them.

TV was not invented. We couldn't afford a radio, or the day-long trip to the nearest movie. So we sang and read aloud to one another. Ever since, I have written for the ear as well as the eye, silently reading back sentences in my head, listening for the rhythm that ought to be there.

There is an image in my memory, as bright today as on that certain evening in 1935. My parents, brother and I are in our miniscule living room by the white light of a hissing gasoline lamp. My father sits in his favourite rocking chair, oak with leather seat, his bald head with its fringe of red hair bent over *The Saturday Evening Post.* My mother, careworn but still beautiful with her strong cheekbones and dark intent eyes, is in the wicker rocker, hands busy as always, mending socks. Larry sits between them on a homemade hooked rug. I am stretched on the davenport-cum-guest bed.

Dad is reading aloud a story by Paul Gallico about two newspaper reporters, Perry Brown and Rusty McGowan. Perry loves Rusty but she's grown tired of waiting and has just married someone else. Then Perry does something so loving and beguiling that Rusty decides to ditch the other guy (who wasn't right for her anyway) and it all ends happily. My father reads with verve, relishing every line; he has a theatrical streak. (Both our parents use proper grammar, in a community where "ain't" and "youse" are common parlance.) We listen, captivated. Good story, good reader, happy family linked by words.

So—by example, environment, osmosis—I fell everlastingly in love with words and the things words can do. My parents neither hindered nor pushed me in this single-minded march toward a vocation. They simply supported and applauded every small triumph. My brother Larry's too, and he, although more modest than I, has been a successful journalist for more than thirty years.

At seven I got into print in the *Torchbearers' Magazine,* a Saturday supplement to the Regina *Leader-Post* and sustenance for prairie kids who longed to write. We called each other "Torchies," and the editors unflinchingly published stories, poems and letters as awful as my first one:

> DEAR TORCHIES:
> WE HAD A DOG NAMED ROVER BUT HE DIED. HE WENT TO SCHOOL WITH ME SOMETIMES. HE WENT HOME WHEN WE GOT THERE. WE HAVE TWO CATS. THEIR NAMES ARE GRAYNOSE AND TABBY.

One Christmas on the verge of the Depression my parents shelled out $1.25, serious money, for "A Toy Typewriter That Really Works" from Eaton's catalogue. It was the Simplex Model A, fire-engine red, royal blue trim, a little tin machine with dial-a-letter alphabet, eight numerals, a comma and a period.

You twirled the Simplex dial until the right letter came front and centre, then punched out one character at a time, capitals only, with a satisfying "click." It was the best gift I ever had. I launched a single-sheet household newsletter. Typing at one word a minute was hard sledding, but there were no deadlines and no urgent news:

> GRAYNOSE AND TABBY HAVE KITTENS
> KUCK, PET CHICKEN, RECOVERING FROM INJURY IN CHICKEN HOSPITAL

At our one-room rural school, I lucked into a teacher, Jean Dempson, who was literate, no-nonsense and caring. She taught me grammar so thoroughly that it became reflex action, although today I couldn't parse a sentence if the CIA held a blowtorch to my feet. She made us read aloud our compositions in class. Sometimes my classmates laughed in the right places. One of my stories was even retold around the neighbourhood. Was this how it was going to be: people reading my stuff, laughing, patting me on the back?

Breathes there a writer who cannot remember that first love, first kiss, first words-in-print and, above all, first money earned for those words? The memory of my first dollar is still vivid after nearly sixty years. It was for "Christmas at the Browns," a three-hundred-word, thinly disguised version of our own family festivities, in the 1934 writing competition of the *Torchbearers' Magazine*. It was pretty bad but I was only ten.

It won third prize–one dollar–in the junior writers' category. When the news arrived by mail I ran from the house screeching, "I won a dollar, I won a dollar!" In 1934 one dollar bought twenty chocolate bars or four decent books. My parents were almost as happy as I. It was not merely the honour. It meant I could actually get paid for doing what I loved.

The summer of '47 was a summer like any other: a tough time for a kid hunting for a job. There were opportunities–Canada was awash in giddy postwar recovery–but for me no ordinary job would do.

A year at university had convinced me that an Arts degree with an English major–although a glorious intellectual awakening after the air force–was, in terms of getting paid employment in writing, about as useful as gum disease. I had to get on a newspaper. Yet here was the eternal dilemma, the Catch 22 of every student job hunt: employers want experience, but how do you get experience if nobody will hire you? I was twenty-two–getting *old*–and desperately needed a first break, that magical moment in life when someone or something starts you down the right path.

I didn't urgently need the money. The Department of Veterans' Affairs was paying my tuition at the University of Saskatchewan, plus sixty dollars a month for school-year living expenses: a grateful nation's reward for my three years of heroic effort as the most tangle-handed mechanic in the history of the RCAF.

Any frugal graduate of the Depression could eke out a living on sixty dollars a month. So I could have spent an idyllic summer on my parents' eight-acre spread at the edge of Shamrock, Saskatchewan, whiling away the drowsy fly-buzzing afternoons with books and daydreams, helping tend the two cows, the half-acre of vegetables and a hundred mindless Barred Plymouth Rock fowl.

Or I could have hired on with a local farmer, pitching wheat sheaves or driving a tractor for fifty dollars a month and all the fried chicken and pork chops I could eat. It would have vastly improved my image among the guys holding up the side of the village pool hall. To them, a grown man who wrote for a living was probably the kind who sat down to pee. But I had to be a reporter. Nothing else would do.

My résumé seemed to me rather fetching as I tapped it out on the clunky Remington portable I'd bought with air force discharge money:

> Editor of Shamrock, Sask., high school paper, 1942 . . . rural stringer for Regina *Leader-Post,* 1941–42 . . . contributor to RCAF newspapers, 1943–46 . . . graduate of the Newspaper Institute of America correspondence course . . .

To any experienced newsman, such credentials were laughable. But I wrote, full of hope, to eighteen dailies and weeklies across the prairie provinces and sat back to field the best offer.

For three weeks the silence was deafening. Then, terse "no's" began trickling in. Panicky, I gambled on a trip to Regina: four hours on the bucking, wheezing CPR local to Moose Jaw, sixty miles from home; another hour to Regina; a night in a cheap hotel near the station, where railroaders and indigent travellers slept to a serenade of chuffing, wailing locomotives.

The *Leader* had not answered my application. Surely that was an oversight, or maybe even a good sign. I would jog the editors' memories: "Remember me? The stringer of '42? Remember that great piece I did for you on the scrap-metal drive for the war effort? . . . " If they didn't, I would woo them with a fistful of winning story ideas, as advised by the Newspaper Institute of America.

"Hire this kid, he's a natural!" a grizzled editor would cry. Nearby, a female reporter with black tresses, heroic breasts and a Jane Arden trench coat (Lois Lane had not yet been introduced to my fantasies) would toss me a lingering glance of admiration and lust.

It wasn't like that. For an hour I sat in Victoria Park across from the Hotel Saskatchewan, scanning the sky and trees for ideas. A funny feature on gophers? . . . A poignant piece on park attendants? . . . A treatise on cumulous clouds? . . .

Finally I trudged the few blocks to the *Leader* on Hamilton Street, empty handed and empty headed. Time has mercifully blotted out most of the details. I timidly approached a long wooden counter, the buffer between newsroom and the yearning outer world. Somebody asked my business. At the *Leader,* a librarian or junior reporter always took time to head off strays at the counter: vengeful advertisers, angry readers, duplicitous aldermen, wild-eyed inventors or nut cases claiming to have the scoop-of-the-month.

I dimly remember a bored editor barely containing his impatience as his deadline loomed. "Sorry. We've hired all our summer help."

It was over quickly, like an execution, and I was back on the train. Saskatchewan is at its tenderest in June. Through the train's open windows the fields smelled of new green life and promise. The twice-weekly local dropped me and the mail back in Shamrock. I scooped the contents from P.O. Box 43. Two letters, but I was in no hurry for more heartbreak. I scuffed down the dusty street, across the railway tracks and into my parents' house. I slumped at the round oak dining table, told them the bad news and listlessly opened my mail.

Another "no." But then, incredibly, a courteous though cautious note from Jack Slaight, publisher of the Moose Jaw *Times-Herald*. He said there "might" be an opening.

I sprang up, ablaze with hope, and repacked the indestructible plywood suitcase I'd bought with cigarettes on the Hamburg black market. I caught the next train out of town which, given the erratic schedule, meant three days later. A five-dollar room in Moose Jaw's finest hostelry, the respectable Harwood—"every guest room with private toilet"—where I'd stayed the night before I joined the air force, was comforting, extravagant and fitting for a future foreign correspondent. In the morning I walked into the *Times-Herald* without an appointment.

Slaight, a harassed-looking man in his late forties, was visibly startled to see me. But it was a simpler time and place. The *Times* occupied the basement, main and second floors of a small apartment building. Moose Jaw, population 23,000, was a farmers' and railroaders' town. In that gentle environment, a publisher took time to talk to a hopeful right in off the street.

"I only said there *might* be a job," Slaight began, fumbling for my letter. A queasy feeling crept into my gut. Then my eye strayed to the application on his desk. There was my name, laboriously typed at the bottom in proper business fashion—but without a signature. I HAD FORGOTTEN TO SIGN MY BLOODY NAME! Well, that was it. Nobody would bother to make a reporter out of an idiot. (Years later I realized that many idiots become reporters and go on to fame as columnists.)

But Slaight seemed not to mind my gaffe. He'd been around newspapers a long time. Maybe he remembered when he was young and nervous. Maybe he admired this awkward sunburned kid for making so chancy a journey.

"Why do you want to get on a newspaper?"

How could I explain the years of scribbling, scribbling, scribbling; the longing to be in print; the love affair with words?

"I've always wanted to," I answered lamely. "There's just nothing else I want to do."

Slaight pondered some more, perhaps relieved that I hadn't babbled the standard response about newspaper reporters meeting such interesting people.

"All right. You can fill in while some of our people are on holidays. Starting July 28. But I can only give you two weeks."

"That's great," I said shakily.

"Eighteen dollars a week," Slaight said, looking at me sharply. Even by 1947 standards, even before it became a Thomson newspaper, *Times-Herald* wages were bottom of the barrel.

"Fine!" I blurted, not admitting I would gladly have paid

him. I floated onto the streets of Moose Jaw. Back home my parents were as jubilant as I.

Four weeks later I checked into a boarding house consistent with my salary–bed, breakfast and dinner for ten dollars a week, just a nudge and a wink and a "hey-there-honey" from the local red-light district. My landlady was tough enough to chew nails and spit rust. There was never enough butter or meat or pie. When the platters circled the dinner table that first night, I was outdrawn by the fastest hands in the West.

My fellow lodgers were local labourers who talked incessantly of sex in the furtive manner of men who weren't getting any. From them, I–who thought the air force had taught me everything scatological worth knowing–learned the most remarkable of the countless synonyms for sexual intercourse: "p-jogging."

On Monday morning, burstingly proud and scared, I scaled the stairs of the *Times-Herald* offices to the second-floor newsroom. It was long and narrow with a pendulum clock on the wall, a reluctant fan on a shelf, a strange high-backed bench forever empty against a wall and a large mirror left over from the room's previous incarnation as an apartment. It smelled gloriously of newsprint, paste pots, clutter and age. I loved it on sight.

The editor, Fred Workman, white haired and courtly, occupied a private cubicle where he wrote editorials and thought great thoughts amid stifling clouds of pipe smoke. The remaining editorial staff of seven, including sports and society editors, sat in the open at old decrepit desks, sharing telephones–except for senior reporter Harold Davies, veteran of two wars, distinguished by a suit with vest and his own phone.

The long, lean sandy-haired managing editor, not much older than I, detached himself from the mess and rose with outstretched hand.

"Nice to have you here," he said as though he meant it. "I'm Jim Lamb. This is Harold and Ruby and Zona and Murray . . ."

They were friendly, unpretentious and tolerant of my gaucherie. Unlike other managing editors I met in later years, most of whom were cursed with chronic gloom and galloping ulcers, Lamb rejoiced in his work. Editing copy at a prodigious rate, tossing out wry or cheery comments on the day's vagaries, jumping up as though on coiled springs, eking out snippets of fact over the phone, he inspired by example.

He never lost his temper yet was always firmly in charge, a legacy from his wartime command of the Canadian corvette *Camrose*. He had come out of the war a lieutenant, taken the very same Newspaper Institute of America correspondence course as I had (he borrowed the entire curriculum from another student and devoured it in a matter of days) and served a short term as reporter for the Woodstock *Sentinel-Review*.

The *Times* was by no stretch of the imagination a great paper, but Lamb's little band, doing a multitude of jobs, filled the pages creditably day after day. That first morning Lamb donned his hat (senior men wore hats; all men wore jackets, ties and short haircuts; women never wore slacks) and guided me to the police station. It was the kind of town where the managing editor could do that and be back at his desk in twenty minutes.

Each morning thereafter I plodded to the cop shop, where a bulky sergeant revealed to me the daily docket of mischief. Then on to court, where good grey magistrates dealt with the dreary misdemeanours of a small city, exchanging in-jokes with arresting officers and meting out patient justice and stern lectures to sorrowful drunks, petty thieves and two-bit gamblers.

Back at the office I wrote my stories, heeding Lamb's advice to "watch for brighteners." I phoned the fire hall which, to my regret, reported not one decent blaze in those two weeks. I black-pencilled the garbled offerings from our rural correspondents and learned to edit wire copy. Spongelike, I eagerly absorbed it all. And I began to learn what every newspaper person knows: much of reporting is tedium or drudgery but, to its practitioners, it is a lifetime addiction.

Then Lamb introduced me to the news feature. He was a born features man himself: insatiably curious about everything from baseball to Beethoven, quick to spot an angle and blessed with a sense of humour. He had brightened the *Times-Herald* with a page of high school chit-chat, a man-on-the-street opinion column and a grab bag of oddities, "Town Talk," to which we all contributed. Now he set me free each afternoon to find features.

From the beginning it felt right. Lamb prodded my imagination, taught me to spot story ideas, helped tune my ear for the bits of whimsy and incongruity that bring mundane subjects to life. I began to learn a skill to be honed for the rest of my life: to set my subjects and myself at ease, to probe for quotes, to fish for what might have happened and then triumphantly hear the interviewee say, "Funny you should mention that. Yeah, one time that did happen . . . " And I wrote and rewrote far into the evening. None of us knew anything about newspaper guilds or nine-to-five hours. The work had to be done, we liked it and we were in it together.

My stories, viewed now on the yellow crumbling pages of 1947, were merely adequate for a beginner: an interview with a leading news vendor on what professional people liked to read (doctors, he told me, gorged themselves on whodunits); a piece on the August heat wave which revealed that 90 degrees Fahrenheit could give a goldfish heat prostration but didn't faze a local baker who worked in 120 degrees; and the earth-shattering discovery that water wings were no longer sold in sporting goods stores, causing me to pun without shame, "It is now a question of sink or swim." The *Times-Herald* gave no bylines, but Lamb featured my stories on the city page with lively headings. I was unspeakably grateful.

Financially, the two weeks were a flop. I grossed thirty-six dollars and spent it all, and more, on room and board, lunches, train fare and an occasional beer with the raunchy labourers, who became rather proud of their literary inmate. One Sunday they invited me to join them in an aimless walk around the lifeless city and an earnest discussion of p-jogging.

Though the fortnight left a hole in my bank book, the benefits were beyond price. I began selling Lamb occasional features from my hometown, including one that tickled his sense of the absurd: how the village fathers and mothers housed our summer clergyman in the only available empty space, the jail, there being a chronic shortage of criminals in Shamrock.

That autumn, newly confident, I returned to my digs in Saskatoon and took over the news desk of the university *Sheaf*. Jim Lamb also invited me to write a weekly gossip column for the *Times-Herald*. We didn't call it gossip. It was to be an assortment of "news" about Moose Jaw students on campus, but we knew what that meant.

So began my short unhappy career as Moose Jaw's Hedda Hopper. We called it "All About U" and it was unsigned, which is why I am alive to report on it today. From the outset, getting material on the sly felt sleazy. Avarice won out: Lamb paid me, as I recall, four dollars a column. That twenty dollars a month, combined with my sixty-dollar Veterans' allowance, made me the Conrad Black of the campus.

An affectionate co-ed from Moose Jaw, whom I'd dated a few times, helped feed me tips. Each week I grew more desperate for material and my column grew more inane. But Lamb knew that *Times* readers were interested in names. So I named all the Moose Jaw students attending the Women's Arts and Science dance. I reported that Hal Sisson, Ross Knechtel and George Rathwell played cards every Sunday. Gordie Dobson was "seen preparing to attend a Halloween party." Elva Wheatley was seen "having fun with a gang of co-eds." Gordon Davies was seen "studying industriously" . . . Pauline Fysh scored two points for the Household Science basketball team . . . Lillian Slusar sold poppies on Remembrance Day . . . Mary Bennett was seen typing out an essay for English class. I sank to the ultimate low with Bob Marsh, viewed "just strolling around a corridor." While the students wondered where this drivel was coming from, their parents wondered what if anything their kids did besides play cards, sell poppies and stroll the halls of academe.

Early in the new year Hedda Hopper tried to quit, but Jim Lamb urged me on. More and more of my items were about Moose Jaw's Hank Johnson, editor of the *Sheaf*. He was a big man on campus and good copy. Although my items on him were gentle and discreet, they began to get under Hank's skin. Once as I sat in the *Sheaf* office, he demanded angrily of the world at large, "Who *is* writing that crap about us?"

I kept quiet; Johnson was tall and rugged. But I now reveal Hedda Hopper's identity after forty-five years on the assumption that Hank, if he's around, would not hurt another senior citizen.

A year later I transferred to the University of Western Ontario journalism school in London, which led to a whole summer's work on the Regina *Leader-Post,* a full-time job after graduation with the London *Free Press* and, most important, a meeting with Pierre Berton. Such is the chain reaction of a first break.

In my graduate year, Berton, then articles editor of *Maclean's,* spent a day regaling our class on the art of magazine writing. Then, as now, he was a charismatic figure: brash, towering, booming voice, thinning red hair, small red moustache and riveting blue eyes that skewered you with mingled humour and arrogance. He was a mesmerizing speaker, telling his tales with such zest and total authority that it would be years before I realized Berton was occasionally wrong.

He announced an article-writing contest, just for our class. The winner would get one hundred dollars and a chance to be published in *Maclean's.* With exams almost upon us, we paired up for the competition to save time. Classmate Bill Holden, a fellow Saskatchewanite (and half-brother of the fine actor Eric Peterson), joined me in a stab at a profile of London; city profiles were then in vogue. We won, but our piece wasn't good enough to be published. Berton invited us up to *Maclean's* to discuss a rewrite.

Another classmate, Holden's girl friend Patricia Hamilton, borrowed a car and drove us to Toronto. At 10:00 A.M. we walked reverently into the rabbit-warren offices of Maclean Hunter at 481 University Avenue, temple of Canadian magazine journalism.

Berton looked up from behind his trademark bow tie, amiable but brisk, sharp eyes pinning us to our chairs. It took him only ten minutes to spell out what was wrong with our piece (a lot) and dismiss us with a "good luck." His head was into the next manuscript before Holden and I got out the door. It didn't occur to him that our moment in his holy presence was the highlight of our day.

We bought Pat Hamilton lunch and trekked home, a long drive in the low-tech cars and lower-tech highways of 1950. I tried the rewrite alone; Holden's heart wasn't in magazines. (After some newspaper reporting he became a prosperous bookstore owner in England, where he died in 1989.)

The rewrite failed too, but I had caught Berton's eye. At last I knew what I wanted to do: not chase fire engines, not cover the drones in city hall, never race to the home of some poor wretch killed by an axe murderer or speeding car and snatch the deceased's photo off the mantel before rival reporters got to it. I wanted to graduate from features into this mesmerizing world of magazines: more depth and length, something for a writer to sink his teeth into; typography, art and photography to showcase the words; a national audience; a longer life for the articles (a month or, at least, weeks versus a newspaper's single day).

Jack Slaight moved to the Thomson Newspapers organization where he stayed until retirement. He died in the 1980s. Jim Lamb married Ruby from the *Times-Herald* staff, moved to the Orillia *Packet and Times* and ended up as publisher. He retired early and, with Ruby, now spends summers in Baddeck, Nova Scotia, and winters in Spain, as befits the author of several successful books.

We are still great friends. His curiosity and enthusiasm for life have not diminished one iota. He was agreeably surprised when I told him a while ago how much that job had meant to me. He remembers only that "when Jack Slaight mentioned you, I wanted you because I was very much in favour of ex-servicemen."

Fair enough. That's the final rule for first breaks: the grantor of one should not be aware that it is an epochal event lest the giving lose its charm and spontaneity.

All the same, such things bestow upon their recipients a certain obligation. They are invisible gifts, passed down through the generations. And looking back, I hope that somewhere along the way I've repaid Jim Lamb and Jack Slaight for my first break; that as an editor giving extra coaching to some beginning writer who really cared, I gave that person heart; that as teacher of magazine journalism at the University of Western Ontario and at Toronto's Ryerson Institute, I reached, maybe even inspired, one or two of my truly earnest and talented students with careful critiques written late into the night.

And I hope, through one of them, the ripples go on and on.

2

THE HOLY GRAIL

Sometimes on drear Toronto nights, when the fern-and-quiche bars are closed and the mournful howl of wolves echoes from the distant wastes of Bay Street, I light a fire with the latest Margaret Atwood book review and muse on the merits of procrastination.

Not my procrastination, for once, but an editor's. If William Thompson hadn't dragged his feet, I might at this very moment be a gnarled and wizened deskman on the Regina *Leader-Post*. At the very least my dream of someday writing for *Maclean's* would have seemed much harder to achieve, and maybe impossible, from the distant West.

Early in 1950, about to graduate from Western, I applied for a permanent job at the *Leader*. I'd been happily employed there through the previous summer: working several beats and insane hours, guzzling draft beers at the La Salle Hotel, ogling the teen-queen groupies who clustered like bees around our friend the honey-tongued radio announcer with his dark saturnine good looks, and sharing the newspaperman's endless self-centred talk with Bill MacPherson and Alan Rogers, seasoned reporters who would go on to great careers. The other summer-student reporter, Wilf Kesterton (later a revered teacher of journalism at Carleton University), and I were what kids called "keeners." One week during the Regina Exhibition we wrote so many feature stories that city editor Bruce "Butch" Peacock actually begged us to slow down.

So why not go back? I had no ties in the East (the UWO co-ed of my dreams had just rejected my cowlike devotion and gone home to her boyfriend in what is now Thunder Bay). There was no immediate hope of getting on a magazine. Maybe I could become a *Leader-Post* feature writer, freelancing to magazines on the side.

Managing editor Thompson didn't answer my job application. Weeks passed. Then fellow Saskatchewanite Max Macdonald, from UWO Journalism '49, put in a word for me at the London *Free Press* features department, where he worked. They offered me a job at forty dollars a week: good money. I grabbed it. Thompson came along a month too late with a thirty-five-dollar offer.

The new job was far from pure. Most of our stories were embedded in special advertising sections. If, say, Sparton of Canada, maker of radios and "phonographs," marked an anniversary, the *Free Press* ran four or five pages of advertising wrapped around stories on such then-amazing developments as the LP record or the history of music. It was hardly subtle.

But it was worth being at the *Free Press* just to share a roof with editor Arthur Ford, a great newspaperman in every sense of that overworked word. He personally knew all the important people in early Canadian journalism, had been everywhere, done everything, *covered* everything from the sinking of the *Titanic* to the birth of the United Nations. At heart he was still a reporter, shunning the editor's ivory tower to go dig out stories and to write lively weekly columns of insight and anecdote.

London was a picture-postcard city: thickly treed with lush gardens, snug solid homes, stately university and easy pace. The *Free Press* had a stranglehold on most of southwestern Ontario and on this fat, smug city, which reportedly had more millionaires per capita than any other in Canada. But it was a thorough and reputable paper, despite the handicap of monopoly, because of Ford and the good people who were attracted to him.

Ford, at sixty-nine, seemed ancient to me. I rarely spoke to him and always as "Mr. Ford," but his tall rumpled figure was a familiar sight throughout the old building on Richmond Street: cigar ashes dribbling down his vest, battered hat worn at a jaunty angle as though he might rush out on a story at any moment. Down-and-outers regularly dropped into his office to tap him for a dollar or two. He always obliged. Arthur Ford was a gentleman.

Another true gentleman, Glen Hancock, the department's

senior writer, took me out on my first assignment (something about the manufacture of house paint) and pronounced me fit. Hancock's talents were wasted on the tainted features of our department. His penchant for deep thought, discussion and debate led him naturally, in time, to the editorial page. But he also had the born writer's childlike curiosity, playful spirit and delight in almost everything—all the requisites for *true* feature writing.

Glen was infinitely more mature than me, although only four or five years older. He had a wife and two daughters—a crushing burden, it seemed to us singles—and an indefinable air of dignity and authority. Such was his modesty that for years I didn't know he'd been an RCAF Squadron Leader with fifty-nine bombing missions over Europe. Had I known, my inferiority complex from having spent the war as a noncombatant leading aircraftsman might have marred our great friendship. Probably he sensed that, for he was a kind and intuitive man.

That autumn Glen and I merrily drove all over southwestern Ontario in a *Free Press* car—luxury in a time when few of us could afford one of our own—living in two-dollar hotel rooms, eating twenty-five-cent meals and developing the writing of community stories into an art. Our formula: a quick drive through town to spot signs of progress—new skating rink, community hall, civic building—for the main story, then a search for some genuine local feature. The *Free Press* logo on the car made me feel important. We represented the dominant newspaper in southwestern Ontario and doors opened to us, despite our frayed cuffs and pitiful salaries.

Back at the office my desk in the features' bullpen faced a drawing board. Behind it lurked a stubby man with round features, a pug nose and the eyes of a naughty child. He hummed, cackled, cracked terrible jokes and drew with wit and heart. Merle "Ting" Tingley was in the third of his forty-five years as *Free Press* staff cartoonist.

In a profession packed with massive egos, the modest Ting never quite understood how good he really was. I instantly took to his humour and compassion, and soon we abandoned our respective digs to share a rollicking upper duplex on Piccadilly Street with radio announcer John Dickins and a salesman named Al. Sometimes Al had vicious migraine headaches, which the rest of us caused.

We dined incessantly on pork chops cooked to death in a pressure cooker. We threw weekend parties that attracted *Free Press* hordes and itinerant out-of-towners. We sang, danced and played silly games. Reporter Larry Holmes taught me the ukulele. My girl friend of the moment gave me a voluminous Mexican hat with a brim that drooped to the knees. One night reporter Gordon Sanderson, full of party spirit, strolled home inside my hat. He was stopped by the local constabulary–a sombrero out on its own was uncommon in London–but his exquisite English manners saved him. Sanderson went on to an impeccable forty-year career as *Free Press* columnist, ombudsman and Ontario legislature correspondent, simply proving that the hat makes the man.

It was a happy, innocent time and could have gone on forever. But after nine months I was learning nothing new and getting tired of pseudo-features. I was twenty-six. The war had robbed my generation of precious years. It was time to move on.

I was labouring over a freelance *Maclean's* piece on the Ontario tobacco town, Delhi–I'd queried Berton and to my delight got approval to try it on speculation. Early in 1951 I answered an advertisement for a magazine job in Toronto, mentioning the *Maclean's* connection. Soon managing editor Jean McKinley of Maclean Hunter's *Canadian Homes & Gardens* magazine invited me down for an interview.

"What's a good cheap hotel in Toronto?" I asked Joe Arnold, a London journalism pal who had won the DFC over Europe and therefore, in my view, could do no wrong. "The Ford, corner of Bay and Dundas," he said briskly, doing wrong.

It was a quiet night at the Ford–no broken-chair fights in the halls, no hookers at my door–so I went to my breakfast interview still unaware of its one-star reputation. Miss McKinley, about to become *CH&G* editor, met me in the upper-drawer Royal York Hotel. She was an attractive thirty-something in stylish tailored suit and a jangle of rings and bracelets.

"You're staying here, of course?" Jean said casually, as a conversation starter.

"No, at the Ford," I said suavely.

"The *Ford?*" cried Miss McKinley, holding the words at arms' length like yesterday's kippers. Only then did I realize that the

Ford was not part of *CH&G*'s world, or even universe. Despite this fall from social grace, Jean hired me as assistant editor.

Back at the *Free Press* I went for coffee with my boss, Jimmy Burns. I hate good-byes. I explained apologetically that I had to leave, but not because I was unhappy. Jimmy smiled wisely.

"I'm sorry too, but of course you have to go," he said. "You won't know for ten years what you really want to do in life."

He was right. Who knew where I'd be in ten years? On magazines, I hoped. I'd never owned a home or the exotic kind of garden that *Canadian Homes & Gardens* held dear, but it *was* a magazine and I was edging closer to *Maclean's*.

Toronto in 1951 was an overgrown small town, despite its metropolitan population of 1.4 million. To residents of more sophisticated venues–in those days, Montreal–Toronto-the-Good was Toronto-the-Tedious. "I spent a week in Hogtown last Sunday," Montrealers jeered, referring to that day in Toronto's week when the only thing open was church.

You could count the decent cocktail bars on one hand. Packs of men huddled in dingy, soul-destroying beer-slopped beverage rooms; women went docilely next door to the equally depressing "Ladies and Escorts." A dining-out thrill was an Italian restaurant with red-checkered tablecloths. Budding bohemians carried home the straw-encased Chianti bottle to create a wax-streaked candle holder on the coffee table.

The subway was still a-building. Farmers' fields lay where huge subdivisions sprang up a decade or two later north of Highway 401 (which didn't exist in '51). Yet for all that, Toronto was exhilarating. It was the big time, as big as English Canada could offer, full of life and zest compared with slumberous London.

The UWO journalism school young-boys' network embraced me. We roomed in cheap unfashionable joints befitting our economic level. Sometimes we were stacked like cordwood in double-decker military bunks. I had one roommate who could burp explosively on command while pointing his finger like a pistol, and another who greeted each bright new day by lighting a cigarette and plucking a warm bottle of beer from under his bunk. I shared with ex-classmates Austin Winch and Bill Gingell of the Toronto *Star*, then with ex-classmate Jack Brown and an apprentice lawyer. We had a flat on a street so grungy I dared not even whisper its name to Miss McKinley. Kids on the block rubbed handfuls of gravel along the sides of parked cars, for fun. In the flat overhead, our brutish landlord and sluttish landlady had nightly fistfights, ending in snarls and yelps when she put her guard dog on him.

Each workday morning I gratefully left this gritty milieu for the island of civility that was 481 University Avenue. This was the home of the Maclean Hunter publishing giant with *Maclean's, Chatelaine, Mayfair, Canadian Homes & Gardens* and innumerable trade magazines. *Maclean's* inhabited a venerable building on the University side; *CH&G* was in a newer adjoining wing facing onto Dundas Street. The office decor was Dickensian but never mind: Pierre Berton walked these ancient halls, rode these same arthritic elevators.

For a while, kindly old Frank Crack, the art director, associate editor Alastair Scott and I shared Editorial with six or seven women. The news that I worked for a woman, in an office full of others, drew much lascivious comment from male friends. They didn't know what they were missing. My female work partners were smart, humane and tolerant of my shortcomings in the realm of homes, gardens, decor, design, culture, everything. They were also pleasing to the eye, which you were allowed to say in 1951.

Assistant editor Joan Chalmers, tall and unassuming with a wry sense of humour, gave no hint that she was daughter of Floyd, already executive vice-president and eventually president and chairman of the Maclean Hunter empire. Assistant editor Zena Cherry, who had married money and later became a legendary society columnist for the Toronto *Globe and Mail,* regarded me, correctly, as an untutored savage. Jean Hill, in charge of editorial production, was short, cheery and attractive. My brief romantic interest in her fizzled out the day I mispronounced Pagliacci (PAG-LEE-ACKY instead of POLLY-AWCHEE). She laughed, and I knew I was culturally out of my depth.

As always on magazines of the time, sparkling well-educated young women were languishing in jobs far beneath their talents. Editorial assistant Carol Frankel (later Sprachman) was saddled with such menial tasks as fetching McKinley's forgotten gloves from a restaurant; by 1992 she was president and a founding member of the nationwide Canadian Federation of Friends of Museums. Editorial assistant Patricia Lamont (later Fillmore) rose from that dogsbody job and ultimately became a TV Ontario executive. Editorial secretary Heather McCallum went on to become head theatre librarian of the Metro Toronto Public Library and in 1992 coauthored a book on Canadian theatre archives.

Like most of the rank and file, I had a cubicle with half-walls, a step up from the *Free Press* bullpen. My first task was to glorify grass. I titled it "Your Lawn: An Outdoor Carpet" and began: "Home gardeners tenderly cultivate it. Poets write flowery verse about it. Everyone in fact admires a velvety green lawn. . . ."

After that there was nowhere to go but up. I edited "How to Make a Fitted Valance," "Getting More Uses from Your Electric Drill," "Awnings for Every Purpose" and "There's an Art to Good Digging." I enlightened readers on how to "Let a Bookshelf Hide an Ugly Window," "Keep up Your Eavestroughing" and "Plant Bulbs Now for Spring Colour." An occasional editorial mission took me to the home of contributing food editor Norah Michener (disguised as "Janet Peters"). Had I known that her husband, Roland, would someday be governor general of Canada, I would have more effusively praised her Green Pepper and Celery Jelly or her Sicilian Cookies with Palermo Ice.

The most interesting part of *CH&G* was McKinley herself. It was surely not easy for a woman running a magazine in that patriarchal organization, but Jean exuded confidence, held her own in male company and lunched regularly with the likes of Berton and Floyd Chalmers. She had a *CH&G* kind of apartment in a regal old house in classy Rosedale (one room was a turret, the kind I've always wanted for a study).

Robert Fulford, who joined *CH&G* the year after I left, wrote in his memoirs that "at some point or other, every man who worked for Jean fell in love with her, if only for ten minutes." Certainly she was attractive, intelligent and charming when she chose. She had a peculiar habit of fluttering her eyelids when asking a favour. My mother would have called it "batting her eyes," but I didn't for a moment think she was flirting with her most junior editor.

The notion of loving one's boss, even for ten minutes, was beyond my ken. For one thing she was an Older Woman (I was too gauche to realize what wonders and advantages that might entail). For another, she was light-years beyond me in style and sophistication. And like editors of either sex, Jean could be extremely domineering. Over two years I watched her grind down several other staffers, men included. Male employers had done that to women for generations; being on the receiving end must have come as a shock.

Regardless, Jean was always fair and usually pleasant with me, perhaps because I was obviously a transient. She knew I longed for bigger and better magazine fare and that Berton had an eye on me. From time to time he boomed through the *CH&G* offices tossing me a nod of recognition. By now I had sold him "Tobacco Town" for a princely two hundred dollars. When the sharply edited version appeared I was deflated, but overall it was one of the highlights of my life. I had touched the Holy Grail of magazine writing.

Miss McKinley knew I was getting bored when, after editing "They Kept the View with a Baffle Wall," I made fun of it in verse for the private amusement of the staff. Doggerel became my refuge ever after when jobs became trying:

'TIS SAID THAT MR. AND MRS. MCCOLL
NOW WISH THEY'D NEVER DESIGNED IT
THEIR KITCHEN IS HID BY A BAFFLE WALL
AND NOW, DAMMITALL, THEY CAN'T FIND IT.

With Jean's blessing, I eased back from "The Drill Press, Your Willing Slave" and "How a Garage Became an Extra Room." She encouraged me to write as many articles as we could dredge up within *CH&G*'s limitations: on home-and-school associations, product design, African violets and a profile of a dear old party whom we headlined "Canada's Lady of the Lilies." Once Jean sent me to Calgary, ostensibly to find a gracious home to write about, but really so I could spend Christmas Day with my parents in Saskatchewan. My choice of Calgary home was so execrable that we quietly scrapped it.

Under Jean I first became aware of the memorandum as an instrument of terror and torture. Her memos, some of which I've kept, were little fireside chats with ominous undertones, designed to make better people of us all. Many of the subjects could have been dispensed with in one minute at a staff meeting, saving much time and many trees.

One of them ticked us off for being late. "To have staff drift in at any old hour indicates one of two things: disinterest on the part of the individual in his responsibilities, or overstaffing. I would not like to be forced to assume either of these points."

Another put an end to office coffee-making but grappled with a counterplan: "Miss McCallum or Miss Hill might take orders at 10 cents for coffee brought from across the street, for those who wish it. This represents an expenditure of about 8 minutes with practically no disruption of the office."

The mother of all memos to Staff ordered us to record all our daily activities and to make a point of getting out of the office "for a certain amount of time," thereby making us "a little sharper, quicker with our desk work."

"I think each of you should make a point of systematically seeing people of importance in your field," Jean added, "at least a person a day and preferably two."

We mulled it over. At two a day, most of us would run out of important people by Friday. Were we ourselves important enough to qualify? I offered to take Staff, two a day, to my favourite eatery, a takeout counter across the street manned by a surly ethnic named Big John, who wore a cap all winter and a hat all summer. There were no takers. My favourite canned salmon with vinegar and pepper on rye did not tempt my feminine colleagues. The memo soon faded and died as do they all.

Meanwhile, I was freelancing as fast as my feet and fingers could fly. Heeding the advice doled out to all beginning writers–"Write what you know"–I queried *Saturday Night* about a piece on UWO's fledgling journalism school, and sold it. During two years at *Homes & Gardens,* I also sold six more articles to *Maclean's* and four to *Mayfair,* an erstwhile society magazine getting a facelift under a tough *Maclean's* alumnus, Herb Manning. Cracking *Mayfair* wasn't difficult. Its office was just down the hall from

CH&G, Manning had heard good things about me from his *Maclean's* cronies and soon I was not only writing for him but sharing the occasionally boozy lunch.

In leftover time I took a night course in radio broadcasting; began writing and reading freelance items for CBC International; joined the Toronto Camera Club and learned to make prints and enlargements; bought an oil-gulping secondhand Studebaker and met a slim blonde dental nurse, Ruth Dillon, on a blind date.

I was not particularly driven, just eager to make up for lost time and to learn, learn, learn. Part of my learning hunger came from my parents (also explaining the dozens of night courses I've taken in a lifetime), but most of my generation was imbued with the same work ethic. It felt good to be making a living from words (my *Maclean's* article rate rose to four hundred dollars). *Maclean's* managing editor John Clare, one of the triumvirate then editing stories, told someone that I was "going to be the best magazine writer in Canada." All this, two years out of journalism school, was heady stuff.

Now I wanted to get married like other normal folk and have a decent apartment where the landlady didn't set her German Shepherd on her spouse and the spouse didn't call the landlady "a fuckin' Nova Scotia apple-knocker."

Ruth wanted that better life as much as I did. She'd come from hard beginnings: parents separated when she was a child; at age twelve she was cooking meals for her brother and sisters; before eighteen she was working. Highly intelligent, she had enlarged her education through reading. I had no idea how tough her early years had been; she stoically kept much of it to herself. Neither of us realized, either, that a writer's life–so much more solitary, demanding and mundane than meets the eye–can strain a marriage.

By June 1952 I had about five hundred dollars in the bank, which seemed a sumptuous sum for launching into married life. Ruth was Catholic; I was Protestant. I took instruction for a Catholic marriage, but at the eleventh hour, we both found the Church's strictures so stifling that we opted for a small United Church wedding.

We rented an apartment so new and clean it still smelled of fresh plaster. Ruth, with a flair for decor, painted it dramatic green and white. With hindsight we realized that dark green walls in a below-ground apartment facing north are slightly suicidal. Otherwise our basement was perfectly acceptable; even Pierre and Janet Berton had inhabited one early in their married life.

For the honeymoon we drove out West and back in two weeks—a kind of Iron Man-and-Woman Marathon typical of my tendency to bite off too much. We took a partly American route because the Trans-Canada highway wasn't completed. At one point, back in Canada, the road literally disappeared and we entered a Kafkaesque night scene of gouged earth, lumbering earth movers and shadowy workmen (workers actually worked at night in that prehistoric era). At a checkpoint in Saskatchewan we were pulled to the side of the road and sprayed for hoof-and-mouth disease, which was epidemic that year.

By the time we reached my parents' Shamrock home, our nerves were twanging like my ten-dollar ukulele. Everyone tried their best, but it was tense. Ruth, city-raised in a modest but immaculate household, found my family's casual country ways (and lack of indoor plumbing) trying. Her unease, in turn, came through as imperiousness. As the first ash blonde in Shamrock's history, she also attracted uncommon attention whenever we passed the local pool hall.

We drove on to Banff for a respite. It was July. We had no reservations so had to bunk in a private house. On the way back, unable to find lodging in Noplace, Montana, we slept one night in the car. The shock absorbers on the weary Studebaker clapped out in Noplace, North Dakota, draining most of my remaining cash (credit cards weren't invented). No wonder that for the last three hundred miles Ruth and I weren't speaking.

But we were full of love, hope and good intentions. I bought a newer used Studebaker and we soldiered on into married life.

By the early 1950s every magazine writer or would-be writer in Canada knew something magical was happening at *Maclean's*. It had emerged from a fusty prewar style to become this country's first truly national magazine. Editor W. Arthur Irwin, after shepherding it through the war years, astutely chose his successor: Ralph Allen, thirty-six, a brilliant cranky redheaded ex-sportswriter, ex–war correspondent. Respected by all, idolized by many, understood by few, Allen was the acknowledged genius behind this journalistic renaissance.

When he became editor in 1950, Ralph had already written one novel and was part of an erudite panel on a CBC radio intellectual quiz show. He was also a fervent nationalist when most of us were still groping in our minds for what it meant to be Canadian. He breathed his vision, his idealism, his love of country into *Maclean's*—not in the blatant, self-conscious spend-a-million-buy-a-patriot manner of modern federal bureaucracies, but with tough editorials and by revealing Canada in its infinite variety through fresh, vital magazine writing.

Allen inherited from Irwin some of the country's best writers and editors: Pierre Berton, John Clare, Blair Fraser, Leslie Hannon, Gerald Anglin. Fiction editor W. O. Mitchell was soaring to fame from his 1947 best-seller, *Who Has Seen the Wind.* Others came when they saw what Allen was building: Fred Bodsworth, Sidney Katz, David MacDonald, McKenzie Porter, Ian Sclanders, Scott Young—a Who's Who of Canadian journalism.

All the editors wrote articles on occasion, and wrote well, which had a salutary effect on contributors. It is difficult to lip off at an editor who has proven he/she can do it better than you. Staffer Les Hannon, an acerbic, darkly handsome New Zealander, once wrote so passionate and evocative a piece on singer Lena Horne that after forty years I still recall it as a model of the magazine profile.

As well, the men all seemed impossibly big and macho. Did Ralph Allen order them to size from some exclusive Testosterone Catalogue? Their centrepiece was Berton, six-foot-four and rising, towering over us other mortals with a voice like cannon fire, confident, unbelievably prolific. Pierre said he could write a full-length article in one day. I never doubted it. In 1951 he went to the Korean war and produced at least five vivid stories and an editorial, plus his own striking black-and-white photos (one of which became a cover) and a page of his own pen sketches. Was there anything the man couldn't do?

Clare, a dark pipe-smoking bear of a man, could pin you to the floor with his unswerving stare. Underneath that impassive exterior, he was a celebrated wit. Everybody quoted Clare-isms.

Once Clyde Gilmour, prowling the *Maclean's* halls, asked Clare, "Which way to the john?" John gave him the look and said through his pipe, "Around here we call it the clyde."

Big associate editor Herb Manning (later of *Mayfair*), with pale blue Icelandic eyes, was cut from the same mould. Big Eric Hutton, the definitive rewrite man, could turn a snivelling writer's feeblest prose into poetry. Big Jerry Anglin (later seconded to *Chatelaine*) with rugged good looks and a voice that carried for miles was, it goes without saying, a fine writer and editor. Tall, slightly stooped McKenzie Porter, latterly of Fleet Street, was a bon vivant, raconteur and–what else?–prolific writer. He'd also won the Military Cross and wore suede shoes and tattersall shirts.

Articles editor Ian Sclanders was gentle of heart and small of stature but could write and toss back rum with any of the big guys. And let us never forget the importance, for most men of that generation, of downing booze in Hemingwayesque fashion. It was a point of honour and a rite of passage. (It took me years to grasp the folly of it. When I finally cut back to one glass of wine per day, my liver gave me a standing ovation.) There were unwritten rules for 1950s' drunks: raucousness, raunchiness and boorishness were acceptable, indeed admired, but real men neither fell down nor upchucked–at least not until they got home to their long-suffering spouses.

Ralph Allen was neither as tall nor as burly as some of his troops, but he could write and drink head-to-head and toe-to-toe with any of them. With his reddish freckled face, thick pursed lips and hard appraising eyes behind unflattering spectacles, Allen was a dominating presence, clearly the leader of his unruly talented band. He was much less comfortable around women. They, in turn, carefully avoided displays of emotion in his presence. "I always went to cry in Pierre's office," one told me years later. "Never in Ralph's."

There were fewer women on staff–this *was* the fifties–but those who broke through the Macho Curtain were exceptional. Eva Lis Wuorio, a gusty, fair-haired Finn, wrote about social issues. Dorothy Sangster (married to Katz) was a solid freelance contributor. Barbara Moon, young, brainy and elegant, had moved from the steno pool to Research but was too good a writer to languish there long. Janice Tyrwhitt, fresh out of University of Toronto, excruciatingly shy and self-effacing, tiptoed into this den of raucous chauvinism as secretary. (Eventually she won the fiction editor's job when Bill Mitchell left and discovered five unacknowledged manuscripts stuffed down behind the ancient radiators; manuscripts so purely awful that W. O. hid them, hoping they'd go away.)

And there was June Callwood, with the impossibly wholesome good looks of a Hollywood girl-next-door, who could write better than most of the men. Potential predators quickly discovered she was happily married to the lean dashing Trent Frayne, who was also a *Maclean's* writer, for godsake. For a snotty-nosed youth fresh out of journalism school, it was all rather daunting.

I finally met Ralph one suffocating Toronto summer day, after turning in a freelance article about a department store detective who caught shoplifters. The detective had insisted on a pseudonym, a practice that *Maclean's* and most other good magazines deplored (it lends a fictional tinge to a piece). I asked John Clare what to do. After some rumbling, he said to go ahead.

Now Allen had caught up with this perfidy and wanted my head on a platter. He was shirt-sleeved, red-faced and snappish in the heat oozing through his open window. There was no air conditioning; Maclean Hunter had probably not heard of it, else it would have instantly launched a trade magazine called *Conditioner & Vent*. Allen looked up from my offending article through his ugly spectacles and curtly asked why I'd used a fictitious name.

"He wouldn't talk otherwise. And Clare said it's okay."

It wasn't the answer Allen expected; he'd assumed I had knuckled under on my own. Nor was he willing to take my word. He called in Clare. John, imperturbably sucking his pipe, fixed Ralph with a stare that would burn holes in sidewalks. It was a good story, he said; too bad about the phoney name, but better that than no story.

Ralph grunted and dismissed us. He had called me upstairs strictly for this exercise in power. The story ran, but the lesson was etched in my soul. Whether or not *Maclean's* ever used a pseudonym again, I never did.

I feared Allen much more than I liked him but desperately wanted to be on his magazine. One of his ways of bringing Canada to his readers was with staff editors posted far from self-centred Toronto, living in and reporting intimately on their regions. Nova Scotian ex-newsman David MacDonald, for instance, was admirably suited to his Maritimes post. The urbane Barbara Moon went to the prairies.

In spring 1953, word came down the grapevine that Moon was returning east. Rumour had it she was fed up with viewing dusty little prairie towns "through fly-specked windows." I'd grown up with those windows. I wanted that job.

I phoned Allen immediately. He hired me over one sit-down in his office. I would be based in Calgary at four thousand a year and must leave as soon as possible. Our first child was imminent and it would have been nice to delay so major a move. But I dared not blow this big chance, a job most writers of my age would have killed for, and Ruth agreed.

So, two weeks after baby Lesley Anne was born, I headed for Alberta alone to set up a home for our little family. Each dawn I was on the ribbon of highway in the bullet-nosed Studebaker, pounding through Michigan, Illinois, Minnesota, Wisconsin, North Dakota and the great aching emptiness of Montana. From the radio and every road-stop juke box, Patti Page asked, "How Much Is That Doggie in the Window?" and Hank Williams wailed "Your Cheatin' Heart" and Kay Starr sang "Wheel of Fortune." Was the wheel about to spin for me?

Three days and 2,200 miles later, I reached Calgary, cross-eyed with fatigue. It felt good to be back amid all that space, sky and pure prairie air. The future seemed scary but limitless. I had a beautiful wife and daughter, and I was western editor of *Maclean's*. I had grasped the Holy Grail.

3

WHO HE?

For a few golden weeks in that first *Maclean's* autumn, life was like a Disney movie: nothing but happy endings. My first story, a profile of Medicine Hat, rolled out of the bouncing old Remington portable in three weeks.

The people of The Hat had been forthcoming and friendly. By now my basic training under Jim Lamb–shored up by three years of newspaper, magazine and freelance work–was paying dividends. I'd discovered that every good interviewer is a bit of a chameleon, adapting him or herself to each new subject or situation. There's nothing devious about this if you are honestly curious. In Medicine Hat it wasn't hard to become enthused over Mayor Harry Veiner (who liked to have footraces with other mayors and once beat a horse in a twenty-five-yard dash); or the woman who captured live rattlesnakes for circus sideshows, or the pioneer ranchmen in the Cypress Club, who loved me because I loved their tall tales.

Interviewing was not easy for me but, like most shy "performers," I hid behind a pose of assurance and confidence. (That front worked with strangers but fell apart under the blinding glare of the *Maclean's* egos.) The Medicine Hat story went through Murderers' Row in Toronto with barely a Who He. Obviously, regional editing was going to be a piece of cake.

Calgary was still a cowtown–friendly, low-slung against a bowl of sky, fringe of mountains to the west, steaks and French fries everywhere, genuine ranchmen on the streets rubbing elbows with poseurs in clean glossy boots and unstained ten-gallon hats. Calgary was also nouveau riche with its six-year-old oil boom and more expensive than I expected. I found a basement apartment, adequate until Ruth and I could search for another together, then drove through the Rockies to visit my parents for the first time in two years.

They had just moved to British Columbia, every dry-belt person's dream. Their little town, Haney, was green, wet and fragrant with burning sawdust. My tough adaptable mother had instantly planted a vast garden, joined a church and made friends. My father—once the extrovert—was now lonely, adrift without purpose in the new community, visibly aging at seventy-two and touchingly glad to see me.

Then it was late August and Ruth stepped down in Calgary from a Trans-Canada flight, cool and chic in a powder blue suit, carrying the blanket-clad morsel that was Lesley Anne. We found a pleasant two-bedroom, main-floor apartment in a two-storey building of dazzling white stucco on Calgary's western edge, a couple of blocks from the Bow River.

Then the Disney movie ended.

Lesley had acute colic and cried much of every night for three months. We took turns getting up to rock and soothe her; none of us slept much. The Studebaker froze solid on the first subzero night. Ruth's father died in Toronto and we could not afford to send her back for his funeral. We were so perilously low on money that when the Studebaker's speedometer went dead I drove ten months without one.

Finally I asked Ralph Allen for a raise. Testily, he granted a fifty-dollar monthly office allowance, which we had to use for household expenses. My office was a makeshift desk in the bedroom. I never escaped the daily small crises of home; I was always in my family's hair.

Nonfiction writers need uncluttered time as much as novelists and poets; peace of mind to go inside ourselves for the graceful phrase and original thought. Now, after forty-odd years, I can shut out most external distractions. Then, every problem preyed upon me: sick baby, lonely wife, shortage of money.

And fear of failure—because suddenly the job was going wrong. Story ideas dried up. Stories bounced back for rewrites.

Everything was done by slow mail. I posted articles to Toronto and held my breath, ten days, three weeks for reaction-by-mail. If an 9x12 brown envelope came back, as it nearly always did, my heart sank. It meant "rewrite." Articles editor Ian Sclanders, kindly middleman, did his best in covering letters to tone down the snarky Who He's from Berton and Allen, but there was no denying those jeering black comments in the margins. My fragile confidence fell apart.

Sclanders scratched up head-office chit-chat to give me a sense of belonging. Everyone at *Maclean's* was taking French classes, he said (something to do with launching a French-language edition). Bodsworth had just published his first book, the soon-to-be classic *Last of the Curlews*. Book-of-the-Month Club had taken it; it seemed that Fred was headed for fame and fortune. Eric Hutton, looking out his side window onto Tator's junkyard, had invented a mythical family for Tator: Dick Tator, the son who went to a Caribbean Island and made good; Gess Tator, the daughter who was always pregnant; Imi, the Tator who could never make up her own mind.

Sclanders's well-intentioned bulletins merely compounded my isolation. I was the little match girl, nose pressed against a very thick windowpane–2,200 miles of prairie and Canadian Shield. I visualized *Maclean's* editors Who He–ing my copy to ribbons before lunch, then rollicking out for bowls of spaghetti and gallons of Chianti at Old Angelo's, then enjoying a little illicit sex in some downtown hotel room, then winding up the day partying in each other's homes, talking gruff editor-talk and drinking rye whisky.

Only once in five years did they invite me back to head office. I do not remember receiving one phone call from *Maclean's*, although there must have been one or two. It was bitterly lonely.

Yet it was my fault too. I should have demanded rejuvenating trips back east. I should have played *Maclean's* correspondent, getting my name in the Calgary papers, entertaining, making contacts. Maclean Hunter was notoriously tight-fisted but if I had taken people to lunch, Allen would probably have okayed the expense. Instead, cursed with Depression and wartime mentality, I was afraid to rock the boat.

So I enjoyed none of the *Maclean's* cachet. I was running hard just to survive. I travelled constantly by car or on railway press passes: Saskatoon, Edmonton, Jasper, Regina, Brandon, Pincher Creek, the Northwest Territories; to an oil rig in the northern Alberta wilderness over frozen rutted trails that snapped car springs like twigs; to a Cree reservation at Hobbema, a radio station in Yellowknife, the sugar beet fields of Lethbridge. Once, mired in mud while driving deep into the Alberta foothills to interview a professional cougar hunter, I was pushed out by a carload of Boy Scouts (putting the lie to the adage, You can never find a Boy Scout when you need one).

I ate in Chinese restaurants all named Paris Cafe or Elite Cafe or Gem Cafe. The proprietors gave the customers what they wanted and deserved: endless vistas of pork chops, sausage-and-mashed, scorched steak and black-fried eggs. And while the customers got acid indigestion, the chefs gorged themselves in the kitchen on delectable moo goo gai pan and subgum chicken chow mein. Or such was my fantasy.

I stayed in country hotels where wind-burned codgers hovered over spittoons in the lobby and a coiled rope lay beside the bedroom window for a fire escape. Once, arriving late at night to a deserted hotel desk in the Okanagan Valley, I helped myself to a room key from the hook—as a printed message invited—and paid up in the morning.

Back home I was writing, writing, writing—or trying, trying, trying. Writing is never easy. For me, it became a fanged monster. I heard that Sid Katz typed, clipped and pasted up his notes in sequence to help him organize the muddle. I did the same, on long strips of newspaper. It sorted out my research but did nothing for my creativity.

Grappling with successive stories on the city of Lethbridge and the Cypress Hills, I rose at 3:00 A.M. to sit over them at the yellow Formica kitchen table, absorbing the latest punishing critique, trying to get it right. Some days I drove the Studebaker to a quiet place beside the Bow River and scribbled leads, over and over, until the footwell beside me was full of crumpled balls of yellow copy paper.

It was my only serious case of writer's block. I've always believed there is a very fine line between the dreaded block and simple sloth. Once the late Isaac Asimov, who had already written

125 books without working up a sweat, heaped scorn on the alleged Block.

"It's the kind of thing that gets encouragement when you give it a name," Asimov told *New York* magazine. "Calling someone a blocked writer is nicer than saying he'd rather drink than produce."

He offered a simple solution: "Sit down and start writing." Exactly. That's how I fought through my Bow River Block, rewriting four, five, six times until it came out right.

Finally that first awful winter turned to spring. Lesley outgrew her colic and became a pink, cheery small person, gurgling her delight to the world at large. Ruth and I found friends: a bridge-playing trucker and his wife next door, and Ed and Grace Brook, a congenial couple with a young family whom I'd met during an assignment.

I had a few newspaper friends or acquaintances–Norman Ibsen of the *Albertan* from UWO Journalism '51; columnist Ken Liddell and reporter Bruce Phillips of the *Herald*. (Phillips, the last I heard, was making $140,000 a year as Canada's privacy commissioner, proving that there is life after journalism.) But we didn't socialize with them. Ruth was ill at ease with newspaper types, partly because she felt (correctly, often) that they patronized nonmembers of their inbred club.

Missionaries passed through from the East: Norval Bonisteel, *Maclean's* gentle production manager, for his first glimpse of the Rockies; Doris McCubbin (later Anderson) on assignment for *Chatelaine;* photographer Paul Rockett, who demonstrated the art of doing a major magazine shoot in a single day with time left over for partying at night. John Clare attended a Banff meeting of the Canadian Authors' Association with a clever ginger-haired young publisher named Jack McClelland. From all of these travellers came the scraps of media gossip and trivia that are the meat and drink of a writer's life.

Peter Varley, art director of *Canadian Homes & Gardens,* stopped in for an evening. I counted this a compliment because Peter was a sensitive, solitary fellow (made more so, I felt, by the long heavy shadow of his famous Group of Seven father, Fred Varley). As we sat in my kitchen sipping a little whisky and catching up on Jean McKinley, Peter remarked, "I hate saying good-bye."

"Me too. So what do you do?"

"I say, 'See you tomorrow.' "

It struck me as a deft solution for an age-old problem. We pondered it over some more whisky. Then Peter got up and said, "See you tomorrow." I didn't see him again for twenty years.

A *Maclean's* specialty, through the regional editing system, was its stories of unsung Canadians doing extraordinary things. It gave readers a new slant on their country and a modicum of national pride.

I loved those assignments. In later years I interviewed assorted "celebrities": Honest Ed Mirvish, author Morley Callaghan, Father Athol Murray (the quixotic genius behind Saskatchewan's Notre Dame college), singer Tommy Hunter, Ed Sullivan ("Hew's everything up there in Canada?" Ed asked me in the strange contorted way he pronounced "really big shew") and Joey Smallwood (who began each lengthy anecdote with "Weee-ll!" savouring the word, unrolling it like a welcoming red carpet). But I remember with equal fondness lesser-known subjects from those early *Maclean's* years, extraordinary people quietly making their mark without fanfare.

People such as Jonas Applegarth of the Cree community of Hobbema, Alberta. For a few glittering months in 1953–54 Jonas was a bit player in Hollywood (playing, predictably, a Hollywood Indian for which he had to unlearn his good command of English); mingling with the likes of Aldo Ray, Van Heflin and Alan Ladd; even signing autographs. Yet when I bade him good-bye Jonas said, "Before you go would you buy me a case of beer?" I did, keeping an eye peeled for the local Mounties and reflecting on the irony of it all. Because in 1954 Jonas Applegarth, who for a while earned four times as much per week as *Maclean's* magazine was paying me, was not allowed to buy a bottle in a liquor store.

People like missionaries Jim and Mary Orr, who in 1955 drove themselves and seven children twelve thousand miles through jungle, desert and the Andes from Brazil to Alberta in a Land Rover. People like Irish-born Gretta Graffin, a Manitoba teacher who in the mid-fifties made a six-month, three-thousand-mile pilgrimage through Europe, living in poverty—begging for clothing, shelter, bread and water—as a form of penance.

And people like Dr. Mary Percy Jackson of Keg River.

Travelling 125 miles of gravelled Mackenzie Highway north from Peace River, Alberta, was no big deal in the summer of 1954. It was the last nine miles of dirt road into Keg River Post, and the next mile and a half to Frank and Mary Jackson's farm that were, as the locals put it, the "beater." It was pouring rain and the rental had no all-weather tires. I slithered into the Post just as the rain became a cloudburst.

Keg River actually *had* been a trading post generations before. Now it was a huddle of log and white-frame buildings—Hudson's Bay store, government telegraph and weather office, public school, Catholic church, a few houses. I sloshed into The Bay. A handful of good old boys taking shelter from the elements stilled their gossip and stared. If I'd had antennae sprouting from my forehead and a flying saucer parked outside, they couldn't have been more thrilled.

I clicked into my stubble-jumper mode: "I'm tryin' to get to the Jackson place." ("Place"—never "home" or "house.") The boys pricked up their ears. Mary Percy Jackson, alias Mrs. Frank Jackson, had been their doctor and angel of mercy for twenty-five years. She was a legend for a hundred miles around.

"They expectin' you?"

"Yeah."

"You the writer?"

I hadn't fooled them. I should have known. There were no phones up here. I'd arranged the interview by mail and telegram, and one of the boys was the telegrapher. There was a pregnant pause while they sucked on hand-twisted cigarettes.

"You'll never make it in that car today," one said, spitting delicately. "Or tomorrow."

"Guess I could walk. It's, what, mile and a half?"

The boys ruminated on that.

"Helluva walk, day like this. 'Course . . . ," sidelong glances under the bills of their caps, " . . . you could take the tractor."

"Tractor?"

"Yeah." The boys examined me carefully. "You know how to drive a tractor?"

"Yeah."

The boys studied me with delight. *Damn! This was gonna be fun. City boy gonna try to drive a John Deere!*

"Soon as she clears a bit, we'll fix you up," they said happily. As soon as she cleared, they did. They loaned me a suit of coveralls and put me and my suitcase on the monster, which, inexplicably, was waiting outside The Bay.

"How'll I get this thing back to you?"

"Frank Jackson'll get 'er back. *If* you get there. . . ."

What the boys didn't know was that—although my father could never afford a tractor for his farm and, anyway, considered it an instrument of the devil—I had driven one during a university vacation for our neighbour, Palmer Munns. Tractor driving did not require a towering IQ; just the ability to steer hard and distinguish between clutch and brake. I had tilled Palmer's field without taking down any of his fences, an achievement that amazed and gratified us both.

I lumbered out of the Post in a shower of mud; the monster had no fenders. The fact that I didn't turn 'er over or stray into a field only slightly dimmed the boys' pleasure. I was still the most fun they'd had all week.

By the time I reached the Jacksons, I was a mud-man: hat, face, coveralls, shoes, suitcase. It seemed like a hell of a way to make a living, but Ralph's and Pierre's watchful eyes were on my back. At the side door a tall robust woman with greying hair and a fresh pink English complexion greeted the mud-caked apparition with aplomb.

"Why it's Mister Collins," she said, in the same matter-of-fact tone that, I suppose, Stanley used on Dr. Livingstone.

Frank Jackson was a Master Farmer, a coveted title awarded by the province for proficiency. He'd built their three-bedroom farmhouse himself and installed hot-air heating, electric lights, plumbing and a green-tiled bathroom. Scrubbed, changed and dry, I stayed with the Jacksons two days and gathered the story of a remarkable woman.

Mary Percy had graduated from the University of Birmingham in 1927 with the scholarship given for the best all-round student of her year. Everyone, including her professors, assumed she would soar to a glittering career in her specialty, obstetrics.

Instead, she read an advertisement from Alberta for "English, well-qualified woman doctors, physically strong and capable of taking complete charge of any type of emergency with no hospital. The ability to ride a horse would be an advantage."

Mary Percy decided to take the job for a year. She travelled by ocean steamer, train, river barge and the last eighteen miles by wagon to her first northern practice. She lived in a 14x20-foot shack, and drank water from a river in which a woman upstream washed shirts and a bridge-building gang took baths. She often forded rivers and occasionally fell in. And she was life itself to the few hundred trappers, farmers and natives for miles around.

The nearest hospital was more than a hundred miles away. Once she took a patient there by sleigh in subzero weather. Another time she escorted an appendicitis patient to hospital by automobile; twenty hours through deep mud. During one eight-day period she spent only one and a half nights in bed, rode 180 miles on horseback and made the killing trip to hospital with a patient on a sleigh hauled by caterpillar tractor.

In 1931 she married Frank Jackson, who shared her toughness and love of the pioneer life. But she kept on doctoring, from a neat, well-stocked little clinic in the farmhouse. They had raised three children by his earlier marriage plus two more of their own.

I was developing the interviewer's sixth sense—a mixture of hunch and hope. *What do doctors do when they need a doctor?* I wondered. So I asked one of those seat-of-the-pants questions that sometimes pay off: "What about your own kids? Who took *you* to hospital to have them?"

Dr. Jackson smiled. She hadn't planned to mention it but . . . well, as it happened, her youngest, John, had caught them by surprise, six weeks premature. It was January 15, 1935, minus 60° F outside. So—with Eva Harrington, the telegrapher's wife, following orders—Mary Jackson supervised her own childbirth, gasping out instructions until four-pound John arrived at 2:00 A.M. in a rather delicate breech delivery.

My jubilation must have shown in my idiotic grin. There it was, beckoning me: the "lead" that every writer strives and strains for; the article's beginning that must irresistibly lure the readers on. The story ran in a special northern issue of *Maclean's*. Ralph and Pierre must have liked it because they didn't Who He me once.

Thirty-five years later I was writing an article on the Order of Canada for Imperial Oil *Review*. Dr. Mary Percy Jackson, by then eighty-five and more or less retired, was receiving the award. I phoned her in Keg River.

"You're the one who started all this!" she said, and over the faint connection to Toronto I couldn't tell if she was pleased or miffed. For she was as modest as ever. "I don't think I'm in the same class as the rest of the recipients," she said.

As soon as we hung up I re-read the list: politicians, CanLit types, media celebrities. She was right; she was not in the same class as the rest. Two-thirds of them weren't qualified to carry Dr. Mary Jackson's satchel.

Earlier that year I called on Emil Strand of Readlyn, Saskatchewan, who had been running his 320-acre farm for twenty-five years with only the help of his sister, Lena, and one hired man. Nothing strange about that–except Emil and Lena were blind.

He rode horses, fixed fences, stooked wheat sheaves, shovelled grain, pitched hay. He walked from house to barn each morning, crawling through a barbed-wire fence en route. About the only thing he wouldn't attempt was running machinery. His longtime friend, Alex Strubeck, did that. Lena cooked and kept house.

It seemed like a natural but, as always, the mishmash of fact had somehow to be stitched into a logical whole, ending with a smile, or tear, or tug of the heart, a final truth that might leave my readers in quiet contemplation or cause them to murmur inwardly, *Yes, of course, that's what it was all about.*

I talked to Emil's friends and neighbours. I followed him around his farm for a day as he showed off his prowess. As always I was watching, listening, fending around in my head for the lead and the ending or "tailpiece." I'd seen my blind farmer galloping full tilt, bareback, that morning; it seemed a suitable beginning.

Just before dark we went indoors. The drab little farmhouse was dim. Nobody bothered to light a lamp. Alex, a man of virtually no words, sat silently to one side. Shy Lena laboured in the kitchen. Emil had one more feat to show.

"Maybe you'd like me to read for you?" he said hopefully.

He meticulously scrubbed his hands, brought out a thick green-bound Braille edition of the Bible and found his way to

Revelation 22, verse 5. Then the blind farmer began to read aloud softly in the darkening room, his fingers flickering over the symbols, a contented half-smile on his face:

> *. . . and they need no candle, neither light of the sun;*
> *for the Lord God giveth them light. . . .*

That night I went away down the rutted country road with my story, reciting the writer's prayer: *Thank you, Lord, for giving me the tailpiece.* Did Emil choose that passage by accident or design? I never knew, nor wanted to know. Some gifts must not be questioned.

To reach Readlyn I had taken a train to Assiniboia. There, lugging suitcase from station to hotel across a dirt street baked hard by sun then slickened by showers, my feet flew out from under me. My pratfall gladdened the locals watching behind rain-streaked windows, but ruined my only decent pair of pants.

I made do with a wrinkled spare until I got back to Regina and a dry cleaner. There, my pal Glen Hancock, ex–London *Free Press,* was ensconced in the Hotel Saskatchewan, Regina's finest in the spring of '54. I was booked into some cheap joint near the railway tracks. Glen had recently joined Imperial Oil's public relations department and was travelling across the country by Trans-Canada Airlines on an orientation tour.

Like all journalists of our time, he and I had been taught that PR men were disciples of Satan, seducing honest newsmen with their sinful food, diabolical drink and fraudulent press releases. Still, Glen's precious soul seemed intact and he certainly wasn't wearing pants with accordion pleats in the knees.

As he treated me to a T-bone steak in the dining room, we recalled our *Free Press* days—the two-dollar hotels, the twenty-five-cent dinners. I was now rich in prestige but still at the poverty level. After dinner Glen lit a thick cigar and ordered liqueurs, courtesy of Big Oil.

"Bob, get out of that rat race," he beamed. "This is the place to be!" Imperial Oil surely looked tempting as I took the night train back to Calgary and braced myself for another round of Who He's. But how dared I lust in my heart for PR affluence when I could be falling down in the mud doing honest writing?

Furthermore I was finally on a roll. Stories poured out of my arthritic portable. Who He's dwindled. *Maclean's,* in a show of faith, unclenched its wallet and sent me a Remington manual typewriter, as black, heavy and noisy as a railway locomotive, and a Rolleicord camera. Would I become a two-way man like Pierre, sending dramatic stories and photos from the western front?

Allen awarded me the first of two raises over nearly five years with a handwritten note: "Don't spend all this on expensive whisky. The cheap stuff tastes just as good and goes twice as far." I was as thrilled by the letter as the money. Ralph, joking a guys' joke with me!

In our eternal search for perfect lodgings we had moved into our fourth Calgary home, a fine upper duplex with a view of the Rockies if you leaned hard against a window and craned your neck. I had the luxury of a separate room for an office. Our landlords invited us downstairs to watch the 1954 Grey Cup game when Jackie Parker and the Eskimos ran amok over the Alouettes. We cheered lustily. We were westerners. Our second baby, on the way, would be Alberta-born.

Lesley Anne now knew her parents by name, that point at which all fathers become smitten. "What a beautiful little girl," strangers said as she beamed up at them with angelic blue eyes. She was a blonde gentle child, alternating between her own dreamy private world and flurries of domesticity. A family of tiny ceramic skunks lived atop our bookcase, the baby no bigger than your pinky fingernail. One day Lesley, bustling over toy dishes and toy stove, was preparing make-believe dinner for her family of dolls.

"What's cooking?" I asked rhetorically. She opened her oven door and proudly displayed in lieu of pot roast *la specialité du jour,* the littlest skunk.

On sunny days we walked on a grassy hill across the street: I, expounding on nature and other wonders of the world; she, in her trademark pink overalls, gravely absorbing my wisdom while picking and sniffing dandelions. She thought I was the greatest man on earth and, with her, I was.

I was also becoming a pretty good magazine writer, largely thanks to Berton. To this day I regard Pierre as my mentor and he, although not given to overt sentiment, sometimes remarks with a glimmer of pleasure that he "discovered" me at Western. Pierre was never easy on me or anyone else. He was a master of the Who He. But of all the *Maclean's* editors he best had the knack of getting instantly to the heart of a writing problem and explaining clearly and succinctly how to fix it. There were other ways to do it, but Pierre's was a good one to follow if you expected to get ahead at *Maclean's*.

You could argue with Berton and he enjoyed it but, of course, expected to win. He was born in the Yukon. In the 1950s he wrote two definitive books about the Canadian North. A writer risked his life venturing into Pierre's Northwest territory. Once he stomped all over a story I wrote about the town of Yellowknife because it lacked frontier colour. I argued back by mail that I'd just been there, Yellowknife wasn't frontier any more and *that* was the story. I lost. *Maclean's* killed it.

Pierre had the extraordinary ability to always seem right. He never said, "I think" or "Maybe." He made pronouncements in his basso-profundo voice like Moses to the Chosen People. Once in a Winnipeg restaurant with Ruth, writer Marjorie Earl and me, he announced, "This is the best buffalo steak in Canada." It never occurred to us to say, "Pierre, you're full of shit. It's tough old Red River cow"–partly because we were eating spaghetti, partly because I wouldn't have known buffalo if it stampeded over me, but mostly because he was Pierre. Pierre knew about the North and buffalo and, well, everything.

In later years I viewed my mentor with clearer eyes. Once *Reader's Digest* considered picking up a piece Berton had written for *Weekend* magazine about railways. In it he cried, "Who can reckon the number of babies conceived [by couples awakened at night by a railway engine whistle]?" This seemed fulsome, I wrote to *Digest* editor Charles Magill: "Setting aside the fact that the railways operated at night only on main lines (thus sparing a sizeable segment of the population from the 'mournful cry of the steam whistle'), who can also reckon the number of babies conceived as the result of (a) tomcat fights on the back fence, (b) raccoons over-tipping garbage pails, (c) warring neighbours, (d) motorcycle backfires, (e) fire truck sirens and (g) cramps in the left foot?"

If I live to be 100 I might even get the best of Pierre (who would then be 104 and turning a little frail). One morning in 1986 we met accidentally on the same radio show in Victoria, to be interviewed about our latest books. The host had the bright idea of letting Berton, celebrated radio and TV personality, interview his protégé. Pierre took a quick glance at the introduction to *The Long and The Short and The Tall,* and we were off.

After a few pleasantries he thundered, "Now then, Bob, what's all this about you 'researching' this memoir? I've just written a memoir and I took it all from memory."

Thinking fast on my feet is not my long suit, but this time the words came.

"But, Pierre," I said sweetly, "*you* taught me to be a much better researcher than that!"

Amusement, maybe even approval, flickered through the sharp Berton eyes. The interview ended smoothly. Afterward Pierre, who is nearly always in a hurry to be someplace else, led the way to a leisurely breakfast in the Empress Hotel. We had a great visit over kippers and toast and parted on a wave of goodwill.

During the *Maclean's* period Berton regarded me, I think, more as promising writer than friend. Over the years as he mellowed and I gained confidence, I sensed more warmth. We are part of a dwindling company that has fought the magazine wars long and well. A while ago, he, David MacDonald and I drove north to visit the then-ailing John Clare, Pierre at the wheel attacking the road with his usual vigour, the three of us talking about writing and writers like old cronies. More recently when I received a prize at an awards' ceremony, emcee Berton introduced me as his "old friend."

We will never be bosom buddies. I have rarely visited his splendid home near Kleinburg, Ontario, which he built, expanded and relandscaped with characteristic energy and flair. (Pierre, God and the citizens of Saskatoon are the only ones I know of who have created their own hills.) But I regard him with affection and owe him much, not the least of which is the thick skin—built up with scar tissue from those *Maclean's* years—without which no writer can survive.

In the spring of 1955 Ralph Allen came to Calgary. *Maclean's* was doing a special issue on the Saskatchewan/Alberta fiftieth jubilee.

Allen, born in Oxbow, Saskatchewan, was working his way through the provinces with artist Franklin Arbuckle to prepare the lead story. I hadn't seen or spoken to him in nearly two years.

Early one morning Ralph's muscular voice came over the phone from the Palliser Hotel. "Come on down." I went, with fixed smile and churning stomach, nervous as a parish priest about to kiss the Holy Father's ring. He was eleven years older than me, but age wasn't my hang-up. It was just that he was *Ralph.*

The happy-go-lucky Arbuckle, known as Archie, promised to be great company. Ralph was friendly in his no-nonsense way; small talk was not part of his being. We sat around his room drinking rye whisky and planning their local itinerary. I would drive Archie to the Drumheller badlands the next day, for background sketching and photography.

We kept at the rye whisky. There was some desultory talk about lunch, which my stomach applauded. Archie sensibly went away to eat. Ralph and I did not. I wasn't about to make the first move and lose points.

The rest is hazy. We kept drinking and trying to sustain conversation. I suppose Ralph was trying to get to know me. He asked penetrating questions about Alberta, not all of which I could answer, causing me to nervously refill my glass. Archie came back for a while. Others probably came and went. Sometimes Ralph was on the phone with cronies, for he was known and beloved by newsmen all over the land.

Around mid-afternoon I fled to the bathroom, lost everything I'd consumed in the previous forty-eight hours and collapsed. From time to time Ralph called out crankily, "You all right?" His tone of voice said he didn't really care. *What kind of a writer couldn't hold his liquor, for christsake?* I was too sick to move. Finally he shouted through the closed door, "I'm going out."

Later I emerged, weakly. It was night. I rested for a while on Ralph Allen's counterpane, then went home, where I neither expected nor received sympathy. The day's awful events kept replaying in my head: *I had barfed in Ralph Allen's bathroom!* Nothing, nothing could be more humiliating.

Ralph phoned at eight the next morning, jerking my chain. I was up, pale and ready with black coffee under my belt. Archie and I had a fine day at Drumheller, bringing back many photos and a cactus for his Toronto garden. A day or so later, before they moved on, I invited them to our apartment for drinks.

From the moment they arrived Ralph, although courteous, was fidgety. I poured them hearty ryes and a very light one for myself. Archie exclaimed, "What a beautiful child!" and took a picture of Lesley, dreamy-eyed beside a window, which is still in our family archives. Ralph downed his drink and said they'd better be going. "What's the hurry?" said Archie, who was enjoying himself. Ralph kept nagging and led the way out with polite good-byes and obvious relief.

Ruth and I were left forlornly wondering what we'd done wrong. True, we were not adept conversationalists. True, Ruth was not a member of the club. And I, alas, was a man—hardly deserving of the name—who couldn't hold his whisky. I suppose those were reasons enough.

Ralph's lead story in the jubilee issue was a masterpiece, a prose poem. I wrote two articles for the same issue—one a funny piece on gophers. Ralph and Pierre, unlike Queen Victoria, were amused. As a little treat they assigned me to a fishing trip in northern Saskatchewan, hosted by the provincial government. Allen, a fisherman of note, had been there himself with W. O. Mitchell and other cronies.

I was appalled. I had never fished. I had no interest in learning. "Have a wonderful time," wrote Ian Sclanders. "Ralph says the fishing is phenomenal."

Great! That was all I needed. If I didn't come back with fifty dead trout Ralph would know it wasn't the fishes' fault. Yet if I admitted this latest defect so soon after throwing up in his toilet, I might as well apply for a posting to *Chatelaine*.

In desperation I snivelled, "I'm not a fisherman," to Sclanders by return mail. Ian thought I was joking.

There was one more chance. Harvey Dryden, the Saskatchewan government tourism man, was an ex-sportswriter friend from *Leader-Post* days. Maybe he could get me off the hook (as fishermen are wont to say). I splurged on a long-distance phone call.

"I'm no fisherman, Harv. I might spoil your junket," I pleaded. Harvey chuckled. What a joker, that Collins. Every man fishes. It is one of man's duties and responsibilities, like fornicating and holding your rye whisky. With heavy heart and brand-new rod and reel, I headed north to kill fish.

My companions turned out to be an agreeable lot: a newspaperman and a rich manufacturer both from Detroit, a Montana outdoors writer, freelance photographer Mike Kesterton from Regina who'd worked with me before. And there was Ted Trueblood (truly!), a tall loose-jointed American from Idaho with a soft western drawl. Trueblood was dean among us. He wrote for all the big-name U.S. outdoors magazines. He told us he considered life wasted if he did not hunt or fish at least one day out of three. He and Ralph would have been soul brothers.

Kesterton was no fisherman either, so as soon as we reached the North and the others sprang for boats, Mike and I walked downstream out of sight and practised casting. That's what he said it was, anyway.

You don't learn to fish in an afternoon, but I learned how to tangle line in bushes. There was nothing left to do but wait and pray. We flew from Lac la Ronge to Careen Lake, Cree Lake, Black Lake. We met quaint weather-beaten guides and ate stupendous meals in lodges. Trueblood, the rich guy and the other writers were ecstatic. Northern Saskatchewan was fish Heaven.

I stalled as long as possible but finally had to cast a line. My companions kindly looked the other way. The eager fish sprang to the lures. Later I wrote of Cree Lake, "Here I caught my first fish, an eight- or nine-pound northern which seesawed back and forth under the boat, nearly tangled my line, and gave me a dirty look as I turned it loose." It sounded as though I knew what I was doing.

With that sort of literary tap-dancing, plus a fine collection of big-fish tales and general northern lore, I wrote four thousand entertaining words, which the Saskatchewan government reprinted by the gross. Ted Trueblood sent me bemused congratulations, expressing mild surprise that such a piece (by a piteous nonfisherman, he meant) could work so well.

But that's the way of the generalist writer. We sail through life knowing a little about everything but not much about anything. We take on an unfamiliar subject, gather a fact here, a fact there; become experts of sorts for a couple of months, put it all in a file folder and move on to something new. I never fished again.

4

LAYING A GHOST TO REST

My *Maclean's* assignment to cover the treaty payment at Fort Rae in the Northwest Territories seemed simple enough, in that summer of 1955. I would fly to Yellowknife, board the federal government boat *Peter Pond* for a sixty-mile ride northwest along Great Slave Lake and view a ceremonial remnant of our country's past.

The annual token payment to Canada's treaty Indians–five dollars for every man, woman and child, fifteen for councillors, twenty-five dollars for chiefs as laid down in treaties decades before–had become in most cases a straightforward mercenary affair. But the Dogribs of Rae, nomadic fishermen and hunters who lived much as their ancestors had, rounded off every treaty day with a traditional feast, games and dances. It would be a quaint colourful show. In a day or two I'd be back home, writing about these happy primitive folk. And the sooner the better; our baby was due within a month.

I was gone nearly ten days.

Ever since the CBC discovered Indians, many Canadian whites have wallowed in the national guilt without ever seeing a native person in the flesh. My evolving views of the "problem" come from writing about Indian people and subjects off and on over forty years. There are rights and wrongs on both sides. The incident at Fort Rae was a classic example of the eternal chasm between whites and Indians–a yawning gulf in thinking and understanding.

From the moment the *Peter Pond* pulled into Rae (thirty whites and a floating population of five to six hundred Dogribs), something was obviously wrong. No crowds greeted the money boat. Ivan Kirkby, superintendent of the Yellowknife Indian Agency, soon discovered why. The Dogribs, temporarily affluent from a superb muskrat catch the previous winter, had no immediate need of cash.

Kirkby, a conscientious civil servant, was frustrated by the native reaction to government largesse.

"A man likes to feel he's accomplishing something at his job but that's nearly impossible here," he said wearily. "The more help the Dogribs get, the less they'll do for themselves. They've lost all initiative and thrift." He ticked off the free health coverage, treaty money and family allowance. "We give them free fishing nets and rifle shells. They use a few shells and gamble the rest away. They say the fishing is no good around Rae and they're right. But they won't bother to go fifteen or twenty miles down lake to some of the best whitefish water in the world."

Whether or not they lacked the initiative Kirkby was looking for, they were quick to capitalize on the situation. They had a problem: Chief Jimmy Bruneau and one of his men were in trouble. The young man had shot a beaver without a hunting license. The chief had been nabbed with the pelt. The Dogribs (who would have made fabulous poker players) were about to call the white men's bluff.

At council that evening Chief Bruneau, seventy-three, sat in the front row, a dignified small man in a government-issue navy blue suit with gold braid at collar and cuffs, a coronation medal on his lapel and a black plug hat square amidships. His shrunken face inscrutable, he delivered rapid bursts of Dogrib in a dry reedy voice. Michel Bouvier, tall and grizzled, a dead ringer for the actor Anthony Quinn, boomed out the translation. And an hour or two of hilarious dialogue (which I avidly scribbled verbatim) boiled down to this: the chief and his people wouldn't accept treaty until he was off the hook in the matter of the illicit beaver pelt.

Kirkby was over a barrel. He'd brought three Ottawa medics to test for tapeworm and tuberculosis. If they didn't corral the Dogribs for the treaty payment, they'd never get the medical tests.

Reluctantly, he flew in a magistrate from Yellowknife. The beaver poacher got a two months' suspended sentence; the charge against Chief Bruneau was dropped. Now the Tailbones, the Murphys, the Apples, the Footballs, Elizabeth Chocolate, Pierre and Madeleine Judas, all cheerfully lined up for their money.

Outside on a hilltop young men were already gambling their money at "short stick," a guessing game.

The women set out bannock, rice, caribou and kettles of steaming tea at long tables. Behind-scenes a few men nipped at "24," a mild home brew of raisins and yeast, named for the number of hours they allowed it to mature. Johnny Simpson, known as Johnny-the-Fat, shouted, "*Kolah!*" meaning, approximately, "Let's go." The chief made a little speech in Dogrib.

"The other day I was in a little trouble, but now, thank the good Lord . . . ," with a pious glance at the Oblate priest who was translating for me, " . . . everything is all right. Now we have a good feast, good dance, everything all right, thank the Lord."

The priest smiled and blessed the food. Afterward the old women lit their pipes, the young women divided up leftovers and the men moved to a huge flat rock.

"*Kolah!*" cried Johnny-the-Fat again, shoving his hands deep in his pockets, and began the tea dance, a measured shuffling sidestep. Instantly a dozen men were beside him, shoulder to shoulder, shuffling clockwise and chanting a tuneless "hey heyheyhey, ha hahahey."

Suddenly Father Jean Amorous towered among them in black cassock and beret, gravely shuffling to the rhythm. The dancers chortled with glee. Huskies howled. People nudged into the circle and out again, perspiring, but the dance went on and on—"hey la hey la hey lalala, hey hi hihi hihi ho"—in the eerie perpetual twilight of the northern summer.

I concluded my article with:

> The Dogribs were still dancing and chanting in the rosy dawn when the *Peter Pond* slipped out onto Great Slave Lake at 2:00 A.M. It was a merry aimless dance with no particular meaning or objective, much like the lives of the dancers. The Dogribs were happy. Their stomachs were full. They had money to spend. Within a month they could be penniless again and by

autumn they would be very hungry. But nobody worried about autumn or next month or even tomorrow. Tomorrow would take care of itself.

Well, of course (I say now with the wisdom of hindsight), the dance was meaningful to the Dogribs and of course their lives had meaning, as do all lives. They were people caught in a time warp. They wanted to live as they had always lived. But time does not stand still. The white men were trying to perform their mandate: make the Dogribs into twentieth-century people. Neither was succeeding.

Today, my editor-daughter prods, "Couldn't you have known the dances or their lives meant more by asking more questions? Or was it simply the attitude of the times?"

True, I tell her, I *could* have stayed to dig out more, with a translator, but I'd have missed my boat—and missed her birth. But, also true, most whites in 1955 viewed most Indians as drunks or lay-abouts and placed little stock in Indian culture. *Maclean's* was delighted with my coverage. When the Dogrib piece reached Toronto, Ralph Allen sent me the only telegram of my years under him:

CONGRATULATIONS. TREATY DAYS STORY AN OUTSTANDING JOB OF REPORTING AND WRITING.

It felt like a knighthood.

On July 31 Catherine Mary was born. After a few frightening days of transfusions to counter an Rh blood factor, she was home, a tiny vibrant force soon to fill our lives with delight. That autumn *Maclean's* held a fiftieth anniversary party in Toronto. Outlanders (but not their spouses) were invited. With Allen's telegram still hot in my hand, and nineteen completed articles in two years, I felt I'd earned this one and only invitation to head office.

At Winnipeg, *Tribune* columnist Ann Henry, a *Maclean's* contributor, came aboard the eastbound train. She was a gutsy, sexy woman of the world. As we sat in the club car, watching the Canadian Shield blur by, she regaled me with stories of people she'd interviewed on the entertainment beat. Once, sharing a taxi with Louis Armstrong, the legendary trumpeter invited the comely Henry back to his hotel room. She declined. There was a flash of white teeth in the darkened cab.

"But, baby," cried the gravelly voice of Louis Armstrong, "think of the memories!"

McKenzie Porter, now covering British Columbia, flew in by way of Trans-Canada Airlines. (I, with my CPR press pass, recognized my place in the *Maclean's* pecking order.) We settled into the Royal York Hotel and–although I hadn't met Porter before and he outranked me in age, experience and fluidity of writing–we hit it off famously. That this surprised me was a measure of my tenuous self-esteem. Porter, with his lean florid face and bright mischievous eyes, was a superb raconteur. One afternoon he told, with assorted comic accents, how he and his company routed a bunch of German soldiers in Italy, winning himself the Military Cross (the Monkey Charlie, he called it; his insouciance impressed me profoundly).

At the *Maclean's* formal dinner the Toronto male staffers went militantly nonformal. Porter and I rented tuxes from a well-known local emporium, inspiring John Clare to dub us "The Sid Silver Twins." It felt wonderful to be included in the banter. In a hospitality suite the scintillating Moon, Callwood and Henry were surrounded by admirers (on the train ride home Ann Henry would amuse me with stories of famous writers who'd been hitting on her that night). Davidson Dunton, head of the CBC, almost fell off a bed in hysterical laughter as Ken Porter acted out a story about a man on a camel.

David MacDonald–open and friendly, with a handsome craggy profile–had recently transferred from Nova Scotia to head office. We had both become regional editors as relative newcomers to magazine writing, and knew the problems, pleasures and agonies better than most. We formed an instant bond and have been friends ever since.

The farewell party at Pierre and Janet Berton's Kleinberg home was awash with glittering magazine people of the time: Allen, Clare, Clyde Gilmour, Blair Fraser, Lionel Shapiro, Scott Young (who complimented me on my gopher story). This was the *Maclean's* I'd dreamed about back West. Yet, perversely, I turned down a chance to be part of it. Allen and Berton said it was time for a change. They offered me a transfer to Toronto, their preference, or Winnipeg. I chose the latter. I still felt cowed by the Toronto egos. I loved my western freedom. I'd succeeded in Calgary; why not in Winnipeg?

It was a bad choice.

Socially, Winnipeg was an improvement. On our second try we found the best home of our western years, what would now be called a townhouse on Academy Road. Former *Leader-Post* cronies Bill MacPherson and Al Rogers were on the *Tribune*. Through them I met a host of other superior newsmen in this lively two-newspaper city: Ted Byfield, Peter Desbarats, Garth Hopkins, Peter McLintock, Bob Metcalfe, Jack Wells and *Trib* managing editor Eric Wells, worshipped by his reporters. Ralph Hedlin, a sometime Winnipeg *Free Press* writer, was trying freelance, and often we met in his house or mine to swap experiences, hopes and dreams. The Press Club's famous annual show, "Beer and Skits," was in its twenty-third year and I had a role as a spear carrier.

Ruth discovered cousins she'd never known, Pat and Bud McLaughlin, who became friends for life. Their kids and ours hit it off. Cathy was evolving into a dark-haired imp with a radiant smile and enormous presence. Family snapshots told the story. Cathy at eighteen months, dropping her drawers just for laughs; Cathy in a high chair, face smothered in goop, laughing uproariously and brandishing her spoon; Cathy clowning in a pair of my shoes; the two girls snuggled together in a big chair: Cathy grinning hugely (*Hey world, here I come!*), Lesley, sedate and composed, head cocked, eyes on her sister, proud but frankly amazed.

But again the job went sour. Was I burning out? It was not uncommon to have an occasional story killed at *Maclean's,* but in my first year in Manitoba I lost four out of five, a crushing blow for me and for my sources whose time I'd used and brains I'd picked. I pounded around the West trying to regain my touch. The newest mega-hit, "Little Darlin'" by The Diamonds, was blaring from every radio and juke box. Six years before, the lead singer, Dave Somerville, had been my closest friend at radio night school. Now he was an international star and I was beating my brains out in little prairie towns. Maybe I should have learned to sing soprano.

Musing on some of those lost *Maclean's* stories, I know I could sell them if I went back in a time machine with today's experience. Toseko MacMillan, for example: a Japanese girl who married a soldier from the Korean War and came home with him to the foreign world of Medicine Hat. A poignant story, but my skills at the time couldn't plumb its subtleties.

And Dr. W. J. McNeill of Empress, Alberta. That one didn't get beyond the proposal stage. My masters saw it as a mere vignette because I failed to outline the gentle, moving story that I dimly sensed. Some stories demand attention, like clanging bells. Some, such as Doc McNeill's—a life of quiet achievement and broken dreams—beckon softly like temple chimes. Even if I had sold the idea to *Maclean's,* I hadn't yet mastered enough nuances of writing, or living, to pull it off. I suppose Doc is gone now, but I wish he were alive to read this, a boiled-down version of the article that might have been.

Empress, when I visited McNeill in the fifties, was a town of five hundred in the confluence of the Red Deer and South Saskatchewan rivers, ninety miles north of Medicine Hat. To reach it you crossed the river on a hand-propelled ferry. Dwarfed by towering bluffs, far from the beaten track, Empress seemed at first like a prairie Brigadoon.

I couldn't have been more wrong. It had a twenty-bed hospital, a new community hall and one of the best electrical power plants anywhere, all largely thanks to Doc McNeill—because the doctor was also a qualified electrician. The tipster who put me on to him said, "When you see Doc going out on a call you never know if he's going to tape a sprained ankle or replace a burnt-out coil."

I found him alone in the cluttered basement examining room of his home. A big brusque cigar-smoking man in a red sports shirt, he reluctantly told a little of himself. He had gone to Empress in 1927 with an MD and MSc from two universities, a course in electricity and a summer holiday's experience with an electrical firm. He had planned to stay only four or five years, then take postgraduate studies in medicine. But the community needed him . . .

"The hospital only had six or eight beds," Doc recalled. "The operating room was also a kitchen. There wasn't enough power to operate a stomach X-ray machine. The Depression came and there was no money–but the sick were as numerous as ever."

Finally, tired of sending X-ray patients to the city, he converted the old lighting plant to 110 volts. The district was elated; it'd never had an electrician. Doc was immediately swamped with requests for power. He needed a bigger plant. He found some secondhand equipment in Calgary. Empress farmers and businessmen promised to raise the cash.

That summer of 1932 the farmers were hailed out and the financial backers pulled out. Nobody would have blamed McNeill if he had left to continue his studies. Instead he bought the equipment on time and installed his own power plant.

"From then on I was tied down," he said a little wistfully. "I never did get to do that postgrad work."

Within six months the plant was jammed to capacity. Everybody wanted power. Over the next twenty-two years Doc raised the system from forty-three horsepower to nearly five hundred, and increased the generating capacity to three hundred kilowatts. He wired the entire town. It took him two days every month just reading meters.

The work became overwhelming. In the fifties, after refusing previous offers, Doc sold out to Calgary Power. He didn't leave town, though, because he had a new tie: the community hall. It had begun as a volunteer building effort. Sometimes only Doc, the druggist and a farmer were on the job. They built mostly at night, until maybe 2:00 A.M. It took seven years. Doc helped wire it, of course.

When I visited him he was still dabbling in electricity the way some men play golf. A typical day had him at the hospital in the morning, in his private practice in the afternoon and at night out wiring somebody's house "just to break the monotony."

The basement office grew quiet, and Doc's cigar butt grew cold. He added as an afterthought, "I wanted to go into the army during the second war but they told me to stay with my community." I said, obviously the community had no regrets but what about him–he who had given his heart and life and labour to this little town? Would he do it all over again? Doc McNeill's eyes lit up.

"If I was younger I'd go to the Peace River country," he said. "If I could get the electrical franchise."

By late 1956 I had written three freelance pieces for Imperial Oil *Review,* the company's excellent magazine for internal and external readership, full of well-written general-interest articles. Now a whisper came down the grapevine: Imperial wouldn't raid *Maclean's,* but if I were to apply for a job its door was open. In December I sent a cautious feeler. Public relations manager George Lawrence promptly replied and soon came through Winnipeg with his right-hand man, Adam Marshall, a *Maclean's* alumnus. A month later they made me an offer, but I decided to not yet give up on *Maclean's*. It was still a coveted job, even though I was in a bad patch.

The work troubles were exacerbating our marital differences. My office was organized chaos; my wife was compulsively tidy and clean. My presence behind closed doors sometimes inhibited normal family life ("Quiet, Daddy's working"). Ruth hoped for interesting conversation from me at the end of a day. Often I was too tired or frustrated and, anyway, had been nowhere more interesting than inside my head.

Our senses of humour clashed: my habit of saying, "Eyes Right!" as we drove past the Javex factory was not appreciated. My closeness to my parents—we exchanged letters every week or two—seemed unnatural to her. Ruth was a persistent critic, on the premise that criticism is good for everyone. I was already getting my full quota from 481 University Avenue.

Afterward, she speculated that the *Maclean's* years turned me into an introvert. In fact, they simply aggravated my insecurity. Once during a Berton visit to Winnipeg, I was in his hotel room with Ruth, writer Marjorie Earl and Sid Katz, and found myself totally incapable of conversation. I felt I had nothing worth saying. It was a paralysing evening.

Worst of all, my father was slowly dying. I went to see him three times in 1956 and 1957. He was in and out of Vancouver's Shaughnnessy veterans' hospital, his body and memory failing. On the last visit I found him attached to a mass of tubes. For an instant his eyes opened and flickered with recognition. Three weeks later he died.

There were a couple of sympathy notes from head office, but I had downplayed his lingering illness and its debilitating effect on me. I felt certain Ralph Allen would not approve of a man who let family matters interfere with the job.

As I soon discovered, it didn't matter. My *Maclean's* days were numbered.

Friday, November 22, 1957. I was in Regina doggedly scouting new story ideas. Around noon, sitting on the edge of my bed in the Hotel Saskatchewan, I phoned home to say I was staying one more day.

"There's a letter for you from *Maclean's,*" Ruth said, "marked Private & Confidential."

It sounded ominous.

"Better open it."

She did and at my urging reluctantly read it over the phone. I was fired.

I kept the letter, in the masochistic way war veterans save shrapnel dug out of their legs. "I hope the reading of this letter won't give you as much distress as the writing of it is giving to me," Ralph Allen began. (Was he kidding?) My performance in the past year had been "disappointing." (In fifty-seven months on staff I wrote thirty-nine articles and many lesser items.) He had the highest respect for my ability and character but perhaps "the rather special and sometimes unreasonable demands of the magazine business aren't your dish."

No rush, but he hoped I would leave sometime before April 1; would give me a month's severance and any references I might care to have. He hoped I would continue "to think of *Maclean's* as a place where you have many friends, of whom I hope I'm still one."

Numb inside but superficially cool, I told Ruth, "Don't worry. I'll be home in the morning."

I took the overnight train–it didn't occur to me to stick *Maclean's* with an air fare–and reached Academy Road around breakfast time. My little daughters, oblivious to our crisis (and we kept it that way), swarmed me with glad cries. Ruth was looking distinctly strained but, to her great credit, offered not a word of reproach.

"It's all right," I said with more conviction than I felt. "It's not the end of the world."

That day I wrote to George Lawrence at Imperial Oil, asking if the job was still open. It was. George flew me to Toronto one weekend and hosted a splendid lunch in the Ontario Club with his lieutenants, Adam Marshall and Bud Charlton: portents of a better life ahead. We agreed I would start work on May 1, 1958.

Before then, in a fit of rage, I did three more stories just to show Ralph Allen, then left *Maclean's* a little early, curious to try some freelancing. Over six weeks I swept across Alberta and Saskatchewan and sold six small stories with photos to various magazines for a total of $750–as much per week as I'd been earning from *Maclean's*.

It might appear that job loss had galvanized me. Sometimes it *is* the dash of cold water that arouses a sleepy life. But a move to *Maclean's* in Toronto would have had the same effect, if Ralph had offered it, and I would have gladly swallowed my earlier fears of head office. Nowadays getting fired, with the concomitant legal advice, professional counselling and long-term severance, seems commonplace, although it is no less traumatic. Then, it was a shameful experience that festered for thirty-five years.

For a while I told myself that Allen was losing his grip. Earlier that year he'd committed a colossal gaffe: on the eve of the 1957 federal election he wrote an editorial assuming a Liberal victory as a fait accompli. By the time it was in print John Diefenbaker's Tories had upset Louis St. Laurent's Liberals. Allen had to eat crow, but that was scant consolation now.

Never mind that other good people were let go from *Maclean's* at the same time (in part, for cost cutting). One got the news in a memorandum from Allen, who sat just a few doors down the hall from her and never spoke directly to her about it. Never mind all the misery the magazine had put me through. It was still the pinnacle of periodical journalism and now I was deemed not good enough. I could not discuss it with anyone for long after. Among Winnipeg friends I left the impression that the move was my choice.

Thirty years later, former *Maclean's* man Leslie Hannon speculated with me over dinner at his home in England that–Ralph being a westerner–nothing I could ever have done for him in his western fiefdom would have been good enough. Perhaps. But our problem went beyond that: we were never comfortable together.

Berton invited me to freelance for *Maclean's* and occasionally I did. Back East I ran into Allen on social occasions. We were always polite. Maybe he was sorry for what happened but was too unbending to acknowledge it. Who knew what private demons were gnawing at him? Eventually I stopped hating him.

Berton left *Maclean's* that same year to become the best columnist the Toronto *Star* ever had. Allen himself ultimately left the magazine to become *Star* managing editor. He also left a remarkable legacy: not merely his *Maclean's* (which in my biased view never had as much soul again) but a legacy of people.

The majority of those he hired remained influential journalists for life. Berton, of course, is a national icon. Callwood, Peter Newman and Peter Gzowski (who arrived as a brash kid late in the Allen era) are not far behind. John Clare (who died in 1991) went on to edit *Chatelaine* and the Toronto *Star Weekly*. Anglin became editor of *Canadian Homes & Gardens*, worked on *The Canadian* and, well past retirement age, served again as one of *Maclean's* more valued editors in the 1980s.

Barbara Moon became a senior editor of *Saturday Night* and is still on the magazine's masthead. The names of W. O. Mitchell, Scott Young, Fred Bodsworth and Clyde Gilmour are household words. Robert Thomas Allen, a prominent freelancer of the time, produced elegant nostalgic essays until his death in 1990. Frayne, Katz, MacDonald, Sangster and Tyrwhitt remain nationally known writers.

Most of them acknowledge the profound influence of Allen and the *Maclean's* of nearly forty years ago. For me it accomplished two things: it taught me everything I know about magazine writing, and that nothing would ever again be as hard or hurt as much.

In 1966 Ralph died of cancer at fifty-three in Toronto. I was in Quebec that year and took no part in the mass mourning. A year later Christina McCall Newman—who began as a secretary in the Allen era and became one of the finest writers of our generation—put together a book of Ralph's work interspersed with her own and others' affectionate remembrances. She showed an Allen that I never knew.

Now, thinking dispassionately of those times, of my own deficiencies as writer and person in the fifties, and of Allen's strengths and weaknesses, I wish I could have known and liked him better.

Twelve years after his death I won the National Magazine Awards' most prestigious prize, the President's Medal, for the best general article of 1978. I wished that I could have shoved it under his nose and said, "Look! And you said I had no future in magazine writing."

But I know, too, that his approval—given so sparingly and rooted in his own impossibly high standards—would still have mattered to me. I have kept his one congratulatory telegram all these years. He had that effect on all of us.

And maybe at last, in writing these words, I have laid Ralph Allen's ghost.

5

BIG OIL

To the sour old managing editors of my formative years, forsaking honest journalism for public relations was like selling your sister to a sailor. Even so, a great many Canadian newspapermen of the day respected Imperial Oil's public relations department. There were reasons, only one of which was the splendid free scoff of food and drink at Imperial press functions.

Preposterous as this will seem to younger readers, many Canadians of the 1950s *liked* the oil industry. The magic of Leduc #1–Imperial's lucky strike, after 133 dry holes, that ushered in the western oil boom–lingered still. The subsequent torrent of discoveries had given Canada all the oil it needed, and then some. An eager public was learning that oil is not merely black gunk; it is the stuff of hexane, benzene, toluene and iso-octane, words fraught with wonder in those simpler times. Nobody had heard of oil spills or toxic waste. Imperial sent out PR people to schools and service clubs extolling the glory that is oil-and-grease with visual aids. One such, bearing fabrics of nylon, Orlon and other petrochemical offspring, practically hugged itself with glee at the mysteries and delights within: it was called "The Magic Suitcase."

In a nutshell, Big Oil was respectable and Imperial's brand of public relations was the benchmark for the industry. The department head, navy veteran and ex-Toronto *Star* photographer George Lawrence, was no more a stereotypical PR man than the Pope is Jimmy Swaggart's brother. Not once did I see George slap a back or even grip a bicep.

He was tall, bald and of grave demeanour. His rich mellow voice lay somewhere in the lower register of a Hammond organ. He spoke in carefully measured tones, his words rising evenly like those little balloons above cartoon characters, and so softly that from across his desk you had to lean forward to hear. Many of us suspected that George cultivated the style: nothing so unnerves a junior employee as having to strain for each word creeping from the boss's lips.

Although outwardly urbane, I think George had put this persona together against his true nature, with years of painful effort. For example, he owned a powerful miniature camera, which he sometimes took to parties. It was a novelty at the time and a conversation piece, so George often good-humoredly snapped pictures of the assemblage. Later he labelled the prints for his own use, and so always knew whose name was whose at the next party.

Social intercourse did not come easily to him. His conversations with most of us felt slightly strained. The fact was, the head of the country's biggest oil company PR department was shy. I related to that, especially after macho *Maclean's*. It was a refreshing change from the average PR hail-fellow, and was one of George's strengths. He engendered trust and, among those who worked for him, it was trust well placed. If you were loyal to him, he never let you down.

Another strength was his skill as talent scout. George's men–in the fifties nearly all *were* men–had strong media backgrounds and sterling reputations. Glen Hancock was a case in point: an experienced newspaperman, something of a philosopher and completely honourable. Everyone who worked for George Lawrence knew his prime task was to put a bright face on Imperial, but it would have been congenitally impossible for Hancock to knowingly spread lies.

Long after, Glen remembered Lawrence as the epitome of all that was best in the relatively new field of public relations: "He established for me a code of ethics without which I would never have gone into PR."

Hancock was one of several "field men" (facetiously known as the "field mice")–public relations representatives stationed across Canada: Jack Birt, Jim Rennie, Larry Iveson, Maurice

Crompton, Eric McVeity, Jim Redditt, Frank Spencer, Bernard Brouillet and his bilingual assistant Edna Scott. I had known and admired several of them while with *Maclean's*. In their communities they *were* Imperial Oil.

All of this coupled with the *Review,* the best magazine of its kind in the country, persuaded me that I was not signing a deal with Satan when I packed Ruth, Lesley and Cathy into the Studebaker and headed for Big Oil. Imperial treated us grandly, by Maclean Hunter standards. A paid-for furnished apartment awaited us in central Toronto. Our daughters, weary of one-room motels, raced gleefully through these temporary quarters, exclaiming over the supplies of sheets, dishes, knives and forks. We invited old friends in for drinks; they rejoiced over our return from the wilderness.

Imperial had recently moved to a twenty-storey, state-of-the-art tower on St. Clair Avenue. Although I started out in a three-writer bullpen, the quarters were finer than anything I'd known: air conditioning, modern typewriters, unlimited supplies, stenos to type letters, a transport department to book tickets and hotels. There were people to have coffee with, lunch with, a drink with after work. It was here I discovered the mystique of broadloom.

We worshipped at the altar of Office. Its size, shape and appurtenances marked your position in the pecking order. I knew a man who paced off his new office to make sure it was bigger than his subordinates'. Carpet in one's office marked the first heady step toward Management. Once on broadloom, you could expect to move rapidly through the other symbols of power and status: coffee table and chesterfield at one end of the room, original oil painting on the wall, planter filled with ferns or *Ficus benjamina* and water carafe with clean glasses.

It seemed to me an addiction as serious as drugs or drink. I fantasized about it for *Gambit,* a wacky broadsheet of the sixties, product of the fertile brain of artist John Richmond and including the work of such luminaries as Robert Fulford, Kildare Dobbs and Harold Town.

> For years, when anybody offered me broadloom I said, "No thanks." It was not easy. I missed promotions because of it and

whenever my boss summoned me, I was obliged to stand in his doorway or arrange to meet him in the hall.

Finally he phoned one day to say, "Meet me in the john in ten minutes." There, over the ceramic tile, he thrust out his hand and said heartily, "Congratulations! As of Monday we're moving you up to senior clerk. Now then, what'll you have—Wilton twist or Acrilan?"

"Nothing, thanks, sir," I said with a tight smile. "But you can freshen up my vinyl tile if you like."

"This is getting ridiculous. A little broadloom never hurt anybody. Come into my office."

"I'd rather not, sir . . ."

"I might as well be frank with you," he said quietly. "There's no room in our organization for a man who can't handle his broadloom."

A tense silence. I dropped my eyes and followed him into his office.

Immediately I felt a curious sense of elation. My step grew springier. I felt taller—1 1/2 inches at least. My boss watched me covertly, with a sly smile.

"How do you like it?"

"It's . . . all right," I said carefully. "But doesn't it become bigger than you in the end, sir? Doesn't one come to depend upon it?"

"Nonsense! Oh, I grant you, when I go home I walk on a little broadloom before dinner. Helps me to unwind. And if I'm out for the evening I'll walk on a friend's broadloom to be sociable. But habit-forming! Certainly not! I can take it or leave it."

"Mind if I take another step?" I said.

They carpeted my office the next morning. At first I walked around only once or twice a day, but within a month I was hooked. I began getting to the office earlier each morning, to have a couple of walks before work. I walked it during coffee break. Often I had lunch sent in and curled up on the floor. On days when I had to go out, I would slip over to Aladdin's or Eaton's for a quick walk on the samples.

I begrudged the moments I had to spend in halls and lavatories. At home we had always used braided rugs. Then one Saturday while my wife was at the Red Cross giving blood, I slipped out and cashed the children's savings bonds on some wall-to-wall wool-and-nylon. After that I slept on the living room floor.

The trip between home and office became a ghastly ordeal. I began staying after work later and later, having one last quick walk for the road. I was there in my office doorway one evening, looking out with dread, when the night watchman came down the hall. He looked at me curiously.

"Can't get off the broadloom, eh?"

"How did you know?"

He smiled kindly. "I was general sales manager here once. Became involved in some illegal stock transactions. Company didn't fire me, of course, but they took away my broadloom. I cracked up."

"But you're all right now?"

"I'm cured. I can even walk on other people's, as long as I don't take any myself." He looked at me with clear steady eyes. "I can help you."

The next morning my wife and the night watchman checked me into a clinic. There, little by little, therapists skilfully weaned me off the stuff. They walked me from wall-to-wall down to an 8-by-10 Indian carpet, then to cocoa-fibre matting, then linoleum and finally concrete. In six weeks I was out, fifteen pounds lighter, new lines around my eyes, but fit and strong . . .

Corporate quirks regardless, my new co-workers were surprisingly diverse. There was no sense of having stepped into the bush leagues. Assistant manager Adam Marshall, a Gregory Peck look-alike, was a former *Maclean's* copyeditor and the best I've known; his fertile brain was a cornucopia of facts. Art director Gerry Moses, respected throughout the Canadian artistic community, had spearheaded Imperial's patronage of the arts, acquiring an enormously valuable company collection of paintings and sculpture. Phil Carscallen was an ex-broadcaster. Staff writer Jim Moore had a PhD, a dry, sneaky sense of humour and a thin, pale Irish kind of face; in another life he might have been a knee-capper for the IRA. Kim McIlroy wrote books on the side;

Bruce Powe wanted to (and subsequently published five novels). Chick Childerhose, a peacetime air force Sabre pilot, already had a first novel out. News writer Robert Fenner—tall, dark and swashbuckling, not long out of UWO journalism school—had the talent for books too but opted for money (today he is president of his own communications company).

The most prolific of all was staff writer Michael Jacot who'd come from the BBC and CBC. Although a mainstay of the *Review,* he also freelanced furiously (and, secretly, ran his own company) writing articles and short stories under five pseudonyms. With ten children to support, Jacot could hardly take time off to eat.

Staff writer Mike Pengelley, whose solid background included Canadian Press and the United Church *Observer,* also had that sense of the absurd that is essential to writers (among his many accomplishments was a brilliant imitation of the "woop-woop-woop" call of a wartime destroyer). A dear rumpled, humorous man, Mike had acquired with marriage a handsome home in Toronto's Rosedale—an area awash in stone, leaded windows, Tories, Tudor architecture and Old Money. Rumour had it that a wealthy Imperial Oil director had considered buying Mike's property but deemed the maid's quarters too small. It was then that Fenner dubbed Pengelley "Squire."

The fact that Squire drove a Beetle made it all the more delicious. Misfortune dogged Mike and his Volkswagen From Hell. Once a pipe mysteriously sprang up from an open manhole in front of him causing, as I recall, the Squire to veer into a parked car. Another time a van accidentally hooked its rear bumper onto the front bumper of his parked Volks, smashing the little Bug into another parked car. Finally the boys from Photo lured Mike to a Volkswagen dealer, asked for the worst wreck on the lot, posed the agreeable Squire in the front seat, and turned the picture into an annual Mike Pengelley Crash Award.

Compared with my previous pace the workload was easy. Even on the worst *Maclean's* days I had always found time to play and read with my daughters; help bathe and feed them and change diapers when they were little; and sing them Belafonte songs with my ukulele until they learned to say "no." Now, although I travelled occasionally on *Review* stories there was much more time at home. Ruth and I bought our first house, a three-bedroom bungalow-cum-dollhouse in suburban Willowdale. I planted gardens, laid sod, built a recreation room, became a suburban handyman.

With suburbia comes neighbours. For a private person, avoiding backyard togetherness without being labelled a snob is a delicate art. My neighbours were mostly honest working stiffs. One of them, an aircraft mechanic, was inordinately proud of his homemade sauna. Sitting in a cramped roomful of steam with naked male strangers was never my idea of fun, but one had to be sociable. And even a sauna is fruitful terrain for a professional listener.

During the Imperial years—perhaps because deep in my heart I felt I'd abandoned real writing—I kept random notes on everything, toward some unspecified day when I would write The Great Novel. Travelling on Big Oil assignments, I watched, listened and scribbled vignettes in airports, planes, trains and bars. One day, sitting by the mechanic's hot rocks sipping his cold beer, I listened to my other neighbour, the meat market manager, work up his own head of steam.

Somebody had called him "lucky" because he had a car and a handsome, sturdy two-storey house free of mortgage. He had laid every brick of that house with his own hands and the more he thought about the airy comment, the madder he got:

> Lucky. Christ, she keeps tellin' me I'm lucky! She keeps sayin', "You got only two kids. You're lucky, we got four." Hell we didn't have *no* kids for nine years on accounta we *planned* it that way. She keeps sayin', "Yer lucky to have a nice house. We ain't rich like you." Lucky, *hell!* I remember I usta take the streetcar up from Yonge and Bloor to Stop 9, I usta walk all the way here, mile and a half, there was nothin' here except the basement and it usta rain and I couldn't go all the way back so I'd put a couple of boards over my head and lay a few bricks and then maybe it'd stop rainin' and I'd pour cement, and when it got dark I'd walk back to Yonge and take the streetcar and bus back to Coxwell. And all my buddies, they'd be dancin' at the Embassy, and me and the wife never went nowhere!

It was the *cri de coeur* of every working man who sought no favours (this was long ago, remember), just a little respect.

Among my jottings were countless notes about those most important people, our daughters. Lesley, as oldest, was head girl. Cathy, four, happily deferred to her sister's seniority (a balance of power that wouldn't last). I scribbled:

> *(Lesley climbs a fire hydrant; Cathy tries and can't.)*
> C: I'm too little.
> L: When you grow big you can do it, Cathy.
> C: Okay, Lesuhley.
>
> *(Conversation at* 7:00 A.M.)
> L: (*matter of factly*) Cathy, you are a bad girl.
> C: Okay.

My daughters were improvisers, as I'd been at their age. They had all the requisite toys, but still preferred shoe boxes for dolls' beds, acorns for doll cups and upright copies of the encyclopedia for houses. But certain procedures were carved in granite and no adult dared mess with them. In 1961, the doting father reported on this in a *Canadian Homes & Gardens* freelance column:

> The other day I found my daughters and their friends doing the high jump. Obviously they were going about it all wrong. They'd tied two skipping ropes and one elastic garter into a long sagging line between two posts, and they were running at it head-on, screaming "Trials!" I strolled over in a friendly way and said, "Want me to show you how to high jump?"
>
> An awful silence settled over them. They stood around not looking at me, scuffing the grass with their toes. Finally Lesley, who is seven, looked apologetically at her friends and said bleakly, "We're not doing high jumps."
>
> "But you were jumping over the . . ."
>
> "We're playing Yogi."
>
> "Yoga?" Giggles from the ranks.
>
> "Yogi."
>
> "Oh. Well, it would be easier if you jumped from an angle and kind of rolled your leg over the rope . . ."

"That wouldn't be Yogi, Daddy."

"Well . . . why don't you at least throw away the elastic and make a tight line?"

"You need the 'lastic for Yogi."

"I suppose you do. What does 'trials' mean?"

"It means if you fall down you get another try."

Always a good loser, I went away smiling. But behind me I heard the humiliating whispers, the giggles and then the savage cry of "Trials!"

One day a call came to the office: Ruth's mother had died. I rushed home with the sorrowful news. Later I explained to Lesley and Cathy that their grandmother was dead and, as was the custom, would be laid to rest in the ground.

"Does the world go on?" one of them asked.

"It goes on, darling."

"Are we born again?"

"Nobody really knows for sure. It would be nice if we were. Because it's such a good world, isn't it?"

"Yes," they both said gravely, "it is a good world."

More than anything else, I wanted that to be true for them.

From the beginning I had assumed (although my bosses hadn't confirmed) that I would work full-time on the *Review*. No one else in the department had a magazine background. The work was a snap after *Maclean's*. Over six months I wrote three stories that pleased editor Roy Cottier and assistant Hal Tennant. Not a Who He in the lot. But the *Review* was published only six times a year. Inevitably, I also had to write public relations minutiae: news releases about new products, news features about plant openings, biographies of middle managers on the rise. I loathed it.

One December morning I presented a newly written biography of some red-nosed manager for his approval, as was corporate procedure. He read it aloud while I stood there. Then he ordered changes. I left wondering, *What am I doing here? I've been edited and fired by the best, and here's some no-talent old fart with a face like steak tartare, reading my stuff aloud as though I'm in Grade 2!*

Coincidentally, it was the day George Lawrence threw his celebratory Christmas lunch for men of the department. We took the subway downtown to the Ontario Club for a hearty repast. About two o'clock, replete with liqueur and cigars, we headed back to work in columns of two and by order of rank, swathed in hats and heavy overcoats, resembling a touring Soviet soccer team. Managers George and Adam led the pack. Writers Moore and I brought up the rear. At Bay Street Moore and I made a sharp right turn. The others didn't immediately notice our absence. By the time they did we were toasting Christmas and each other in the Toronto Radio Artists' Club.

Around supper time Moore did the right thing and went home. Still smarting from the morning's humiliation, I moved on to the Knights of Columbus Hall and the annual Christmas party for all Imperial employees. I was the life of it. I wondered, idly, why my immediate boss, W. G. "Bud" Charlton, was watching me with troubled eyes. Or, at least, one troubled eye: he sometimes wore a black patch over his artificial eye, which gave him a piratical look.

Bud had no journalistic background. He had joined Imperial as a fifteen-year-old copy boy, and would stay his entire working life. Although he had edited the *Review* during World War II he had no literary pretensions. Nor had he attended university, which I know he regretted.

Yet Bud was as intelligent and canny as anyone else on staff and if anything his shortage of formal credentials gave him a certain distinction. He stood apart from all us instant-wonders from newspapers, journalism schools or academe. He related to such diamonds in the rough as Imperial's legendary western operations manager Tip Moroney, who once during a raging oil well fire in Alberta spotted a public relations man arriving on scene.

"Well, here comes Cronyn to put out the fire with his typewriter," said Tip Moroney, to the immense delight of the roughnecks around him.

Similarly, Bud brought Everyman's view to our written words. Sooner or later, every *Review* editor, me included, had prolonged screaming matches with him. The aggravating part was that Bud was often right; his company knowledge frequently saved our skins (he'd already been there thirty years). He knew

Imperial's politics, people, sacred cows and where all the bodies were buried.

Bud and I accommodated our differences and came to quite enjoy each other. But on the morning after my transgression he said, more in sorrow than anger, that the senior manager with the raw-meat face had been phoning for me all the previous afternoon. Bud, Adam and George were hurt. I had let down the side. It was the only time I ever did, but the message got through. Within days I went on the *Review* as assistant editor (Hal Tennant was moving to *Maclean's*). The magazine was where I belonged and stayed, from thence forth.

The *Review* had come far from its beginnings as an employee publication in 1917. Then, it dwelt heavily on oil stories and peppered its readers with little homilies: Without an aim, life is mere existence; Beware of the lure of false economy; Your work is your best friend. . . . Be strong, therefore, and do it.

Employees were urged to conserve food by saving bread crumbs, not to waste soap by leaving it in the water and to "feed the mind with wholesome mental food instead of trash or morbid literature that decomposes and poisons your whole life." It was like getting a letter from your mother.

Gradually, the *Review* increased its quota of general-interest subjects, always with a petroleum connection. It remained a hybrid internal/external magazine, officially published for "shareholders and employees." The change to a distinct external came in the early 1950s under Cottier, a former London *Free Press* reporter. Almost from the day he arrived as a staff writer, the feisty Roy—a wartime British commando—began storming management's beaches with prickly memos. There was, he said, a public out there wondering what Big Oil was all about. An external magazine of quality and integrity would reflect well on Imperial. The *Review,* "a valuable tool," should be used to better advantage.

He got a chance to prove his thesis in 1954. His October issue abandoned the "employees and shareholders" label, and pioneered with an abstract cover and inner artwork on a refinery by "a promising young Canadian," Harold Town. Later Town became Canada's best-known and most controversial artist.

After that, there was no holding them back. "It was a good time to be alive," Cottier told me recently. "Imperial became not just 'that bloody oil company,' but a company pioneering in a form of communication, and using the best people in the land to do so."

He and his sidekick Tennant, formerly of the Vancouver *Sun,* were first-rate editors and paid acceptable money for the times (two hundred dollars). Cottier's sharp mind, tongue and temper got on some people's nerves, but if he respected you he was stimulating company. We hit it off splendidly. I learned magazine production and whetted my minimal editing techniques. Like others who've worked both sides of the fence, I was to discover that writing had made me a more compassionate and perceptive editor, and editing would make me a better, more efficient writer.

Within six months Roy, having been editor for five years, wanted to move up the corporate ladder. I took his place. Jean Danard, who had started her working career as Pierre Berton's secretary on *Maclean's,* after a stint in the Navy, emerged from the writers' room to resume her earlier role as assistant editor. We laughed a lot together and produced an outstanding magazine. She was sweet tempered, company-wise and a much better editor than Imperial's chauvinistic male hierarchy ever realized.

The next six years were mostly bliss. Cottier had pointed the new direction, addressing provocative (for a company publication) themes such as school-bus safety and flaws in Canada's educational system. I took it a step farther. In 1960 we devoted an entire issue to the Canadian North–its wonders, prospects and politics–and published some of the first Eskimo sealskin stencil and stone block art. In 1963 I produced another special, on the plight of Canadian agriculture, that reverberated throughout that industry.

We carried a profile of the renowned neurosurgeon, Wilder Penfield, reflecting the company's interest in education and science. Long before bilingualism was de rigueur, I commissioned famed novelist and teacher, Hugh MacLennan, to write for the *Review* on the value of French for English Canadians.

To our bosses, the changing content seemed at first bold and risky. About two years into my mandate, luxuriating in success and the sin of pride, a memo from George Lawrence (addressed formally to "Mr. R. J. Collins" and signed for him by his secretary) pulled me up short. He had been reading the latest issue, he said. "Without taking anything away from the fine job that is being done, I would simply like to ask the question of those who are most directly interested in its production—do we need to take a look at it to see whether we are keeping it as fresh and vigorous in every respect as it might be?"

Shades of *Canadian Homes & Gardens:* the memo as instrument of terror. I examined the issue; it had fewer oil stories than usual. Probably someone higher up in the food chain had been rattling George's cage, a common management ploy. We went on doing more or less as before without further complaint.

Outsiders invariably praised the content. The magazine went free to company employees, shareholders and what we called "thought leaders": senior business people, hundreds of teachers and all elected members of government. The northern issue drew six hundred letters of praise; the agricultural issue brought an even greater deluge and requests for extra copies. Teachers were so enthusiastic that I introduced for them a back-page collection of oil industry miscellany—The Learning Page—and toyed with launching my own magazine for teachers.

Gradually company management unclenched its knuckles, realizing that every subject did not need a specific oil angle (usually there was a tenuous one); that the *Review* could carry stories on almost anything, within the bounds of good taste. Imperial gave us enough money to do the job, to the envy of most other industrial editors.

In my six years there we won fifteen or sixteen national and international awards for writing and editing, and as many again for design. We hired such talented art directors as John Richmond and Ken Rodmell, who both went on to acclaim in consumer magazines and the art world. Our visuals were brilliant and innovative, although the occasional noble experiment didn't quite work. My 1961 December cover doubled as a Christmas mobile that readers could punch out and assemble: three shepherds, two angels and a crib, to be suspended by threads from a multi-pointed star. It was a charming concept. The trouble was, as some readers pointed out, it took a PhD in mechanical engineering to put the thing together.

Prominent freelance artists lined up at our door: Eric

Aldwinckle, Huntley Brown, Graham Coughtry, Theo Dimson, James Hill, Tom Hodgson, Arnaud Maags, Colette McNeil, Leo Rampen, Robert Markle, Michael Snow, Neil Shakery, Walter Stefoff, Lorraine Surcouf, William Winter, Walter Yarwood and Hans Zander. If there were a Canadian Illustrators' Hall of Fame, most of them would be in it.

One day Richmond and I took a tape recorder and bottle of scotch to Harold Town's studio. The famous Town had a hawklike face and angry eyes; even his smile seemed predatory. Our interview was wide-ranging and revealing, but most telling was the way Town paused at intervals to savagely hammer a punching bag, hung in the studio for letting off steam.

We drew top photographers—Harry Rowed, Walter Curtin, Peter Croydon, Horst Ericht—for the same reason we attracted fine artists: the money was good and the *Review* was a handsome showcase for their work. But our photographic core was a superb staff trio—Roy Nicholls, Al Schoenborn and Ron Cole—not always given the recognition they deserved.

I was learning that editing must or should be as creative as writing; that an editor's most difficult task is to give a publication a distinctive personality without harshly imposing his or her style on the contributors. As writer I had viewed most editors as ham-handed louts who read my manuscripts too hastily, asked stupid questions and wielded the black pencil like a broadaxe. I now discovered that many writers—including some I'd idolized at *Maclean's*—were sloppy, lazy and unreliable.

But sometimes I got lucky. One day, to my delight, a manuscript came in from W. O. Mitchell.

The first time I read that Mitchell story of how as a child in Florida he recited the Gettysburg address, badly, on Decoration Day and got his foot caught in a spittoon in the process, I thought it was screamingly funny. That was 1962. W. O. submitted it on speculation and I gladly published it, under my all-purpose "Canadiana" category.

I hadn't just fallen off a turnip truck; I knew W. O. hadn't written that story specifically for me. He was no doubt looking for some fast cash to finance his book-writing habit. Which was fine. His prestigious name graced my magazine. I changed his title (which I think was "The Day I Gave the Gettysburg Address") to "The Day I Spoke for Mister Lincoln."

Bill must have liked my title because I next heard the story, under its revised name, at a 1979 luncheon meeting of the Empire Club in Toronto. Guest speaker Mitchell was in rare form that day. His timing was exquisite. His simulated spitting sounds crackled over the microphone like firecrackers. His audience was in stitches—except for two elderly codgers in double-breasted suits a couple of tables over. I watched their granite features as Mitchell brought the house down. These guys hadn't smiled since the Crash of '29.

Then about midway through "The Day I Spoke for Mister Lincoln" their faces began to crack involuntarily, like the South Saskatchewan River at spring breakup. At the end they were actually laughing aloud. Mitchell the old master had done it again.

The third time I read the Gettysburg Address story was in Mitchell's 1988 novel, *Ladybug, Ladybug*. By then I was pretty damn tired of it but, I supposed, thousands were enjoying it for the first time. And now I guessed what W.O. had been up to when he sold me that story in 1962. Whether or not he knew it then, it was what authors call "work in progress." He'd kept polishing it over the years. Now it was honed to perfection.

Mitchell wrote two more stories for the *Review*. Having him, June Callwood, Ian Sclanders and Sid Katz in our pages was one of the reasons I loved my job. But I had a soft spot for all our freelancers. Solid professionals such as Fergus Cronin, Ron and Sheila Kenyon, Bill Stephenson. Former London *Free Press* friend David Spurgeon, turning into one of the country's finest science writers. Harold Horwood from Newfoundland, who stalked in wildly bearded and steadfastly wearing his parka, as though he might dash out for Labrador at any minute. Grey-flanneled PR men stared in wonder (in those days we were not even allowed to wear sports jackets in the office), assuming I was entertaining some service station dealer, not one of the country's most acerbic and accomplished writers.

Publishing consultant Arthur Hammond strode towering into our midst with high-laced boots, sheepskin jacket and thick flaxen hair (Imperial men with long haircuts risked court-martial, if not the electric chair). I could almost hear the secretaries whispering, *Oh gawd, another one of Collins's vagabond writers!* And there was Thelma Dickman, a writer who liked to shock. (Within moments of our first meeting she was telling me of her life in the Canadian Womens Army Corps, where each morning "fifty women ran for the washroom, their pubic hair waving in the breeze.") When Thelma later came on staff she rocked the corporate boat, but our bosses secretly enjoyed her quick mind, irreverent ways, even her liberal use of the f-word.

She and all the other writers and artists and photographers had a salubrious effect on the entire department, as well as my magazine. No matter how enlightened my employers, Imperial *was* a corporation, as big and torpid as they come. Our artistic emissaries from the real world helped make Imperial Oil public relations an interesting place to be. Rather like migrant flocks of peacocks, cockatoos and humming birds, flying in daily to ruffle some feathers in our corporate chicken coop.

6

ALDERMANIA

Once or twice in an editor's career, if he or she is lucky, comes a writer blessed with such rare and genuine talent that the editor mutters, "Where has this person been all my life?" Such for me was Tom Alderman. As a fringe benefit, he was also the antithesis of everything implied by "public relations," which appealed to the rebellious streak in me on days when Big Oil tried my patience.

He came in 1963, through the eternally revolving door of our writers' room. Our staffers, like all writers, were nomads, continually packing up their little bundles of words and moving on to someone else's campfire. Jim Moore had left for stints with the Saskatchewan government and the LeDain commission on drugs. Powe went to the Ontario Liberals and later into the insurance industry. Fenner was posted to Imperial's New York parent and on to the Middle East. Squire Pengelley took up teaching.

Childerhose switched to the Toronto *Telegram* and eventually to freelance life on Vancouver Island (he has written eight books). The industrious Mike Jacot left to produce CBC radio and TV dramas and industrial films. Along the way he did a five-year weekly stint in children's drama for CBS in New York, and wrote six novels; one, *The Last Butterfly,* became a movie. (In 1992 he was head of graduate studies for film and video at Toronto's York University, and working on more books.)

Jean Danard travelled around the world; later became the longtime travel editor of the *Financial Post.* Thelma Dickman swept in with a flourish as my assistant editor. An able but troubled writer—who in the last days of his tenure habitually drank his lunch, fell asleep in his office behind closed doors and peed on his chair cushion, until the cleaning lady turned him in—was fired.

So we advertised for yet another ink-stained wretch. By then I knew that roughly 90 percent of the replies to any such advertisement can be discarded. Our mailbag overflowed with poignant applications from hopeful has-beens and never-weres. Their résumés tried to beguile us with artful typing, elegant binding and sheer obfuscation—in some cases the most creative work these writers had ever done—but their lack of experience and talent was transparent.

Amid this flotsam and jetsam came a letter from Alderman, age twenty-seven. He had won four scholarships during a three-year course at the Ryerson journalism school; had been a reporter on a suburban weekly newspaper and for almost four years was associate editor (under editor Frank Rasky) of the general magazine, *Liberty*.

Tom was just back from a year in Europe and Africa, de rigueur for young people in the early sixties. His résumé was intelligent and succinct. He didn't want too much money. He looked too good to be true. What was wrong? Did hair sprout from his teeth at moonrise? Was he on the lam? Had he bricked up his mother in the basement? I invited him in to find out.

It turned out he admired the *Review,* heard it was well edited and thought it might be a place to learn. When we knew each other better he explained, "I figured if I could learn to write about oil, I could write about anything." He was skinny and dark, with a laid-back air, a raspy voice that could pierce concrete and a penetrating gaze. A woman who is immensely fond of Tom finds only one disconcerting thing about him: "He has the eyes of an axe murderer."

I liked him instantly. He was clearly an individualist and seemed to be carefully curbing a sense of humour, a commodity in fairly short supply in public relations. I sensed a kindred spirit. His irreverence was bubbling just below the surface, but Tom knew corporate Canada took itself seriously, and he was not about to blow the first interview with some smart-ass remark.

For the same reason, his haircut was corporate-short and his attire was sober charcoal. Although always a natty dresser, dark two-piece suits were not Tom's first choice, but he had shrewdly adopted Big Oil's protective colouring for this occasion. It was warmly received by my bosses, who accepted my recommendation to hire him after looking him over themselves. Later Alderman told me he got the suit at a discount from his cousin the clothier on Spadina Avenue (the Toronto garment district).

It could have been true. Tom was always citing real or mythical cousins for some raffish activity. Regardless, Alderman was a fashion plate and regularly chastised those of us who were sartorially disadvantaged. During one after-work social gathering Tom looked at my feet and said, "Brown shoes after five! I'm sorry. That's not acceptable." I've never felt good about brown shoes since.

Once ensconced in the writers' room, this unlikeliest of PR employees quickly became the joy of my Imperial Oil years. For one thing, he was a wise-guy (in the non-Mafia sense), a kind of latter-day Damon Runyan character. Maybe part of me (I must check this with an analyst) wished I was like Tom.

More to the point, Alderman was the most prolific writer I've known (Pierre Berton included). I would toss him an assignment, like a slab of raw meat, and Alderman would pounce on it, pausing only for a barbed remark if the subject struck him as dull.

Dull or not, he would be back in record time with a lively finished piece and ravening for more. Other staff writers upon finishing stories would, I knew, fake a couple of extra days on their assignments and hide out doing freelance. Tom regularly clamoured for more work.

I thought I was dreaming it. He brightened my days and lightened my burden. In his first year on the *Review* he wrote fifteen stories: two or three per issue, including some under his predictably quirky pseudonym, Burbridge Henry. It became a challenge: what shall I do with Tom today?

Like any good writer, he could become intensely interested in any subject of the moment: salt, retirement, automated car clinics, pollution, moving vans, corneal transplants. His stories required little editing and had some of the best quotes I'd seen. Too good, in fact; I knew how hard it is to eke colourful language out of the average droning interviewee.

"Come on, Tom, you made that up," I'd say.

"Nyeh!" he'd screech. "I said to the guy, 'Isn't this what you really mean?' and he said, 'Yeah, sounds good.'" Sure it did; Tom Wolfe and Nora Ephron couldn't have made the guy sound better. Tom's subjects never complained of misquoting; after he had airbrushed them, even their mothers-in-law thought they were geniuses.

Only once, to my knowledge, did Tom ruffle his sources. We shipped him to the Northwest Territories to do a story on the oil town Norman Wells. Apparently he asked the locals, with genuine amazement, why anyone would want to live in such a godforsaken place. Photographer Ron Cole, following in the writer's footsteps, had to do a little stroking and fence-mending.

Alderman was the kind of writer who must always be writing (I recognized the disease, being afflicted myself). If there were no articles to be done, he resorted to letters or memos. I kept a personal file marked "Aldermania." It includes a memo to me, requesting a rebate from the company educational assistance plan:

> Y'r obedient servant has graduated magna cum laude from "Film: The Medium and Its Techniques" at Ryerson Polytech. Standing first in this course does not necessarily mean something. You'd know what I'm talking about if you could have seen the collection of kulakuhs I led across the finish line. . . .

Like every writer Tom loved and depended on libraries. He could turn a simple book request to the company library into a contender for the Leacock Medal:

> Your obedient servant, much too humble to appeal to you in person, requests a tiny small infinitesimal favour. To wit: I cannot live without a book called the *Geological Evolution of North America*. I cannot possibly exist without it. . . . The only known copy rests in the science section of the Toronto public libraries. And to pry that book loose for more than two months would mean grappling with that dragon who oversees the business conducted there. As you know she is my sworn enemy; on a personal vendetta. I go down on my humble knees before you, I beg, I insist. . . .
>
> P.S. I have powerful friends.

The library ladies could never refuse him and once he rewarded them with a basket of goodies and this accompanying note written in lower-case:

> tom alderman considers it his bounden duty to protect the library ladies from the indigestibles which regularly festoon the coffee-wagons in this building. for in so doing, they perform for him even more excellently the tasks of rounding up stray particles of useless information, strike a blow against heartburn and that feeling that your body is failing to assimilate unpulverizable cakes of soggy cement. try these with your coffee. alderman has just inherited a whole case of the stuff from a sneak-thief cousin, and is trying like mad to unload it before the authorities close in. help him out.

Even his apologies were a hoot. He sent this letter to a man whose name we misspelled in an Alderman story.

> Somewhere in the many processes that bring word to printed page, some boob decided that your name was not Richard but Richmond. He is at this moment being ferreted out from whichever dark corner he is doubtless cringing. He will then be summarily hung by his thumbs till he screams for mercy, and only then will be cut down to write, with crippled fingers, your name ten thousand times.

Like the other nomads, Tom was just passing through. He left Imperial in 1965 and became a star writer on *The Canadian*. That magazine, like so many, is long gone but its survivors all treasure their Alderman stories. Tom and I kept in touch. Happily, time did not change him. In the mid-seventies, after my second ill-fated marriage had gone down the spout, he accosted me at a Toronto writers' meeting.

"Hey, Collins," he said cheerfully, in a voice that could be heard in Chilliwack. "Who you married to this year?"

Later I wrote him a congratulatory letter about *Cityspan*, a short-lived publication he was editing: "I've come through all these years without saying a kind word to another writer/editor–'Let jealousy and envy prevail' is emblazoned on the Collins family crest–and now what I'm about to say causes my gorge to rise. Well, might as well get on with it–oh this is hard, hard–*Cityspan* is the best magazine in Toronto. (Oh god, I can't believe I'm saying this.) The only way I can live with the situation is to tell my friends that I taught Alderman everything he knows."

"Well, it was about time. Sheesh!" Tom wrote back. "I'm telling everybody Frank Rasky taught me all I know. Next time get your plaudits in a little faster."

As of early 1993, he had for several years been an on-camera reporter with "The Journal" and its successor, "Prime Time News." In that youth-ridden organization, he once told me, he is considered an old man. Maybe so. But I'll lay odds that Alderman's leading all those CBC kulakuhs across the finish line.

7

CHANGING TIMES AND OVERTIME

The writers and editors at Imperial Oil were my extended family. We were bonded by common cause and our pride in a profession that most of our bosses and spouses didn't quite understand. At times of disenchantment with Big Oil and society at large, we joined in tomfoolery to let off steam. As with the New Year's Anti-Gaiety League.

The League was born December 31, 1958, when Bruce Powe and I were still restless denizens of the writers' room. Bruce complained that nobody had invited him out for New Year's Eve. Nobody asked me either, which was normal. We went to the Northgate Hotel tap room to sulk about it. A couple of other New Year's Eve rejects joined us. We invented the League on the spot.

The idea was simple in the extreme: we sat around, drank beer and jeered at other people's New Year's Eve revelry. By 4:00 P.M. we felt so much better we all went to Powe's place for Christmas cake. You can imagine how thrilled his wife, Alys, was to see this rowdy gang of four amidst her New Year's Eve dinner preparations. Then I went out to buy a New Year's Day turkey, and mislaid it, causing my wife to later speculate that the wrong turkey got lost, but that's another story.

The next year League membership rose to six. We were pleased to welcome Sam Kirschenbaum, a dentist who had once lived in suburbia, where he grew Golden Bantam sweet corn for a front hedge to aggravate his neighbours. Sam represented the spirit, heart and soul of Anti-Gaiety.

The following summer, unable to wait for New Year's Eve, we founded the Anti-Company Picnic Festival. The premise was similar: eight of us sat around making fun of the Imperial Oil company picnic, while our fellow employees were running the three-legged race on Centre Island. Six months later the New Year's Anti-Gaiety League held another successful sitting, with ten members.

The next summer a large Anti-Picnic contingent gathered in Squire Pengelley's Rosedale recreation room. We were shouting out a ballad our guitarist, Davey Powell, had brought from the U.S., all about the rich, the "pore," a betrayed maiden and a venal southern politician:

She were pore but she were honest
Victim of a rich man's whim
'Till she met
That Christian gennlemun, Big Jim Folsom
And she had
A child by him

Now, it's the rich that gets the glory
It's the pore that gets the blame
It's the same
The whole world, over, over, over
Ain't it all
A low down shame. . . .

Suddenly the music died and everybody looked at everybody. Slowly the truth crept over us: this was gaiety. This was a New Year's Eve party without the paper hats. We had become the very thing we were protesting. We all went home quietly. The Anti-Gaiety League disbanded.

But the antics went on. In my first Christmas with Imperial, frustrated for a creative outlet, I wrote a skit for the departmental party. There had been Christmas skits before my time, in bids to raise the cultural level of that annual event from its licentious round of drinking and secretary pinching. Now, by unspoken agreement, I took them over, sating a lifelong desire to be a lyricist, versifier and Broadway impresario, treading modestly into the footlights to cries of "Author, Author!"

George Lawrence was visibly uneasy as we kidded his department, the company and the oil industry, but I knew which side my job was buttered on. I was careful to cut close to, but not into the bone. It was a success. George relaxed, beaming. Each Christmas thereafter, and soon by request at every farewell party, I bit the hand that fed us, in word and song.

Over seven years I wrote a couple of dozen scripts and hundreds of lyrics. Our volunteer casts came from the writers' room and steno pool. Costumes were minimal: for instance, Bill Young, a tall writer with a noble profile (later a senior vice-president of Imperial Oil) made a striking Prince Philip with the mere addition of a nautical cap. We adapted everything from the works of Dickens to *My Fair Lady* to Christmas carols:

Good King Wenceslaus looked out
On the feast of Stephen
Service stations all about
Prices fixed and even . . .

We reflected the changing nature of the department, the business, even Canadian mores. The times, as Bob Dylan soon would sing, were a changin' and our Christmas frolics changed with them, even to satirical references to drugs and contemporary "hippies," subjects alien to Big Oil.

In a salute to the industry's glory days we celebrated Alberta's riches, to the "Battle Hymn of the Republic," rendered by our "Ernest Manning Gospel Singers."

There's oil upon our highways and there's oil upon our grass
The oil lies underneath us in one great enormous mass
The oil extends from Dawson Creek right up our Crowsnest Pass
The oil just pours and pours.
Glory, glory hallelujah
Glory, glory hallelujah

A little dab of oil would do ya
But ours just pours and pours.

Well that was fifteen years ago, the oil is flowing yet.
We've paid off all of Premier William Aberhart's bad debt.
Just keep the royalties coming, we'll take all that we can get
While the oil just pours and pours. . . .

When a staff man returned from a posting to our affluent parent, Standard Oil of New Jersey, we saluted him to the tune of "The Man Who Broke the Bank at Monte Carlo."

I went walking down 5th Avenue with an independent air
My heart was free of care
'Twas though Jersey wasn't there
And at noon I'd throw a luncheon bash
And then charge it up to petty cash
I'm the man who broke the bank account at Esso. . . .

In the sixties the industry moved into cutthroat marketing. Imperial introduced its original "Put a Tiger in Your Tank" campaign with ersatz tiger tails handed out at the pumps. Sears and Canadian Tire sold gasoline. Imperial retaliated in ways that we celebrated one Christmas with three make-believe Esso dealers singing to the tune of "We Three Kings":

We three things have come from afar
Bearing stuff to put in your car
We're from Esso?
Yeah, I guess so
Wish we was in a bar
Ohhhhhhohhhhhh
  Esso sheets so crisp and white
  Thermos jugs and Christmas lights
  Drills and dryers, no-skid tires
  Heating pads and three-wheel trikes

Honest Ed thinks Esso's gone nuts
Birks and Eaton's hate our guts

They're complaining, we're retaining
Markets with fair price cuts
Ohhhhhohhhhhh
Esso sheets so crisp and cheap
Cots and bags in which to sleep
Clocks and dolls and kids' footballs
How did we get in so deep?

All this was an antidote to the nagging realization that I now worked for a company where commercialization had displaced the pure (if it had ever been) and romantic business of oil finding.

What with the skits (which I wrote on my own time) and the *Review,* my creativity was working overtime. Once I asked ace photographer Roy Nicholls to picture a refinery's pipes and towers as an art form. The result, titled "And Night Begins to Work Its Magic," was poetry in colour images. Another time we took Harry Rowed's action photos of roughnecks on a drill rig and showed how, close cropped, they became a kind of ballet. I called it "Fantasy on the Drill Floor." I can only guess what the roughnecks were calling me.

Yet again I invited two poets–one of them Earle Birney–and an artist to picture or write whatever came to mind after visiting an oil refinery. The results were genuine artistry. Birney's poem, for example, began:

Under the breath of the first dragons—
those spell binders who watched over gold-hoards
—whole fields of warriors wilted
Even hero Beowulf died in the hot blood gushing
from the firedrake's mouth
But this hugest of beasts
though he winds back a thousand miles
leaping and leaping from unimaginable deeps
beneath Alberta's plains
is led to these shores at last and hour
by hour engaged . . .

Hardly what you'd expect in an "oil" magazine.

But some of my brain waves went berserk. One day Chick Childerhose and I got to talking about psychic phenomena as applied to plants. I'd heard of a professor in India who said flute music made plants grow faster. A couple of high school students in Toronto claimed to have demonstrated that green beans germinated faster to the wails of Elvis Presley than to the keening of Johnny Mathis. Childerhose remembered scientific papers from McGill University about a faith healer who claimed he could will plants to grow.

We decided he'd write a piece about all this. (Farmers use oil products so agriculture was within our purview.) Chick would plant two batches of seeds, direct hatred at one and heap love on the other. If all this psychic stuff were true, the loved ones would grow bigger and we'd have a first in Canadian journalism.

Childerhose planted tomato seeds in two flat boxes in a sunny bedroom window in his house in Oakville. Each morning before work he stood over them for maybe fifteen minutes, methodically loving A and hating B. Seedlings sprang up sturdily in both boxes.

"I think I know what's wrong," Chick said one day. "The tomatoes are in the same room as the baby. We all love the baby. Some of it is spilling over onto B."

They moved B, but it kept growing tall and strong. Childerhose said he thought June, his tenderhearted wife, was sneaking into the room by day and giving B a little loving on the sly. I reminded him of great husband-wife partnerships throughout the history of science. "Eve Curie didn't mess around with the radium behind Pierre's back," I pointed out. Chick promised to speak to June.

But a week later he slumped into my office, drained from fifteen minutes of sustained hate followed by thirty minutes of driving the Queen Elizabeth Way. "B is pulling ahead," he said bleakly.

We pulled the story out of the lineup. Childerhose transplanted the seedlings into his garden. He reaped a fine crop of tomatoes that fall, although half of them were uncommonly bitter.

One of my pleasures was taking my dear daughters to the office on a Saturday. Big Oil filled them with awe and glee. There were rituals. After we'd parked behind the twenty-storey building, they would scrunch up against it, crane their heads back and squeal with pleasure and vertigo, convinced it would fall on them. While I worked they played hard, using infinite supplies of paper and coloured pencils and flushing the corporate toilets over and over. Before leaving we always climbed the stairwell to the rooftop observation deck, another deliciously terrifying treat that turned their legs to jelly.

Also on Saturdays, we brought home armloads of books from the public library for story sessions. Until they could read–too soon for me–I vied for their approval with dialects, funny faces, squeaky voices, all the hammy things that fathers indulge in. The legacy of reading, passed on to them as mine was passed on to me, stayed with them evermore. When they were older one of their favourite made-up games was "Library": hours of filing books from their own bookshelves, stamping them out to each other, taking them in, filling out library cards. Twenty years after that Cathy was a writer and editor, and Lesley is a bookstore habitué. Holidaying with me in England once, she sat down in a hushed and sunny nook among the ruins of an abbey and exclaimed in pure delight, "You could sit here all day and read a book!"

Having turned away from the Catholic Church at marriage, Ruth and I agreed that our daughters would be confirmed as Anglicans, about as close to Catholicism as Protestants get. On Sunday mornings, Mother slept in while I made cereal, bacon and toast for the girls and invented new chapters in the continuing saga of Elizabeth Anne, who was five-going-on-eleven and had a veritable Einstein of a dog, The Amazing Spooky. Her friends the Wibbledywoos, small rosy-cheeked doll-like people, inhabited a make-believe world and had an adventure every Sunday morning. Our favourite involved The Blue Witch, who was finally vanquished when Elizabeth Anne threw Javex on her, turning the witch white and harmless. We all related to Javex.

At church Canon J. de Pencier Wright, a great billet of a man with ruddy face and booming voice, swept the choir down the aisle ahead of him. Then Lesley and Cathy went downstairs to Sunday School while I daydreamed through the sermon. I wrote to myself:

> The little girls wriggled to the edge of the pew and, as their classes filed by, peeled off like dive-bombers to join them. But one of them clung to my arm for just a moment and the other sent me a wave and a brilliant smile. And for one sharp lovely moment I thought how good that time was, and how I wished it would stand still forever. And for a while I could not see to read the hymn.

George Lawrence moved to the American parent company and Scott Fyfe, a former assistant PR manager who had been serving time in Advertising, replaced him. Scott was tall and urbane with a twinkling eye; a firm but good-humoured leader with the uncanny knack of knowing everything that was going on in the department, and who was doing what to whom.

He became my friend as well as the best boss I ever had. One of his first questions was, "How did you *live* on the money *Maclean's* was paying you?" Scott got me up to sixteen thousand, more than double my parting salary at *Maclean's*.

He also had the soft, well-modulated voice that was standard issue for senior PR men. Ron Cole and I dealt with this at a company party, posing as George and Scott in a song I wrote to the tune of "Whispering":

> G: Whispering . . . hope that you can hear me
> S: Whispering . . . wish you'd move up near me
> G: Whispering . . . you don't come through clearly
> S: That may be true . . . but I still can't hear you
> G: Whispering . . . *mouthing words*
> S: Whispering . . .
> Both: Life here would be so much more cheery
> If only I could hear from you.

Looking back, I realize I had become a workaholic. When in 1960 I went to hospital with Werlhof's Disease and was eventually relieved of my spleen, I kept editing stories and dictating letters from my bed, convinced I was invincible and indispensable. Yet I also felt more vibrant and alive than at any previous time in my working life. I loved what I was doing.

As long as I kept up my office work, Imperial was generous about travel. I've always believed working editors should write, to keep their hands in. So I roamed the length and breadth of Canada and into the Northwest Territories on assignments. I lived for five days on a geologists' boat moored at Aklavik. Once I hitched a helicopter ride into the Mackenzie Delta, that vast geographical jigsaw puzzle with water in the "missing" spaces. In the distance the blue haze of the Arctic Ocean fanned out to infinity. The pilot dropped me at a geological camp beside a small stream in a deep gorge. The geologists were out at work. It was ghostly still, only the whisper of wind through scrub willow and the murmur of cold, pure water trickling down from the Richardson Mountains. It was like world before man.

One of the many endearing things about Canadians north of the 60th parallel is that they care not a whit for timetables, rules or restless ulcer-ridden southerners. Ron Cole and I traipsed the length of the Mackenzie River for a *Review* story. One morning in Fort Simpson I tried to phone Toronto. No one was working the hotel switchboard and there was no direct-dial service. Grumbling like a southerner, I joined Cole in the coffee shop and, lo!, there sat the switchboard operator slugging back coffee and gossip.

"I called and called and there's nobody on the board," I complained.

"Go back to your room and I'll put you right through," she said agreeably. It took three minutes to make the circuitous walk back. I rang. No operator. Back to the lobby. She was back at her coffee.

"You said you were going to the switch board," I snapped.

"I went there, right after we talked," she cried righteously. "And I rang your room and there was nobody there!"

My bosses rightly believed that if an employee had a high profile in his or her specialty it reflected well on the company. So I joined the American Association of Industrial Editors and International Council of Industrial Editors, both headquartered in the United States; got into executive work, made speeches, helped plan conferences, organized editorial judging programs.

The *Review* kept winning honours, culminating with one of

the two top awards for industrial magazines worldwide. This pleased Imperial's board of directors, guaranteed our budget for another year and insured that I could travel just about anywhere in North America.

I roamed to editors' meetings, awards' nights and conferences from New York to Miami to San Francisco. For the first time I met the people, vernacular and attitudes of the deep South: the segregated washrooms, drinking fountains and restaurants; the hatred. And, of course, I made notes.

The American northerners were appalled at the South's hatred of President John F. Kennedy simply because he was facing up to the race issue. The southerners considered the northerners naive with no real understanding of the problem: "Would you like youah daughter to marry a Nigra?" A gentle, well-educated man from South Carolina lamented: "Befoah they push this integration the Nigra was always smiling, happy, like a chile. Now he nevah smile no more."

The trouble was, of course, they wanted to keep the Negro like a child. As the lone Canadian among them I felt remote, watching a family quarrel through a neighbour's kitchen window, and smug because in the 1960s it was a peculiarly American problem. Surely, I thought, it would never come to Canada.

There were few really innovative industrial magazines in either Canada or the United States and, given America's greater numbers, I found more like-minded spirits there. One was Don Erickson, editor of a chemical company magazine. He was young and a bit arrogant, with the blond, imperious good looks of a Nazi SS officer in a World War II movie, and impatient with slow-witted fellow editors. During meetings we hung around together because we cared about what we were doing and respected the other's work.

By the mid-sixties Erickson and I were restless. We'd done all we could in industrial editing. I was ready to return to consumer magazines; Don wanted into them for the first time. One day he phoned from New York with pure joy: he'd been hired by *Esquire,* the ultimate in magazine journalism at the time.

By the mid-seventies he was editor-in-chief. I looked him up in New York. He was modishly dressed in the ankle-length overcoat and broad-brimmed hat of the period. We wandered through *Esquire*'s rabbit-warren offices and went out for a drink. Although still friends, distance had grown between us. He was editing some of the best periodical writers in North America; I was writing for *Reader's Digest*.

Don resigned from *Esquire* in 1980 after a change in ownership. He edited a public television magazine until the money ran out, then joined *The New York Times Magazine*. He was there in 1988—still relatively young, still a shining talent—when he died of a brain tumour.

Ruth and I were also painfully moving apart. Thirty years later it is difficult to remember why something that began with such hope and goodwill should fail. If I could have taken to those times the patience and wisdom and maturity of now, it might have been different.

We shared most of the same values, but increasingly realized we had radically different personalities, interests, senses of humour. I was no longer the introvert who had left *Maclean's*. I was valued by my employers, respected in my field, had won numerous honours, had new friends all over the continent, could speak in public with only a trace of sweaty palms. By 1965 I was president-elect of the American Association of Industrial Editors.

Yet I tried not to neglect my family. We socialized often with Ruth's relatives. One memorable night a small limber niece taught all us adults The Twist. In the morning we regretted it, when our screaming back muscles reminded us that rye whisky and delusions of youth do not a Chubby Checker make. We took family trips to fall fairs and to Prince Edward Island, New England, Mexico and North Carolina. After working nights, days and weekends to complete a special issue on agriculture, I told my bosses I was going away mid-week to explore some Ontario caves with my daughters. They acquiesced, in puzzlement. What kind of PR man wanted to go in a cave?

We moved to a comfortable two-storey in Toronto's Leaside area, where our daughters had safe sidewalks and a school nearby. It was a quiet, green neighbourhood where crickets sang merrily on summer nights. When I heard later that Margaret Atwood had lived in Leaside and now scoffed at it, I knew I had made the right choice.

During the Imperial years I had two editing job offers. One was in New York. I'd often travelled to that rude, awesome city; its cabbies bawling, "WATCHIT, WATCHIT!" when you opened a taxi door; its waiters trying to shame you into a bigger tip ("Sir, you forgot your change"); its hoteliers oily and pseudo-French; a city not giving a damn about the rest of the world. It was still fun to visit in the sixties, but I couldn't conceive of raising children in or near it.

A major oil company in a small Ohio city also offered me an editorship and flew my family down in the company aircraft for a weekend. Having one's own plane with solicitous steward for a few hours is beguiling. The Ohians were hospitable to the extreme. It would have been lucrative. But the claustrophobia of a one-company town can smother families. Further, none of us wanted to give up our country.

The gap widened. Once Ruth and I went to New York for one of my meetings. We planned to stay the weekend. By the Saturday night we sat in the hotel bar, together yet alone, realizing with enormous sadness that we had nothing left to say. The next morning we flew back early to the only and most precious things we had in common, our daughters.

The company didn't regard the *Review* as a career job. I had held it nearly six years and latterly also headed up the whole publications division. I had the requisite big office with clunky prestigious furniture and Margaret Temple, devoted secretary and friend-for-life, who guarded my door like a lioness. I was standing taller on my own rich pelt of broadloom. Imperial began sending me on management training courses. It was time to decide whether to be a grey flannel suit or an editor/writer for life. The monetary rewards were alluring–I was just getting into company stock options–but there was really no choice.

In Montreal a move was afoot to beef up the Canadian *Reader's Digest*. Douglas How, an outstanding journalist, was now its editor. My *Maclean's* pal Dave MacDonald had been there more than a year and urged me to join them.

In my first meeting with *Digest* president Paul Zimmerman, I was so low-key as to be almost invisible. Zimmerman, a big, aggressive self-made businessman, had no time for shrinking violets. MacDonald begged him to give me a second chance, then pleaded with me to sell myself. Always more articulate on paper than in person, I sent Paul a letter that made me sound like the Second Coming, and was hired.

So at the end of 1965 I bade Imperial Oil farewell. It had done the impossible: mended the damage done by *Maclean's*, helped make my family at least financially secure, tapped depths of creativity I didn't know I possessed and restored my faith in myself. A most uncommon public relations experience.

8

WALKING THE HIGH WIRE

After one unhappy year with *Reader's Digest* in Montreal I fled back to Toronto. The job had been inconsequential and boring. Its only pluses were friendships in the Canadian *Digest*'s small editorial family: editor Douglas How, roving editor Dave MacDonald, editorial secretary Phyllis Cockfield, art director Louis Hamel and a few other kindred spirits.

Nearly everything in the magazine came from our U.S. masters at the Pleasantville, New York, headquarters. Each month a distinctly *un*pleasant emissary named Adrian Berwick visited Montreal to view the next editorial lineup and to rattle my cage. Berwick disliked me because, I suppose, I was unhappy and therefore reticent, not a gregarious yarn-spinning, good-buddy Digester. I loathed him because he was rude and sometimes boorish. A fellow editor from that time remembers Berwick eating an order of fried eggs with his hands.

In autumn of that year Doug How was pulled off the magazine to begin the *Digest*'s celebrated two-volume history of Canada in World War II. I took over the Canadian edition. It required scant creative effort. There was maybe one original Canadian article per issue. Sometimes I was allowed to write a two-hundred-word Canadian sidebar for an American story, but Berwick horned in even on those.

Worst of all, my marriage had broken up. It was a cruel time for all four of us, the blackest time of our lives. The *Digest*'s Paul Zimmerman, who'd become a true friend and supporter, urged me to stay, but I had to return to Toronto and somehow lessen the misery for my daughters.

One afternoon former boss Scott Fyfe came to Montreal and invited me to dinner in the Ritz Carlton Hotel's Maritime Bar. It turned into a long, enjoyable and boozy evening. Scott had somehow found out things were going badly for me (if Churchill had used Fyfe during the war Britain wouldn't have needed radar). I said I'd always wanted to freelance but it was too risky with a young family, and alimony and child-support in the offing.

He immediately offered me a five-thousand-dollar annual retainer to be earned mostly by writing for Imperial Oil *Review*. It was the kind of assured basic income every freelancer dreams about, and must have to succeed. Never mind that I was launching into one of the most precarious jobs on earth. It felt like an anvil had been lifted off my foot.

Not long ago I heard a greying man proudly tell a roomful of other writers that he was now a full-time freelancer, was supporting a family, and had doubled his income in each of the previous six years. This glittering success story won a robust ovation from the other strugglers.

Some quick math would have told them that, since his acknowledged first-year income was six hundred dollars, the poor soul was still hovering near the official poverty level. All the same, he deserved the applause. He was already head and shoulders above most others of his kind. The average freelancer's income, according to the Periodical Writers Association of Canada, is about fourteen thousand dollars a year.

Freelance writing, fraught with rejection and failure, is like walking a high wire over Niagara Falls without a net—yet thousands of Canadians yearn to do it. The words have a splendid romantic ring, rather like "knight errant." Once published, just once, they wear the freelance designation as proudly as the Order of Canada. Most have another paying occupation or a spouse who works. As genuine working freelancers know, it's no way to get rich.

"Nobody can truly understand freelance life unless they've done it, which may rule out your entire editorial staff," I once wrote to a *Reader's Digest* editor. "If you hitch your star to one market, and lose a story, it's a major dent in a very modest yearly income. Every critique looms larger. Every letter or phone call becomes overly important. Every delay and silence is magnified. Every perceived hurt is blown out of proportion."

Why, then, would any sane person do it? Why did I in 1967 forsake a secure job for this "high-wire" act at such a stressful time in my life?

For the possibility of success, which, being so difficult to attain, is all the sweeter for having. In my first three-year freelance stint, by working flat out all the time, I earned more per year than ever as a salaried employee. That was good for my morale and for my family's well-being.

And for the freedom to partially control my destiny, away from the confines and stifling protocol of company offices and people. Since that heady beginning in 1967 I've spent only two years in a conventional office. I squander no time in traffic jams or mindless meetings. I shop and bank when I feel like it, meaning when the fewest others are there.

I do not, as did the orderly and mega-selling author Arthur Hailey in his formative years, get dressed in shirt, tie and jacket before starting work. Usually I am a fashion statement in jogging suit or slacks and T-shirt. Occasionally I've gone directly to work in a white heat of creativity in my pyjamas. Author Maggie Siggins once told me she too sometimes worked in pyjamas. She looks a lot better in them than I do, which was why her mailman insisted on passing her the mail by hand instead of through her letter slot.

When I feel like it, I stop and pick tomatoes or take a walk with my dog (who recommends the freelance life to other dogs). Or I go to a movie, mid-week in broad daylight, or watch last night's taped PBS show, or reruns of "The Rockford Files." I may sit out on my patio of a sunny day, editing stuff I wrote indoors on rainy yesterday. I may work Saturday and Sunday but take Monday and Thursday off. More than once I have worked by choice on Christmas morning, feeling not at all deprived.

But this freedom requires the strictest self-discipline, which for me now comes by reflex action. Illusory freedom has dragged many a writer down the drain or into the Press Club. Like most successful freelancers, I work much harder—sixty-hour weeks are commonplace—and am infinitely more efficient than the average nine-to-fiver.

There is an element of swank to successful freelancing. It shows your journalistic friends you can still cut it. It baffles the hell out of your neighbours—in itself, reason enough for doing it. My pleasant neighbourhood lacks the anonymity of apartment developments. When I moved in I sensed neighbours' eyes and furrowed brows behind drawn blinds. *He doesn't drive out in the morning or go to the bus. He cuts his lawn by day, when decent breadwinners are at work. Bearded men and bohemian-looking women sometimes come to his door. Is he a bookie or a drug dealer or what?* Later, accustomed to my curious profession, they sometimes said fondly, "We saw your light burning last night. You must have been Writing."

Freelancing is the supreme test; the hardest kind of writing life. Few survive, fewer do really well. Successful freelancers are the elite of the writing world.

In a sense, that first full-time outing was not a total gamble. I'd been flirting with the high wire all my working life. Freelancing is to me as salted peanuts are to Weight Watchers and marriage is to Elizabeth Taylor. At the London *Free Press* I freelanced to the *Family Herald and Weekly Star.* While at *Canadian Homes & Gardens,* I was selling to *Maclean's, Mayfair* and the CBC.

For six months in that period I also freelance-edited "Parade," a *Maclean's* back-of-the-book collection of supposedly original anecdotes submitted by readers. The stuff came in garbled torrents. Sometimes an identical "original" joke came from opposite ends of the country. Sly contributors were always trying to fog old chestnuts past us. A perennial favourite was about the construction foreman in Oakville (or Winnipeg or Montreal) who drove his cement truck into his own driveway and poured a full load into the open convertible of the fancy man in the upstairs bedroom who was pleasuring the foreman's wife. (In some versions, the convertible turns out to be not a seducer's but a surprise gift to the foreman from his wife.)

While on staff with *Maclean's,* I wrote and broadcast more items for CBC Radio International, did a few articles for Imperial Oil *Review* and wrote a TV documentary. At the *Review* I did an occasional piece for *Maclean's,* wrote and hosted a two-part show on agriculture for a Montreal TV station and, with Michael Jacot, wrote lyrics and story treatment for a stillborn musical. During the *Review* years I also freelanced for the Toronto *Star Weekly,* where *Maclean's* alumni Dave MacDonald and John Clare were then ensconced–and moonlighted as travel editor for *Canadian Homes & Gardens,* then edited by *Maclean's* alumnus Jerry Anglin.

I also discovered that pleasant perquisite, the "writing holiday," enjoyed by thousands of scribblers loosely designated as "travel writers." It permits trips to fun spots for the sole purpose of describing their delights and, too infrequently, their drawbacks. The writer is usually paid a pittance, enough to cover basic expenses. More accomplished practitioners also diddle their fare, lodging, some meals and maybe a U-drive out of airlines, hotels, restaurants and rental agencies. (How much these writers know of the ordinary traveller's problems is a moot point.)

In 1960, after recovering from a splenectomy and realizing I was mortal, I took the family to Mexico for a fortnight. It was insane, given that we had a tenacious mortgage, Lesley and Cathy were only seven and five respectively and Mexico was noted for Montezuma's Revenge.

But most of us had a wonderful time in Guadalajara, Puerto Vallarta (before Elizabeth Taylor and Richard Burton spoiled it for ordinary folk) and Mexico City. Along the way I did a *Star Weekly* cover story with colour photos about the overall trip, another on Mexican food, and others for *Canadian Homes & Gardens* on travelling with small children, the town called Tequila and Guadalajara's open market. It paid our way.

With that background and excellent contacts, my 1967 freelance plunge paid off quickly. Editor Jim Knight of Imperial Oil *Review* poured jobs my way to work off the retainer. The *Star Weekly* assigned me to write a whole issue of that magazine on Expo 67. Later that year I covered the Royal Tour for the same magazine, feeling like a newspaperman again; jostling for position among the reportorial hordes; shaking the Royal hands in a kind of journalistic conga line; mingling with the Royals in informal groups at Government House: Philip relishing the thrust and parry of questions, the Queen bravely making small talk and secretly wishing she were home with the corgis. Then, sitting up half of a night writing the story, telegraphing it from Montreal to Toronto (pre-fax, pre-computer times) and waking up the next morning to receive congratulations and a job offer from an appreciative editor.

The *Star Weekly*'s John Clare, who'd awed me with his physical presence and imperturbable ways at *Maclean's*, now felt more like an equal, although he remained as impassive as ever. One winter day we lunched in Toronto's Victoria Hotel. Over a few drinks we solved several of the world's problems. Around 3:00 P.M. we rose, put on our hats and coats, and fell downstairs. Well, slipped, lost our footing. It was just a short flight. We did ourselves no lasting harm. Our hats rolled down ahead of us. *Now,* I thought, *surely John's veneer will crack. He'll at least say, "You all right?"* He did not. He rose with dignity, caught up with his hat, nodded curtly and went back to work.

Today, with magazines closing, or struggling and leaning on staff writing, freelance prospects are bleak. There were many more writing markets in the sixties and the variety was part of the charm. I wrote about Canada and its centennial for *The Lamp,* American counterpart of the *Review,* and received a kind note about it from Bruce Hutchison. I interviewed comedians Frank Shuster and Johnny Wayne for *en Route* magazine, about their frequent travels in California and discovered that rarity—stars who were genuinely nice guys. They were also compulsively funny. During the interview they played a kind of verbal Ping-Pong polished over a lifetime of partnership:

> Wayne: Once I rented a house in L.A., a place worth about $200,000, I got a very good deal . . .
> Shuster: Yeah, you sold your children . . .
> W: I was roughing it in a two-and-a-half acre place with an Olympic-sized pool . . .
> S: The Olympics were on at the time . . .
> W: And as usual Canada did not get a gold medal. . . . But nearly everybody has a pool, you see . . .
> W: [California] is so good you sometimes have the feeling it can't last. Once I was sitting poolside with my son and said, "Mike, would you please get me a lime for my drink."

He climbs a tree, so help me, and picks one! I kept waiting for lightning to strike me down or a large voice from the skies to say, "I WILL SEND A FLOOD TO DESTROY YOU! YE HAVE LIVED TOO LONG ON THE FAT OF THE LAND."

S: Of course some Californians in certain religious sects think they *will* be struck down, or an earthquake will dump the whole state into the Pacific . . .

W: That's why Howard Hughes is buying up Vegas . . .

S: So he'll have waterfront property . . .

Working with Wayne and Shuster, then and on a later story, reminded me how much I yearn to make people laugh. As must be apparent by now, I am a frustrated humour writer. In daydreams I see myself being kissed on both cheeks by Sandra Shamas as she pins the Leacock Medal to my chest–although actually (and here goes my last chance for the Order of Canada) I don't find the revered Leacock nearly as funny as Joey Slinger on a good day or Garrison Keillor on any day. I also think CBC radio's clever "Double Exposure" has it all over the hoser humour of "The Royal Canadian Air Farce," just as the aforementioned Shamas is light-years funnier than Dave Broadfoot.

It's a matter of taste, of course. Humour is wildly subjective, which is why it's such slippery footing for its practitioners. While always pleased and relieved when some editor accepts any of my work, I'm pathetically grateful whenever one takes a flyer on my alleged wit. Such as the time Ann Rhodes, editor of *FP* magazine, bought my fantasy piece about being a back-of-the-book man.

"Back of the book" is jargon for magazine back pages that sometimes carry book reviews, a horoscope, crossword puzzles or a column by some deep thinker or struggling humorist. Others, the ones that fascinate me, are full of small noisy advertisements for trusses, erotic literature, aids to a faltering sex life and other gadgets designed to make you a complete person. "Dreaming of a Better Me" was composed from advertisements of that time:

. . . I was walking along in a dream the other evening when I met my mother whom I hadn't seen in weeks.

"Why, son!" she cried. "You're . . . you're taller than I remembered."

I laughed her a big rich laugh. "It's my Elevators, Mom! I'm two inches taller. Craftily constructed, they Get Me Up Where I Belong. And also, they Keep A Girl On Her Toes!"

"Your hair," my mother said. "It never used to be so dark . . ."

"I touch it up with Top Secret, same as Jan Garber, the famous dance band leader." And I laughed my thunderous laugh again.

"Your voice is different, too, son. It used to be sort of thin and reedy like the Queen's . . ."

"YES. But even you can have a HE-MAN VOICE, Mom. Write to the Perfect Voice Institute in Chicago. They'll send you a free booklet and No Salesman Will Call." I thrust my face toward her. "Notice anything else?"

"You're not the wrinkled little boy that I remember," Mother admitted.

"Why Do You Have A Poor Memory?" I teased. "Maybe you should write to Mundelein, Illinois, for a simple technique for acquiring a powerful memory that can Pay Dividends In Business And Social Advancement. . . . No, no, I'm kidding you, Mom. My skin isn't dry and fatigued any more, because there REALLY IS AN ANSWER TO AGING SKIN. I slosh on Super Shape every day, after I crawl out of my Personal Sauna Bath."

"And what are you working at now?" my mother asked cautiously.

I automatically dropped to one knee, pulled out a pencil and clipboard, and looked around for a smashed car. "I earn up to $1,000 a month as an Accident Investigator," I explained. "A half-million accidents a year create a Wonderful Money-Making Opportunity for men like me. And I'm also training at home for a Big Income Career In Accounting. They gave me a free electric adding machine. On top of that, I'm earning $3 to $6 an hour in my basement, filing saws with my Foley Automatic Saw Filer. And in the kitchen, which is where they tell you to do it, I'm operating a Profitable Rubber Stamp Business using an ordinary electrical outlet."

Then, in the dream, we walked over to my pad (which is what back-of-the-book men live in). My mother examined my

> paint-by-numbers reproduction of a Roman orgy, and the Talking Toilet that jokingly says, "Hey, I'm working down here!" when you sit on it. In the living room she said, "What's that funny-looking radar kind of thing by the window, son?"
>
> "It's my Snooper-Ear, Mom. Works on the same principle as the fabulous missile trackers. Picks up voices too distant to hear. At night I point it across the courtyard, or against the wall of the chick in the next apartment. Best part is, you can plug a tape recorder into it and take everything down . . ."

My working home during that first venture onto the high wire was appropriately bohemian. I answered an ad soon after returning from Montreal. The stairway was dim and moody with heavy oak risers, panelled walls and a big metal-clad door at the top, the sort you should rap on three times and say, "Rocky sent me." I cranked an ancient doorbell that uttered a guttural "drrring" and a wisp of a woman peeked out.

She was a handsome sixty-something with white hair, mobile face, an impish smile and brown eyes that went warm or cold depending, I learned later, on whether she was lovingly planting a petunia bed out front or raging at insensitive bureaucrats in City Hall. But on this particular morning in 1967 she resembled a comic figurine in her baggy Chaplinesque pants, a woollen tea-cosy hat, cotton work gloves and beat-up tennis shoes.

She fixed me with the wary look of someone who has been conned by door-to-door salesmen. I put on my best smile and said I'd come about the studio/room.

"Come in and walk on the newspapers and take off your shoes," she said briskly. "I do all the cleaning myself, so we must not track on the stairs."

It felt like Grade 1 again, but I obediently kicked off my Hush Puppies, padded over the Toronto *Star* classifieds through a hall glowing with polished wood and a garish sign that said SAVE THE OLD CITY HALL, and into Sophie Simkin's life. I am grateful now that pride and the hole in my right sock did not turn me away that day. Sophie was one of the most vital humans I have known. She epitomized the mood of the late sixties-early seventies: people breaking out of conventional moulds and life styles. *My* mood.

The moment I saw studio-apartment #1, I wanted it. It was

a big sunny room facing Toronto's historic St. Lawrence Hall, with an original nineteenth-century iron fireplace, a gigantic table, single bed and other odd bits of furniture, lamps and knickknacks. The tiny kitchen was equipped with a shower. The gas-burning stove beside it was at genital height, which made for interesting times.

At first when I said I'd left a good job with *Reader's Digest* to freelance in Toronto, Sophie was uneasy. She discussed my possible income and whether I smoked or drank. But after an hour of wide-ranging conversation (she checked out prospective tenants very thoroughly and, if they were young, liked to meet their parents), the place was mine. I learned that besides Sophie and three cats, the building housed three other tenants, including two long-timers: David Waterhouse, a University of Toronto professor of East Asian studies who also practised the bagpipes at night, and Peter Kopplin, a specialist in internal medicine at St. Michael's Hospital. She habitually called them The Professor and The Doctor like sons who, happily, had turned out well. Over the years she had housed other professors, an Actor, a Science Instructor and a Newspaperman. I think she was rather pleased to add The Writer to her roster.

From then on Miss Simkin–she always called me Mister Collins and I always responded in kind–showered me with kindness. She asked only that I keep the place clean and not burn it down. She brought little treats at odd hours: fresh apples or dark bread from the neighbouring St. Lawrence Market, a bowl of homemade soup, a plate of eggs and German sausage. I never had the nerve to reject her offerings and often went out sluggishly to dinner, my appetite deadened by a whopping piece of apple pie with cheddar cheese.

Each December she made Christmas dinner for "my boys." It was a fairly chaotic event because the rooms were not equipped for gourmet cookery. But by using The Professor's oven for the turkey, her own for potatoes and pudding, The Doctor's for squash and other vegetables, my refrigerator for salads, and by screeching up and down the stairs like a madwoman, Sophie made it work. Warmed by wine and her obvious delight, we men made tentative conversation, although we had nothing in common except the house, greedily accepted second helpings and retired lumpishly to our quarters, stuffed with dressing like the littlest Cratchits.

About the time I arrived, she was turning her empty ground floor into an antique shop, stocking it with furniture and dishes and silver and lamps and God-knows-what-else trundled back from God-knows-where via pushcart or baby buggy. She never made money from the shop but didn't much care. Shoppers might be asked, "Yes, what do you want?" in the same peremptory tone that made me remove my shoes. Once a friend of mine went in to browse. "We don't much like browsers here," Sophie said tartly. Yet she put an old chair on the sidewalk with a note inviting weary strangers to "Sit awhile." And she would have long gossipy chats out front with any congenial passerby, while burnishing copper or stripping a pine chest.

She was under no obligation to fetch wood for our fireplaces but she did: shopping bags brimming with scraps scrounged from a lumberyard. She rejoiced with me when the cheques rolled in. She raised the rent by a mere eight dollars a month over three years. "And if you can't afford it, we won't raise it!" she insisted. "I know it's difficult for a freelance writer." I said it was okay, I'd just sold a book to McClelland & Stewart. Miss Simkin was visibly relieved and plied me with home cooking for a week.

Little wonder that I was productive in that yeasty environment. I don't mean to imply that freelancing was or is a breeze. There are more losers than winners. As an exercise in humility I keep in a yellowing scrapbook the form-letter rejections from articles and short stories unsold some forty-five years ago. But there were no rejections (just rewrites) in that first tour of serious freelancing. I simply couldn't afford failure.

Nor could I afford to be sick or hurt. A freelancer friend, Dean Walker, was once pottering about his house when a window fell on his fingers. He lurched toward his wife, hands gnarled in pain, in search of solace. She said, "My God, Dean, how are you going to type?" I stayed away from open windows.

I also kept my fingernails clipped very short so I could type really fast. Once a woman of my acquaintance, an aggressive amateur psychiatrist who was always probing for my soft spots, cried hopefully, "Why do you bite your nails?" I smiled enigmatically and beat her off at ninety words per minute. Freelance writers should keep their nails and their relationships short.

And I learned to have many assignments in various stages of dress or undress with more than one market–insurance against the inevitable change of editors and editorial favourites. When Peter Gzowski became editor of the *Star Weekly* in 1967, I knew my freelance days with that magazine were over. Gzowski and I had crossed swords when at *Maclean's,* and he no more wanted to work with me than I with him. Fortunately I had plenty of alternatives.

With those few provisos my freelance experiment was an unqualified success. Through 1967–69 inclusive I wrote forty-eight full-length magazine articles, five books and twenty-four other items: booklets, magazine humour columns, some editing jobs (I tried to launch an editing service, which flopped), a few speeches and a one-hour stage show for an Imperial Oil anniversary party. There were working trips to the Florida Everglades and Cartagena in Colombia.

Over the three years I grossed $60,303, not bad for the times. I learned that most essential of words for a freelancer: "No." Writing is a bit like prostitution: you do it for money and hate to say no because the client might never ask you again. When I was able to say it out loud–being selective in jobs accepted, turning down those I hated on sight, allowing time for other things in life without breaking out in cold sweats at 3:00 A.M.–I knew I had arrived.

It was time for the next adventure. My daughters and I, after the pain and awkwardness of separation, were getting back to normal. (Ultimately Ruth and I would become friendly again.) I had survived some of the worst hurdles of the writing and real worlds. Life was fun again.

9

THE CHIEF

Of all my story subjects during those freelance years, the paradoxical John Diefenbaker was by turns the most entertaining and just plain maddening. He was a frustrating interview, wrenching from me every trick and technique I had acquired over the years. At the mere sight of a note pad or tape recorder he put on his official face, adopted his most sonorous tone and snowed you under with deviation, obfuscation and tales of his prairie upbringing.

If you ever crossed him, or he thought you were going to, he turned to stone. Dief never forgot a grudge. After the 1958 publication of Peter C. Newman's *Renegade in Power,* a candid biography that revealed all the politician's warts, Diefenbaker snubbed the author. Nine years later, writing about Dief for the Toronto *Star Weekly,* I looked up Newman in Ottawa to see if they had kissed and made up. Not so.

Once, during the 1965 election campaign, Peter said, he and Diefenbaker came nose-to-nose in the cockpit of an Air Canada Viscount. The pilot, who liked Newman's book, had asked him up front. The co-pilot, who admired the Chief, as Dief's intimates called him, had invited him.

"I finally said, 'Hello, Mr. Diefenbaker,' " Newman told me. "He just glared at me. At other times in the campaign, he looked through me."

Diefenbaker was an inept prime minister—partly because his decades as a political loner gave him no experience in trusting or managing people. Many journalists and political watchers despised him for that, for his jealousies and for his alleged megalomania. But Douglas Fisher, a former NDP member of Parliament, one of the longest-serving and more astute journalists on Parliament Hill, put it best for me: "I've always admired him as a personality and performer in Parliament."

Exactly. Dief-the-performer, Dief-the-character, Dief who loved the Parliamentary game. Those are the qualities I remember with amusement and affection.

My first meeting with him was for that *Star Weekly* article of '67. He was still Leader of the Opposition and the Tories were having a convention that fall. Would Diefenbaker stand for leadership again? Would the party dump him? He didn't yet know and wouldn't have told if he did. But we wanted a chatty session and some intimate glimpses of this complex, colourful man.

At first he played cat-and-mouse. I went to Ottawa with an appointment. I hadn't seen Diefenbaker in the flesh since a political rally at university twenty years before, but he still looked like his cartoons: the crinkly grey hair centre-parted, the pale blue eyes beneath arched eyebrows giving him an air of perpetual astonishment. He was hard of hearing and had a slight tremor, but the oft-imitated voice still had its resonant cadence.

He had to cancel, he said. A bad day. See my secretary for something next week. If that had happened to me a dozen years earlier, I might have lost heart. But I showed up a second time with a clean shirt and a friendly smile. Dief backed off again on another pretext. I guessed he was testing my staying power, and I'd acquired it in spades. He promised to see me at eight the next morning, a time of day when Diefenbaker was fresh as a newly minted coin and most reporters are at their worst.

Faced with an empty afternoon and evening in the City of the Living Dead, I flew back to Toronto at my own expense. My female friend of the moment was receiving some minor editorial award that night. I would attend, offer praise and win points as a caring, sensitive male.

Instead the evening degenerated into a fight, as our evenings frequently did. I returned to Toronto airport at 10:30 P.M. in a foul temper and a torn suit. The flight was delayed; Ottawa was fogged in. With a clutch of other tired bitchy travellers, all with ten o'clock shadows (well, the men anyway), I hung around until

2:00 A.M. Then, with Ottawa still in a fog, Air Canada flew us to Montreal. There, at 5:00 A.M., the people's airline put us on a bus. A good driver could reach Ottawa in two hours; I could still make my interview.

Our driver, it transpired, had never been out of Quebec. After a false start, he actually found the highway, but at the outskirts of our nation's capitol he threw in the towel. The late Warner Troyer, broadcast journalist and fellow traveller on this voyage of the damned, moved up front and talked the driver into downtown Ottawa. At 7:30 I sprang out near my hotel (I'd kept the room), changed, shaved too fast and ran for the Hill. Bleeding only a little, I got to Diefenbaker's office at precisely eight.

The old Chief was bright as a jaybird. He'd been up since 5:30 answering his mail. He was still getting three hundred letters a week, claimed to read them all and personally answered about half, to the despair of his staff.

"I'm sorry we've had so much trouble getting together," he said, "but this is another bad day. . . ."

Jack Sangster, a big quiet business man from Saskatoon, was lingering in the outer office. *Bad day, my butt! You just want to gossip with your crony!* By now I had grasped one of writing's little verities: be polite to your subjects but don't let them bully you. As *Times-Herald* cub reporter, I would have smiled apologetically and turned away. But this was twenty years later, I'd been up all night and had an Excedrin headache. I stayed put and fixed the Chief with the death-ray glance that my late father had used on Liberals. "This is the *third* time, Mr. Diefenbaker."

Dief decided the game was over. He led me into a small back room, flopped on a couch, wrapped his arms behind his head. "Tell me the kind of things you want." I did. Dief verbally bobbed and weaved for fifteen minutes, telling how his family had driven a wagon to the prairie in 1903 amid old Red River cart trails and bleaching buffalo bones. Having already read this in checking his biographical background, I did not find it mesmerizing.

Then he bounced to his feet and said, "Have you had breakfast?" He led Sangster and me to the Parliamentary dining room, pausing in his outer office to point out his eight-foot-six-inch stuffed marlin staring down glassy-eyed from a wall. In his John F. Kennedy accent, he told how the U.S. president had seen and coveted the fish ("I've spent fifty thousand dollars trying to catch a fish like that"). Upstairs an aide had staked out a corner table overlooking the Ottawa River and Hull. It was a sweet, soft June morning. Diefenbaker tied into his grapefruit, bran flakes, bacon and eggs, and the stories began to flow.

He told of meeting Winston Churchill and how "my life in politics has been worth it if only because I had the opportunity to meet the old man in his various moods." In his Churchill accent, he told how Winston on hearing of an MP described as a wolf in sheep's clothing, had growled, "The Membah is a *sheep* in sheep's clothing." In his Bond Street accent Diefenbaker remembered that British prime minister Harold MacMillan once purged several cabinet ministers, causing a colleague to remark in a twist on the Scriptures that "Harold has laid down his friends for his life."

He interrupted himself to press more toast, milk, coffee upon us, with a kind of warm country hospitality. He told C. D. Howe stories and Paul Martin stories ("I love to make Paul mad. You can do it by saying innocently that no other Member has the ability to compress such small thoughts into so many words").

Then he said, "Excuse me, I'm terrible when I get this way," but none of us wanted the story-telling to stop. There was a little silence. Diefenbaker looked out the window and said softly, "I love this place. If I should ever leave here, I wouldn't come back. I couldn't come back and just watch from the gallery." He had said this before and would say it again, but for once seemed not to be playing to an audience.

Later I got the official interview. It was a flop. Some subjects, I've discovered, are spooked by tape recorders—terrified at seeing their every word being locked into a cassette. More experienced interviewees, accustomed to the electronic media, talk comfortably as though the machine weren't there. Diefenbaker took the taped interview to another plateau: for an hour he simply talked in platitudes.

The moment the tape recorder clicked off, he was transformed. He showed me his collection of cartoons which, although wicked caricatures, mostly showed him in the role he loved: battling pesky Liberals, doubting Tories or unspeakable socialists. He held up a small green dumpy Man-from-Mars figure and said it looked like Paul Martin. He told a new John A. Macdonald story. He followed me to the outer office and produced a letter from a pack of Cubs that had toured his office. Now that I wasn't officially "press" any more, John Diefenbaker seemed reluctant to say good-bye.

Then, more than ever before, I realized that the seemingly peripheral parts of a story can *be* the story. My piece, heavily featuring those informal glimpses, told far more of the man than a dozen formal interviews. The *Star Weekly* ran it as a cover story with Duncan MacPherson cartoons. I guess Diefenbaker liked it–although the subject's approval must never be the gauge of good journalism–because later he gave me one of his autographed illuminated copies of the Canadian Bill of Rights.

There were other Dief-encounters. I wrote a profile of him for *Reader's Digest*; then in 1976 ghostwrote a short piece about his favourite boyhood Christmas for the same magazine. It was a thin premise at best and I got off on the wrong foot by violating a basic precept of journalism: be fit, sharp and awake for an interview. The night before meeting him I called upon journalist friend Hartley Steward, who was visiting his parents on the outskirts of Ottawa. Hartley Sr. welcomed us with some bottles of his powerful homemade red wine.

We sat out back, that balmy summer evening, working on the red and discussing affairs of state. This was no impertinent little wine but a big bossy one that wouldn't take no for an answer. In time we no longer felt the hordes of mosquitoes biting us through spaces in the deck chairs' webbing.

Around 4:00 A.M. the wine was gone and so were we. Hartley Jr. drove me back to my hotel. No one else was on the road. I remember, with shame, that I sang a merry tune while he drove skillfully down the white centre line. I know that Hartley got back alive because he went on to be managing editor of the Toronto *Star,* and later publisher of the Ottawa *Sun*.

After a couple of hours in bed I rose to face the new day with the vicious headache I deserved. I once read a self-help article that said writers should prepare for an interview the way boxers train for a fight: eat a thick steak, eschew sex, avoid booze and get twelve hours sleep. I had broken training on at least two counts.

At nine I reached Diefenbaker's office, zombie-like and writhing with mosquito bites arranged in checkerboard squares across my back and buttocks. Diefenbaker was disgustingly cheerful and seemed pleased to see me. We were on amiable terms from earlier assignments and, as subjects go, Prairie Christmas was about as threatening as a newborn puppy.

His glory days as Prime Minister and Leader of the Opposition were over. He was shoe-horned into a cramped office where we sat virtually knee to knee, surrounded by all the precious clutter of his political life.

My question list was on my lap, as always. I had learned to plan assignments the way nineteenth-century brigadiers planned their jolly good wars. I spend hours preparing for every interview, gathering background on my subject, working up questions in a sequence that flows easily from one topic to the next, making sure the key questions get asked within the allotted time, prepared to follow any deviations that might crop up, but with *enough* questions to keep the whole thing moving smoothly without bumbling pauses. (Planning also prevents the moronic queries so common to sports writers: "What happened?" or "Uh . . . how do you feel?")

While the subject is answering one question I glance at the next–if it isn't obvious or if the topic hasn't taken an intriguing new turn–so there is no sense of reading from a script. Nearly always it comes off like a conversation between two friends.

Except this day, I'd left my brains and reflexes back in the hotel.

"Ahh, I see you have your questions," Diefenbaker droned in his courtroom voice with the sibilant s's. Then he reached across, plucked them from my nerveless fingers and began reading them aloud and answering them: " 'How old were you, the first Christmas you can remember? . . .' Yess . . . Yess . . . our family came west in 1903 in a wagon with the cow tethered behind . . . the buffalo bones were still bleaching on the prairie . . ."

Mercifully, he was called to the phone. I snatched my questions back and regained a semblance of control. Turning it into a passable story required every device of questioning, frantic research and writing I had learned in thirty years. (Sometimes I likened myself to Gordie Howe in his last years of hockey: my legs had slowed but I still had a helluva wrist shot.)

"My First Prairie Christmas" ran as the *Digest*'s lead story that December. As a goodwill gesture, the magazine plated the opening pages and affixed them to a walnut plaque. Editor Charles Magill and I then ascended the Hill like the Magi to present our gift to the Chief.

It was another non-threatening mission and Diefenbaker was thrilled. He looked at the four-colour illustration of his parents, brother Elmer and himself and intoned, "Yess, that's exactly how we looked!" (How could he possibly remember after sixty years?) He retold the story of how Elmer hit the preacher with a volley of BB pellets in church one Sunday. He told all the other stories I'd heard before but Magill hadn't. It was great entertainment.

A half-hour later, we rose politely: Surely Mr. Diefenbaker had other things to do? Apparently not. He escorted us to the outer office where ex-broadcaster and staunch Tory Joel Aldred waited patiently, along with Dief's secretary and a junior MP with large white teeth.

"Look at this!" Diefenbaker showed the plaque around.

"Very nice, Chief," Aldred said in his big, rich radio voice. "When did you write the article?" I waited for Dief to say, "Ahhh, Joel, my friend Collins here actually wrote it, you understand."

Instead, the Chief turned to me, his pale eyes questioning, genuinely puzzled. He said, "Ahh, when *did* I write that article?"

Magill and I laughed all the way down Parliament Hill.

Although the Conservatives dumped Diefenbaker from leadership, he kept winning his Prince Albert seat. Once I attended an election night in that Saskatchewan city, to see Dief yet again accept the plaudits of his constituents, with second wife, Olive, at his side. When he introduced me, Olive smiled with her lips but appraised me coolly with watchful eyes. Media, with their habit of crucifying her man, were not her favourite species.

I last saw John Diefenbaker near the end of his life, from the Parliamentary visitors' gallery during a routine Question Period. He was sprawled in his front-row Opposition seat, inert, eyes hooded, like an ancient turtle slumbering in the sun. Then suddenly he was up, hands swept backwards on his hips—his trademark stance, the old trial lawyer sweeping back his gown—

levelling storm and outrage at the Liberals. It was nothing of import, a small procedural point, but he'd caught the Liberals off guard, sent them scurrying for papers, caused a moment of mild embarrassment.

The Chief settled down, a glimmer of pleasure in his eyes. The Tories around him grinned and nodded and thumped their desks. For a moment he was Dief of old. For a moment he had Parliament in the palm of his hand.

It was all he ever really wanted.

10

THE BACTERIA SHIRT, AND OTHER STORIES OF MY SECOND CHILDHOOD

In the spring of 1970 the planets were in confluence, God was in His or Her Heaven and the universe was unfolding as it should. For me, anyway. My daughters, centre of my personal universe, and I were close again.

The country was still agog with sixties' rebellion and change: drugs, dropouts, easy sex, live-in relationships. Micro skirts, hot pants and bell-bottoms adorned the nation's shins and derrieres. "The Age of Aquarius" and "Bridge Over Troubled Water" rang out from radio and disco. A young Robert Bourassa had just been named head of the Quebec Liberal Party. The ocean tanker *Arrow* spilled 1.5 million gallons of Bunker C heavy heating oil into Nova Scotia's Chedabucto Bay. In October Prime Minister Trudeau would invoke the War Measures Act.

The best of times and the worst of times.

The city magazine, a relatively new genre, was making modest waves. *New York* magazine, in its third year, was already the talk of North American journalism with its fresh ideas, superb editing and the writing of such then or future superstars as Tom Wolfe, Gloria Steinem, Gay Talese, Gail Green, Jimmy Breslin, Judith Crist, Peter Maas and on and on. As a *New York* junkie I began reading the local version, *Toronto Life,* which suffered badly by comparison.

After five years *Toronto Life* was into its second owner and third editor. It was known as a "horsey" magazine, written for the socialite friends of its polo-playing publisher, Michael Sifton. This was not entirely fair. Sifton was a serious and long-established publisher. Editor Alan Walker, anything but horsey, was producing some fine articles by fine writers. But the magazine seemed wildly uneven. There'd be solid pieces on juvenile offenders, the Don jail or slum landlords–and other vague confections on rugger, body building, horseback riding or skiing. Covers often featured cutesy female faces. There was a regular feature on fashion. A monthly photo section, About Town–mostly dedicated to society glitz–reinforced the horsey image.

I thought *Toronto Life* lacked cohesion and identity, and said as much over dinner in 1969 with my university friend Max Macdonald, now editor of the Siftons' Saskatoon *Star-Phoenix*. We both recall that I was angling for nothing more than a fat consultancy to sweeten freelance life. That life was prospering, but I was getting tired of working at a dead run every day.

In October Sifton's right-hand man in Toronto, Preston Balmer, invited me to lunch. Balmer had the mild demeanour and deceptive offhand manner of a farm boy just in from Boondocks, Saskatchewan. In fact, he was a vice-president and canny administrator, and Sifton trusted him implicitly. Balmer listened politely and attentively as I spouted off. He did not even hint at a job but admitted they wanted to improve *Toronto Life,* which was mired in a circulation of around 21,000. When we parted, he invited me to send along any additional thoughts. I happily poured out a two-thousand-word treatise, saying in part:

> . . . *Toronto Life* could do more than offer aid and entertainment to the individual. It could reflect the character of this city; be the voice of this city. I come back, now, to the sickness that infects so many other North American communities. The magazine should in every issue explore one or more of the citizens' and/or city's major problems or complaints. It should treat these in depth, ferreting out the good and bad for praise and constructive criticism respectively. Without becoming partisan it should keep officialdom on its toes. It would be authoritative, forthright, respected. It would be a publication that a majority of Torontonians would feel obligated to read . . .
>
> This calls for strong inspired editorial direction. *Toronto Life*'s editor needs a vast knowledge of, and curiosity about, all aspects of his city from Don Mills to Yorkville, Bay Street to

> Little Italy, Queen's Park and City Hall to the waterfront and Mac's Shoeshine. He should be at least spiritually in tune with many levels and age groups; should be a skilled writer, editor, manager of staff and a superb idea man; should be familiar with the essential partnership between copy, titles and illustrations that make each magazine feature a concerted package and make each issue of a magazine an effective entity. Such a person having demonstrated his ability and trustworthiness to management should be given wide editorial freedom and should be treated and paid as a senior executive of the organization. He should also know the best writers and illustrators, be respected by them and be able, at his discretion, to pay top rates for freelance.

It was fairly clear that I considered myself to be this paragon—no longer the scared self-deprecating creature who'd left *Maclean's*—but I ended on a suitable note of humility:

> . . . Thanks for letting me pontificate. A magazine is, or should be, a living organism, a whole thing with personality and impact, not just a random collection of indifferent writing. For me, too often, *Toronto Life* is the latter. But I wish you luck in your efforts to improve it . . .

Early in 1970 Mike Sifton invited me into Armadale, the family's holding company offices in the Toronto-Dominion tower. A handsome man of thirty-nine, he'd served an apprenticeship on the London *Free Press* under Macdonald. (Max didn't immediately realize that young Sifton was a scion of the newspaper family, and gave him earnest lectures on proper journalism. Mike made notes and years later blithely used Macdonald's own words against him when—roles reversed—they were arguing a point.)

By 1970 Mike was at the helm of the family firm under father Clifford, who in turn was son of Sir Clifford Sifton, the turn-of-the-century Liberal cabinet minister who profoundly influenced western Canadian immigration. The Siftons owned or controlled newspapers in Regina and Saskatoon, a Regina TV station, radio stations in four cities and the community airport at Buttonville north of Toronto.

Blunt and aggressive, Mike didn't beat around the bush, which I appreciated. He liked my ideas, he said, and would offer me a job as editor but was a publisher who wanted to be involved. If I didn't like that we should part right now.

It worried me. I knew Mike was a burr under his editors' saddles but, with the exception of Walker, they had the advantage of distance between themselves and the boss. I went away and thought hard. Somebody was going to get the job; Sifton had made up his mind to let Walker go. If I went I'd at least have a shot at turning *Toronto Life* into a real city magazine. If I turned it down I'd always regret it.

On February 22 I sent Mike a six-page letter laying down my thoughts and hopes for *Toronto Life* and a working relationship with him:

> . . . I'm still somewhat uneasy over the matter of editorial freedom, although you were frank on the point. I think the publisher should care and take part, particularly when he has real journalistic knowledge and experience . . . I think the role of editor has to be clearly defined and carefully preserved. Teamwork, by all means. Policies laid down by the publisher, yes. Specific suggestions from the publisher, yes, providing these are not automatically regarded as direct orders. There may be special cases where the publisher will overrule the editor on a story, for sound business reasons perhaps, but these cases should be extremely rare. The editor should be able to reject suggestions from above, as well as below, if he firmly believes (and can demonstrate) that they are not best for the magazine. It has nothing to do with the editor's ego.
>
> An editor is hired as specialist, not just a caretaker, not a mere editor of copy but a creative and sound individual who can take the policies from above and the offerings from below and distill them into a strong entity, a great magazine, a magazine with a unified voice, purpose and personality. This is more important today than ever before; in fact, it's mandatory to a magazine's survival.
>
> To do this the editor needs creative elbow room. A great magazine is the result of teamwork above and below the editor's level, but the editor has to be free to make the editorial

> decisions. If it becomes necessary for a publisher to directly assign a staffer to a story over the editor's head, for whatever reasons, then the editor should resign. Obviously he has lost the publisher's trust, and trust is inherent in all of this. . . . Editing by committee, no. It never works . . .

This was a balancing act. A good magazine must reflect *one* vision and personality: the editor's. I knew *Toronto Life* would have to mirror mine, but had I said so at this point, Mike would have interpreted it as an effort to undermine him. He already felt the existing staff was conspiring against him.

I proposed detailed content for a revamped *Toronto Life,* and concluded by saying these were the only conditions under which I could be effective. If he chose to not act on them, he was welcome to any of my ideas and I would offer suggestions for other candidates for editor.

On the back of my copy of that letter I scribbled pros and cons. Atop one column was "Challenge," atop the other was "Frustration with Sifton." Lower down I wrote: "His stated views alarm me." I was going into this with eyes wide open, but was arrogant enough to believe I could pull it off.

I got the job, took my daughters on a two-week motoring trip through Florida, and returned to the two most exuberant and exhausting years of my life.

Beforehand, I had coffee with outgoing editor Alan Walker, fair-haired, stocky, thirtyish, with a bespectacled gaze that reminded me of Ralph Allen. Walker was a capable editor simply in the wrong place at the wrong time. He'd been on *Time* magazine (and went from *Toronto Life* to *The Canadian,* then *Maclean's,* where until recently he was a senior editor).

Ostensibly we met to discuss the changeover. In part he was sizing me up for his staff, back at the office nervously awaiting his report. I was forty-six; they were ten to twenty-five years younger. I had written for *Reader's Digest*: was I a small condensed person, committed to articles on "10 Ways to Save Your Flagging Marriage" or "Every Cloud with a Silver Lining"? I was Mike Sifton's choice; was I in the pocket of this wealthy Philistine who'd had the audacity to tell them how to run their magazine? Long after, I discovered they'd been contemplating a mass walkout. Walker sensibly urged against it, although it must have been tempting.

Among Walker's interests were a passion for old Dracula movies and a fondness for casual footwear, especially moccasins. He told his staff (I heard later) that I wore beat-up Hush Puppies at our first meeting so perhaps I was not beyond redemption. We arranged that I would go into the office on the Friday before my starting date. He would show me around. I'd go away, leaving him to his farewells, and start work the following Monday.

When I showed up that Friday morning Alan wasn't there. I couldn't blame him; it was a terrible situation. Managing editor Anne Marshall became my saviour. As the daughter of Adam, my Imperial Oil number-two boss, she knew I didn't have two heads. Tall, slim, red haired, blessed with editorial savvy and her parents' charm and good sense, Anne introduced me to the staff. It was *Earth Creatures Meet Alien* at the Roxy.

I knew they distrusted and maybe hated me. I had unseated their much-loved editor who had (perhaps unwisely) made himself one of them. But they seemed also to love the magazine, which was a start. My job would be to harness their affection to a somewhat different and better version.

Assistant managing editor Mary McIver, the only other editorial staffer, a short brunette with Elizabeth Taylor eyes, was polite but reserved. The sales force greeted me with false heartiness. The art staff, Nick Burnett and Rob Melbourne, watched me closely for portents. Art directors live for the grand splash: lots of photos and four-colour illustrations in extravagant full-page spreads. Editors are their natural enemies, the kill-joys who want to fill the pages with bothersome words.

My tour of inspection ended abruptly. The June issue was close to press. Everyone was looking to me for answers. For the rest of that day I plunged into frantic decisions, hasty editings, heads and decks. I wrote the first of many titles that tickled me, on an article by Marci McDonald about Irving Ungerman, manager of boxer George Chuvalo. The feisty cigar-smoking manager also ran a chicken plant, so:

WHAT'S A TOUGH BIRD LIKE IRV
DOING IN A CHICKEN PLACE LIKE THIS?

Lunchtime passed without lunch. Ten hours later I lurched out of the editor's shoe-box office onto the street. A man from the business side insisted on buying me a drink but it turned out he was angling for favours.

By autumn I was getting a hold on the magazine and over the next eighteen months turned it into something close to my dream. Along with hundreds of service stories we ran articles on feminism (a fairly new phenomenon); the Mafia in Toronto (evidently it didn't upset the Mob because nobody made me an offer I couldn't refuse); kids freaking out on LSD; sexually molested children; on being black in Toronto by a black writer; marijuana, the new "business lunch"; on keeping hysteria out of the anti-pollution campaign; the rehabilitation of a slum; and on the considerable power and curious rules of the Liquor Control Board of Ontario.

I dumped Fashion and introduced "The Itinerant Eater," a monthly feature on good new low-priced restaurants. "Citylife," a new regular feature on miscellaneous helpful ideas, told how to find a nursery school, night school, cleaning woman, foreign movie, dependable taxi firm or grub for a gourmet cat.

Peter Newman wrote us a lyrical guest column on the Palais Royale dance hall and his passion, the music of Stan Kenton. Other fine writers–Tom Alderman, Alan Edmonds, Harry Bruce, Sandra Peredo, Cathy Wismer, Jon Ruddy and Maggie Siggins–were contributors. Marq de Villiers, who'd worked for Walker, continued writing for me; years later he became the longest-running editor in *Toronto Life*'s history.

A brash twenty-two-year-old, Joanne Kates, who'd studied Cordon Bleu cooking in France, took over "Itinerant Eater" in its second year. Later she became the feared and celebrated restaurant critic for the Toronto *Globe and Mail.* Marjorie Harris, noted today for books and columns on gardening, wrote for us on her city garden. Myra Sable regularly floated into my office on waves of heavenly cologne to write of such things as antiques and summer camps, and went on with a partner to market the Sable & Rosenfeld line of gourmet condiments.

Writing for *Toronto Life* did not necessarily contribute to their subsequent success or celebrity. It simply meant that the best available magazine journalists were eager to work for us. It's gratifying, and somehow part of the editor/writer kinship, that most of them have prevailed.

I inherited a mixed bag of columnists. The stylish David Cobb could make even a monthly car column interesting, although he was habitually late ("Anne, tell Cobb if that column isn't in *today,* he's through!"). Toronto *Telegram* staffer Sid Adilman continued his lip-smacking monthly reports on the city's burgeoning ethnic restaurants. When the *Telegram* forbade staff freelancing, a Zelda Bruchner abruptly took over "Ethnic Eateries." No one had ever heard of Zelda but, amazingly, she wrote just like Sid.

Edie Frankel continued her society gossip/photo feature, "About Town." It represented everything I hated, but Sifton loved it and it was impossible to dislike Edie, a blonde divorcée whose effervescent manner, honed on the social circuit, masked a shrewd mind and an earthy sense of humour.

Margaret Campbell, a former Toronto mayor and by then a councillor, wrote a civics column that defied reading. But she was decent and gracious so I interviewed her each month, and tried to manufacture a silk purse from her words. In time she gracefully withdrew. Harold Town, on the other hand, left noisily. The iconoclastic artist had been allowed to write anything he liked. His column was lively and opinionated, but he was a loose cannon on the deck. We got along nicely for nearly a year. Then Town turned in a column on another artist so outrageous and so libellous that we told him it had to be cut.

"Nobody cuts my copy," he said. "If you do, I quit."

"We're going to miss you, Harold," I said. We did, but not all that much.

And I wrote an editor's column that served many purposes, not least of which was to show off my writing. It is useful to let writers know their editor can build words as well as destroy them.

The fact that John Bassett Sr. phoned to chastise me about a piece we did on his *Telegram*; that Clark Davey, managing editor of the *Globe and Mail* (later a good friend) once snapped, "I suppose you're going to savage us in your magazine"; and that Peter Newman called, perturbed over our forthcoming piece on *Maclean's*, indicated we were catching people's attention. We weren't the "horsey" magazine of reputation.

In fact, Sifton became highly sensitive on the subject of

"horsiness" and stopped pressing me to use articles by his cronies. But *Toronto Life,* the only magazine in the Sifton empire, was close to his heart. He stayed involved. Some called it meddling but I had no grounds for complaint, although naturally I complained. He was true to his stated intentions, and it was his money.

Mike took umbrage at a Bill Cameron piece on American draft dodgers in Toronto. We argued about it for an hour on the phone. He considered it pro-dodger propaganda. Cameron (later co-anchor of CBC's "The Journal") indeed showed sympathy for dodgers who had skipped over the border for reasons of conscience. Sifton felt a lot of them were cop-outs and undesirables.

Some publishers, feeling as strongly as he did, would have killed the story. Then I would have had to resign. In the end I ran Cameron's story as he wrote it, and aired Mike's and my differing views in the editor's column. Some days I felt like applying for the Nobel Peace Prize.

In the beginning Mike had specified that he would approve our covers. It was a bargaining chip I'd had to relinquish for my shot at a city magazine. Each month I faced the ordeal of taking transparencies to his office tower, where he'd installed a light box for this purpose. I always took a broad sampling, working up to the one I wanted. Mike debated them all with vigour.

He liked cover photos of pretty women because, he maintained, they sold magazines. I considered this outdated (we'd never heard of "sexist"), wanted covers tied to an inside story but didn't always have a strong contender, which Mike was quick to spot. Many times I got my way, but only after exhausting exchanges that left me feeling as though I'd been hit by a train.

Sometimes we were both satisfied. Our cover story on feminism, for instance, had feminist writer Maggie Siggins arm-wrestling with her boyfriend. Singer Tobi Lark, a vibrant black lead in the musical "Hair," adorned the issue that carried a profile on her. Two fetching cyclists, Shirley Thompson and Barbara Rutledge, rode in mini-skirts on our cover for a special on back-to-work commuting styles. To go with Tom Alderman's piece on where to get Toronto's best shoeshines, our cover showed a pair of long booted legs (not Tom's) with shoeshine at one end and hot pants at the other.

Although not the posed vapid faces of earlier times, they were frivolous covers, to be sure. I was desperately trying to lure readers, frantically trying to find the secret ingredient that makes people buy a magazine at the newsstand. Our best-seller was an unposed shot that I pulled out of a pile of photographic contact prints: two students impulsively hugging in a York University common room.

Rarely did we achieve the kind of cover Mike wanted. Nor, probably, was I ever exactly the editor he hoped I'd be. I suspect that, because I was older, Mike assumed I wouldn't rock any boats and would more often share his views. One evening after work, he took me for drinks at one of the body-painting bars that passed for entertainment in the seventies. We made desultory conversation while bra-less women in see-through blouses served our drinks and a painter smeared colourful designs around a model's bare nipples. Mike was simply being friendly, trying to establish rapport, maybe trying to find out whether I was a normal male who liked bare breasts (I do, in private), but it was all a bit awkward.

Yet I liked him and I think he liked me. Once, when the magazine's business manager fell ill, Sifton insisted that I be general manager as well as editor. It was an impossible combination and after a few months we found a replacement. Still, Mike trusted me enough to oversee all aspects of his magazine.

The staff got used to me. Mary McIver proved to be a fine writer. Skinny Rob Melbourne, with his Jesus hairstyle, tinted wire-frames and psychedelic clothes, became an equally fine art director after Burnett moved to *Maclean's*. Anne Marshall was even-tempered, wise and had excellent contacts, particularly in the arts world. Her desk looked like Toronto after Hurricane Hazel. One night in the early weeks, working long after everyone else had gone home, I went searching her office for a missing manuscript. On top of the rubble lay her half-finished letter to a friend: "... Our new editor is not as vivid as the old one but he seems to have the knack of getting on with our publisher ..."

My "knack" was the reason we all still worked there and why Walker did not, but I never mentioned my illicit discovery. Anne eventually realized that I wasn't totally boring, nor in the publisher's pocket, and that I loved *Toronto Life* with all my heart. She became one of my strongest allies. The other was stocky, dapper John Moore, who rose from the ranks to be advertising manager. Moore and I resolved to bury the usual advertising/editorial hatchet and between us make this magazine a winner. We ended up very close friends.

The entire staff lived and breathed *Toronto Life*. After work we often repaired en masse to the nearest tavern and talked deep into the evening. It was intoxicating (in the intellectual sense), all-consuming and hard on marriages for the few who were married.

There were also endless incestuous media events for anyone with the inclination to attend. I wrote a column about them:

> A number of you have been kind enough to ask me about the social whirl of being an editor. I'm delighted to be able to tell you and you'll forgive the malicious little lift I feel, knowing the envy in your hearts when you hear what you are missing.
>
> Every day two or three invitations to something arrive in the office: to sample a wine, view a new line of clothing, attend the opening of a tower, herald the launching of a book or, once, to view a new strip joint and all the wonders that it entails. Wise men avoid most of these functions, mainly because each has a commercial axe to grind, partly because the booze and hors d'oeuvres are bad for one's arteries and small brain cells. But even attending, say, 10 percent of them, one detects a certain pattern.
>
> For instance, Jack McClelland's Sunday brunch at the Westbury for Pierre Berton's *The Last Spike* was a very fine brunch indeed and I was gratified to see so many familiar faces. Naturally Pierre was there, and his wife, Janet, and Charles Templeton and Peter and Christina Newman of *Maclean's,* and Doris Anderson of *Chatelaine* and Bill French of the *Globe and Mail* and Alderman Bill Kilbourn. And Elsa Franklin, Pierre's television producer and her husband, Stephen, and Mike Hanlon of *The Canadian* and Robert Fulford and Harold Town.
>
> Well, then, at the reception in Ontario Place for Yousuf Karsh's new book I was pleased to see Peter Newman again, although Christina wasn't there, but Jean Wright of *Chatelaine*

> was and so was Pat Murray of CTV. A few nights later at Arthur Hailey's *Wheels* party in the Granite Club it was good to see the Franklins again, and Mike Hanlon and Janet Berton (although regrettably Pierre couldn't make it, being en route home from Calgary). And then there were Jeannine Locke and Lyal and Barbara Brown of CBC, and Frank Shuster, and although I didn't see them I am darn sure Johnny Wayne and Peter Newman and Bob Fulford and Bill French were there too.
>
> As luck would have it, I ran into Lyal and Barbara Brown the very next night at Macmillan's book-launching party, and also Bill French and Bill Kilbourn, and on the way out I said hello to Harold Town who informed me that *his* new book was coming out very soon. Unfortunately I missed that one, and I sincerely hope all my friends noted my absence. But I made it to Captain John's for the McGraw-Hill smash for Hugh Garner and Alice Munro, and was delighted to see Mike Hanlon and Bill French and Pat Murray and Steve and Elsa Franklin and . . . well, you know.

Those were strange, frenetic times. Young people in vibrant colours danced to maximum decibels in the surreal blink of strobe lights. They smoked pot; fell in and out of relationships by the month, or week, or day; made love-not-war; struggled to understand what life was all about.

Free love didn't necessarily make them happy. One glum young woman told me, "I'm so tired of waking up and wondering who the face is on the pillow beside me." A statuesque redhead of my acquaintance decided to spice up her relationship one night: she planned to greet her boyfriend (not me, not me) at her apartment door clad only in whipped cream. He was late. When he finally showed up the whipped cream had run and dried. It was not a pretty sight.

Neither was I, upon arriving at *Toronto Life,* according to stylish friends (suddenly I seemed to have a lot of them). My wardrobe was simple and utilitarian: two tweed jackets, grey slacks, one elderly dark blue suit for special occasions. My haircut was contemporary–collar-length at the back, sideburns to the jaw line–but my "look" was not.

I dread buying clothes. Salespersons bully me. My colour blindness has led to some spectacular gaffes. This time writer Thelma Dickman, whose persuasive powers were awesome, led me by the nose to Harry Rosen's high temple of haberdashery where her husband bought his clothes. Thelma was briefly home on holiday from France, where Charles's company had posted them. Having a temporary Parisienne help choose my new threads seemed a good omen. Rosen's eager salesmen moulded me into a chocolate brown, double-breasted blazer with brass buttons and bell-bottom slacks of green-and-blue plaid, and a double-breasted, electric blue suit with wide chalk stripe and acres of lapel.

Emboldened by this taste of seventies' chic I bought an orange shirt and another of cobalt blue, and two very wide blue ties (with them, a man hardly needed a shirt): one with a chicken-wire pattern in red, another peppered with white dots the size of twenty-five-cent pieces. When I walked shimmering onto Richmond Street, strong men recoiled and mothers covered their children's eyes. Only the *Toronto Life* salesmen were enthused; they all dressed that way.

Then I went right off the deep end and bought a white sports shirt with deep collar and appliqued pattern of red dots and writhing circles that looked like paramecium; the kind of garment that bolder men wore open to the waist with gold chains. Cathy and Lesley called it The Bacteria Shirt and urged me to burn it. They named my chalk-stripe The Nathan Detroit Suit, after the two-bit mobster in *Guys and Dolls*. Maybe I was a Man of the Seventies but I did not look the way they thought fathers should look. They waited anxiously for me to recover from second childhood.

Often they came to dinner in my new lower duplex with its walkout garden on trendy Macpherson Avenue. Usually I cooked my specialty, Roast 'n' Boast (a kissing cousin of Shake 'n Bake). Other Lonely Guys from the seventies may remember it: you threw a pot roast into a plastic bag with ready-packaged seasoning and cooked the whole thing to a fare-thee-well.

"It was before we worried about grease," says Cathy now.

The daughters studied my new clothes, lifted the bell-bottoms and cried piteously, "Ahhh—look at his little sparrow ankles!" A woman whom I'd met once beside a swimming pool was phoning me regularly from California. "What does she see in you, Dad?" Lesley asked earnestly. Although unstinting in the love most daughters have for fathers, they managed to keep me honest.

Near the end of 1970, worked almost to exhaustion, I went to New York for a week, stayed with my friends the Ivens, fell instantly in love and was instantly rejected by their enchanting neighbour Marianne, and called on Clay Felker, editor of *New York* magazine. Felker was one of my idols. I had a half-formed notion that if only I could meet him, some of his magic would rub off. I wrote ahead, then phoned on arrival in Manhattan. A secretary said, come on over. In retrospect, I visualize Felker in the background muttering, *Oh shit, that person from, where, Toronto?*

I put on my Nathan Detroit Suit and went to 207 East 32nd Street. The office was vintage 1940s Newspaper—a great messy bullpen, a slum compared with *Toronto Life*. Felker received me graciously. His office was a cubicle like mine, but without even my floor-to-ceiling walls. But I remember his suit, a tasteful grey worsted, and his air of total assurance.

We talked amiable magazine talk, I can't remember exactly what. He sneaked glances at my suit. Then Tom Wolfe came by—Tom Wolfe, high priest of the New Journalism!!! Every writer of the sixties and seventies was influenced by Wolfe. He revelled in exclamation marks and suspension dots . . . like these . . . and italicized asides. His stories were full of shouts and grunts and other strange noises. In *New York* he once described his landmark piece, "The Kandy-Kolored Tangerine-Flake Streamline Baby," as "vignettes, odds and ends of scholarship, bits of memoirs, short bursts of sociology, apostrophes, epithets, moans, cackles . . ."

Wolfe took outrageous liberties with accepted magazine form. In an *Esquire* piece about Las Vegas he used the word "hernia" fifty-seven times in the lead. In another his entire lead was the name "Harry" spun into a single fifty-syllable wail. His imitators tried to match him dot for dot, exclamation mark for italic, "Wow!" for "Aaaaaggggh!" None ever quite pulled it off. Wolfe's magic could not be imitated. He could drop adjectives like "prognathous" and "infarcted" and "lubricious" and get away with it, because he actually knew what they meant and where they'd fit. Wolfe's superior mind was backed up with a Yale doctorate and some of the deepest research in journalism. He had discovered, as he wrote in 1972, that it was "possible to write accurate nonfiction with techniques usually associated with novels and short stories . . ."

And now . . . here he was . . . yes! . . . the architect of New Journalism! . . . in the flesh . . . before my wondering eyes. Wolfe, a symphony in midnight blue hat and matching ankle-length coat, exchanged a word with Felker and dropped something in his in-basket. Tom Wolfe did not look directly at me but I felt his eyes flicker over my suit. He did not say "Wow!!!! . . ."

Reality washed over me. What was I doing here in this bizarre suit, from a provincial city and a magazine causing not even a ripple in that city? Why were we planning new offices we couldn't afford, while such brilliance flowered in this incredible clutter? I thanked Felker for his time, shook hands and snuck out. I clung to the Nathan Detroit Suit for a while longer. Once it earned a compliment. During intermission at a performance of "Hair," a young actress came over and said, "*Love* your suit!" "And I, yours," I said gallantly. She was wearing a raggedy costume, which she stripped off completely in the final act.

After *Toronto Life* I gave the suit to the Salvation Army. Sometimes, driving past a certain hostel where guys with watered-down hair perch like starlings along the curbs outside, I look for it still. Nothing. The down-and-outers are not that hard up.

But deep in a drawer, a memento of those vivid times, The Bacteria Shirt wriggles on.

We moved a few blocks east to new offices. It was Sophie Simkin country and, lo!, there was my former landlady, larger than life. Sophie and our *Toronto Life* shared many beliefs and values. She was a Downtowner who believed that a city core need not be yielded to bums and muggers at night. She was single-handedly trying to beautify her King-and-Jarvis district which, as Tom Wolfe might have said, was conspicuously Low Rent. She set pots of petunias out front of her antique shop, in defiance of city grime and the drunks who teetered out of nearby beverage rooms, full of beer and bitterness, and kicked over her plants. They never did it in her presence; Sophie would have flayed them alive.

She was regularly at war with officialdom: the City for not

supplying bird feed after she'd spent several winters shovelling snow and stocking a feeding station at her own expense; Bell Telephone for not maintaining the flower bed she'd planted around the phone booth next door.

She was, in short, a magazine profile. I went to interview her and to catch up. She was still running a printing shop out back of her place, going to classical music concerts, NFB films and square dances, and looking after waifs. She'd just taken in a young stage designer because "I think he needs looking after." She'd had some young women from the touring New York Ballet over to dinner.

"It was one way of giving thanks; the price of a ticket doesn't begin to pay for what they do," Sophie said defiantly, as though I was about to challenge her. "They devote their entire lives to their art!" Sitting there across from the historic St Lawrence Hall, we recalled The Day Sophie Nearly Died, when I was her tenant. The Hall restoration was underway and Sophie was darting around the scaffolding like a baggy-pants mascot. It was very nearly her undoing. About five o'clock one spring evening the east wing collapsed after the workmen went home. I had just finished an article and taken a celebratory swallow of beer. When the house began to tremble my first thought was to congratulate Labatt's for a truly memorable batch.

Then dust clouds rose outside the window and The Professor and Sophie joined me at ringside to watch a maelstrom of cops, firemen, TV cameramen, backed-up traffic and spitting hydro wires. Suddenly Sophie remembered she had passed that very wing not fifteen minutes before! We praised God and immediately withdrew to The Professor's quarters for a brandy to celebrate her escape from death.

When the Hall was finished she received an invitation to opening night, and attended, handsomely gowned. "If they hadn't invited me," Sophie said, "I'd have thrown rocks at the place." She would have, too.

My *Toronto Life* story reported all this, and on her newest crusade: to prevent the city fathers from tearing down her building. After the piece came out she suddenly appeared in our offices during coffee break in her tea-cosy hat, with an array of cheeses and a hardwood cheese board from her lumber supply (a gift for me, a little thank-you for furthering her cause) and served the whole staff. Everyone loved her. The young salesmen tried to bandy words with her and Sophie neatly cut them down to size.

The city never tore down her building, and her King-Jarvis corner became a favoured spot for yuppies with a cleaned-up park, flowers, farmers' market and the grand old Hall. Sophie's legacy.

One day Anne Marshall brought in a swarthy young *Telegram* reporter, Hartley Steward, who'd written for Walker. He was a gem. As soon as the budget allowed, I hired him. He was a prodigious worker. When the *Telegram* folded Hartley worked all one night finishing a rush story, the first in-depth report on the death of a newspaper that had been a Toronto institution. I found him asleep on my office couch in the morning.

When Anne married and left Toronto I made Hartley managing editor. He was a born idea man. Once, when nailed for a batch of unpaid parking tickets, he asked if he could opt to serve time in the Don Jail—and write about it. "Let's make sure it doesn't leave you with a record," I said. "If not, and you want to do it, great." He wrote a wonderfully evocative story of the kings and queens and rogues inside the cells—*so* rich and profane that I had to mollify my publisher with a little disclaimer about the language (sort of: the language herein may be bad for your health). It was first-class city magazine journalism, and the pity was that more people in Toronto were not aware of us.

By mid-1971 Sifton, Balmer and I were discussing *Toronto Life*'s future with increasing urgency. It was a bad year for publications: the *Telegram* and *Globe Magazine* dead; *Saturday Night* hanging on by its fingernails and a Canada Council grant. Television, radio and *Toronto Calendar,* a giveaway, were gnawing at the local advertising market.

Toronto Life had lost money ever since Sifton bought it in 1967. In my time we cut costs to the bone (salaries were pitifully low and toward the end I was writing many articles myself to spare the budget). But still we lost money. In my first year we jacked up paid circulation from about 21,000 to an audited 29,000. To us it represented a phenomenal 40 percent increase; to advertisers it was an old story. For when Sifton bought the magazine he inherited a stated circulation of 30,000; it turned out to be much less, and took a long time to verify.

I pleaded for a powerful circulation drive and some audience research to arm our sales people. But Mike had already hung on to a loser longer than most publishers would have although, to the last, he looked for ways to keep the magazine. He also looked for possible buyers and, on the quiet, so did John Moore and I (I called Honest Ed Mirvish, for one, but he politely declined). Moore and I were sure we could make the magazine soar, if only we could find an angel with deep enough pockets.

In mid-December Mike phoned me: "Good news! *Toronto Life* is going to stay alive." He was selling it for a nominal sum to local publisher Michael de Pencier, who felt he could make a go of it. There would be no job for me but maybe for the rest of our staff. The next morning Sifton announced the sale.

Although characteristically frank, he was clearly hurting. In a strange way the staff had never felt closer to him. Then de Pencier announced he already had seventeen people in his operation with scant room for more. Existing *Toronto Life* staffers could reapply for their jobs if they wished but there were no promises.

After they left we shut down the office and had a wake. Big Tony Sokol, retail sales manager and ex-policeman, brought in cases of beer. John Moore, who had not taken a holiday in two years, sat like a stone, too hurt and angry to be consoled. A man from head office phoned to say he was coming to take inventory of the furnishings; I persuaded him to wait until the corpse had cooled. Outsiders couldn't understand how much it hurt—not just because of jobs lost but because we all cared, so much.

A young man from the art department sat down beside me, put his head on my shoulder and wept, for all that was and might have been. Our new circulation assistant, on the job just two weeks, cried as hard as her boss, Heather Godfrey, who had been on staff five years. All of us had literally loved and nursed and sat up nights with *Toronto Life*. It was like having your kid run away from home, just when you thought he was going to be Prime Minister.

Some writers sent me thank-you notes for helping them grow a little. A gracious letter came from Alan Walker. I had job prospects. Mike Hanlon, editor of *The Canadian,* had something. Max Macdonald, now executive vice-president of the Regina *Leader-Post,* was looking for an editor; was I interested? Martin Goodman, editor of the Toronto *Star*—who had offered me a job in mid-*Toronto Life*—invited me in again, offering carte blanche.

I opted to return to freelance. Hartley Steward eventually became managing editor of the Toronto *Star;* then a publisher in the *Sun* newspaper chain. Rob Melbourne became art director of Calgary's city magazine. Mary McIver moved on through *Chatelaine* and *Maclean's* to become managing editor of *Homemaker's* magazine.

A few years later, Alexander Ross, one of a string of subsequent *Toronto Life* editors and one of the best, wrote me to say with some surprise that he'd been re-reading my issues with admiration. Later still de Pencier told me he'd liked my work, but had felt obliged to wipe out all vestiges of the Sifton era and its "horsey" label. He and Ross confirmed what I'd known in my heart.

At the time Mike Sifton confided that he considered it a bitter personal failure. So did I. But I was also proud of what we'd achieved. It was an exhilarating time, one of the many seasons in a writer's life. I wouldn't have changed it for anything.

11

MY MOST UNFORGETTABLE MAGAZINE

Once upon a time there was a man named O. K. Armstrong (I'm not making this up) who wrote for the U.S. edition of *Reader's Digest*. A former conservative Congressman from Missouri and an acquaintance of Chiang Kai-Shek, Armstrong was a Digester to the core. So much so that when Mrs. Armstrong died, he placed in her hands as she lay in her coffin a copy of the world's most famous little magazine.

And why not? The *Digest* inspires cradle-to-grave devotion in most of its readers and some of its writers. Besides, if Heaven really *is* Heaven, you'd better take your *Reader's Digest* with you. There won't be a dentist's office.

The *Digest* is the world's most widely sold magazine: 28-million circulation in thirty-nine editions in fifteen languages around the world, including Russia. Close to 2 million Canadians, French and English, buy it and they are not all little old ladies in tennis shoes. One-third are over fifty but, by the last survey I saw, 27 percent are ages thirty-five to forty-nine and 38 percent are younger. The average reader is forty-two.

Surveys claim it is not only the most widely read magazine in Canada, but that readers pick it up more often, spend more time with it and hang onto copies longer. One couple saved their *Digests* for forty years.

This is sometimes difficult to comprehend. Among all my friends in larger Canadian cities, I rarely find one who admits to *buying* the magazine. At most, they say they browsed through a copy at the doctor's or dentist's. The *Digest* is more closely aligned with oral hygiene than Crest, Stim-U-Dents or flossing after meals.

Readership figures to the contrary, the little magazine is not universally loved. I can think of no other publication, with the possible exception of the *National Enquirer,* that attracts so much derision, particularly from other journalists or "intellectuals." Some resent or despise it for predictable content, simplistic style, a Pollyanna view of life and hackneyed titles. The titles often *are* banal. Even staffers smile, albeit thinly, at the old joke about the perfect (mythical) *Digest* title, embracing all things the magazine holds dear–religion, animals, anti-Communism, consensual sex and the personal pronoun: "I Fucked a Polar Bear for the FBI and Found God."

In smaller cities, towns and rural Canada, it's quite another matter. There, where being culturally correct matters not a whit, respect and affection for the *Digest* is awesome. Those people openly love the magazine for its wholesome family values, inoffensive jokes, self-help and articles that generally put a bright face on life. (Canadian editor Alexander Farrell once stated his view of *Digest* values more elaborately: "The sanctity of life, human courage and resourcefulness, marriage, comradeship, education and self-improvement, the entrepreneurial spirit, cheerfulness and good humour, charity, political democracy, the stability of the social order and a certain reverence for nature.")

In my travels outside major centres, people seemed as pleased to encounter an actual *Digest* writer as they would be if they'd found a rare Small Whorled Pogonia under a bush. Once, in Arnold's Cove, Newfoundland, I was invited to address the congregation from a Salvation Army pulpit—partly because I was writing a book about the Army, mostly because I'd written a *Digest* article on it (to a vastly wider readership than my subsequent book).

The magazine's relentless optimism does not always reflect the real world, but a world as most people would like it to be. It is also an easy read, belying the enormous research that goes into most of its articles. You can finish a whole issue in the time it takes to read half a blockbuster in the *New Yorker.* The *Digest* has also done deep investigative stories, which its critics prefer to overlook.

Nonetheless, the "small wonder," as some have dubbed it, is the butt of endless jokes. It is such an easy target. How can you take seriously a magazine that runs articles called "I Am Joe's Bladder" and "I Am Jane's Ovary"? Millions *do;* the thirty-two-part Joe and Jane series was wildly popular. When its author J. D. Ratcliff died, many of us hoped that Joe and Jane had run out of steam, if not bodily parts. But soon the *Digest* was back with a new author and a rejuvenated Joe: "I Am Joe's New Heart [transplant]."

Sooner or later every minor critic and second-rate columnist, on those desperate days when his brains run dry, takes a shot at the sitting-duck *Digest*: "A magazine for bores, by bores about bores"; "specializes in making a bland cake-mix of the world"; "Victorian Valentine sensibilities tempered with a touch of 1970s' parlour psychoanalysis." The CBC once offered a definition of "brain-dead": "Someone who enjoys *Reader's Digest.*"

Little wonder that RD staffers sometimes feel as if they're working in a leper colony. At first they are puzzled by the invective heaped upon them, mostly by Toronto's pseudo-intellectual media. Any attempt to defend the *Digest* brings swift ridicule, pity or contempt (one takes on the CanLit Mafia at risk). It matters little that some of the critics have tried writing *Digest* articles themselves for the supposedly easy money, and failed—unable to withstand the rigorous editing and checking.

Eventually Digesters settle into stubborn disregard, doing their jobs proficiently within the limits imposed upon them. Yet they wonder: *Why are we always being picked on?* Because the *Digest* keeps asking for it. When in the 1980s the parent company had the temerity to condense the Holy Bible—the *Bible,* for godsake—those of us on staff headed for our foxholes. The onslaught was predictable and massive. I couldn't resist inventing my own tiny joke for anyone who'd listen:

> Q: "What's the Condensed Bible version of the Ten Commandments?"
> A: "No, no, no, no, no, no, no, no, no, no."

The British humour magazine *Punch* topped us all, telling how the *Digest* would *market* the new Bible:

> Miraculous Introductory Offer!
> Open to purchasers of the New Bible ONLY!
> BUY FIVE LOAVES AND GET TWO FISHES
> ABSOLUTELY FREE!!!

and

> Introduce a friend to Jesus, get a wine-making kit for yourself, FREE! . . .
> Introduce TWO new converts and we will send you, COMPLETELY FREE, a handsome folding bed you can actually take up and walk with!

My unhappy year on staff in 1966 did not preclude doing the occasional freelance piece through the latter sixties and early seventies. No freelancer could afford to ignore *Digest* rates. In 1972 I was getting $550 to $600 for an article in *Weekend* magazine and $2,000 from the *Digest*. (Later, other magazines caught up.) The Canadian edition had few of the cumbersome procedures that came later with its growth. Ralph Hancox and his assistant, modest young Charles Magill, were agreeable editors. When in 1973 they offered me a $5,000 annual retainer plus fees per article to be contributing editor, I grabbed it. I was still paying alimony and, with some sort of death wish, venturing out again on the marital limb.

At *Toronto Life,* I'd met Leigh Richmond, dark, vivacious and twenty-odd years younger than me. After three compatible years we thought we could permanently surmount the age spread. We joked that Pierre Trudeau and young wife Margaret were our role models (which turned out to be a bad joke). We married in the summer of '73.

Soon I was reminded again that the hand-to-mouth introspective, isolated freelance life can shrivel a marriage. Compared to the swirl of *Toronto Life,* where I was always at the eye of the storm, my freelance life and I were stupendously boring–rather like Heinkel Trocken versus draft beer. That, along with personality differences and the age gap–I seemed to grow older and Leigh increasingly younger–did us in. After twenty months of wedded bliss she left abruptly.

When the dust settled my mother, not meaning to be cruel but shooting from the hip as usual, said, "Well, Son, I guess she didn't love you enough." She had that right. When the divorce nisi came through my lawyer reminded me that I couldn't marry again for three months. I said I would try to restrain myself. In fact, I decided to quit while I was behind. A miniature schnauzer is now my constant companion. You know a dog will always be there when you get home at night.

I was now sans wife yet wrapped in the *Digest*'s comfortable wife-support. In 1976 came an even better offer of a "roving editor" job, the euphemism for staff writer with salary and benefits. It was like freelance without terror. The money was nowhere near the salaries paid to blow-dried talking heads on television, but I could live and work where I chose, write about virtually anything and travel wherever the subjects led.

It was a sweet deal but, with one less family responsibility, I hesitated. Did I really want to be tied to one magazine, especially *that* one? In the end I accepted and stayed in Toronto, with its excellent research facilities, within easy range of East or West and close to my daughters.

My first impulse here was to put down something glib and facile, endearing myself to all those who'd made sport of the *Digest* and me for so long. But in re-reading a dozen years of letters and files, I am reminded that the *Digest* people I worked with were, almost without exception, honest, well meaning and decent. Some were of considerable talent; some of little or no talent, about the same as on any other magazine or in any other business. So this is not to bite the hand that once fed me—although loyal Digesters might see it that way—but a sorting-out of my ambivalent feelings toward this oft-maligned publication.

Vancouver writer Paul Grescoe once said, correctly, that mine seemed to be a love/hate relationship. On the one hand, *Digest* editors were among the most considerate I have known. Feisty Nova Scotia writer Silver Donald Cameron once told them, only partly in jest, "You people are so reasonable that it's difficult to have a good donnybrook." On the other hand, the magazine's ways drove me and many others (including Cameron) into fits of rage and frustration.

For many years the *Digest* prided itself on being "a writer's magazine"–not because it was the repository of great writing but because founder DeWitt Wallace regarded writers as special people, and paid and treated them better than did most editors of his time.

Every *Digest* staffer knew the Wallace legend: how as a teenager he conceived the "digest" idea; how as a soldier convalescing after World War I he began condensing magazine articles; how in February 1922 he and wife, Lila, started *Reader's Digest* on a shoestring. That first issue, a plain self-cover in black and white, was otherwise remarkably like today's magazine: one condensed article of "enduring value and interest" for every day of the month, including "How to Keep Young Mentally," "What Kind of Husband Are You?" and "Watch Your Dog and Be Wise." It sold for twenty-five cents.

By the early 1930s the Wallaces, not finding enough ready-made articles they liked, began publishing a few originals written by their growing staff. In 1933 the first signed one appeared. Originals were condensed, of course. The *Digest* has always believed that anything can be cut down into an acceptable–no, a *better*–piece. Subsequently, staff writers were named "roving editors" to help maintain, I was told, the illusion that all *Digest* content was picked up from other sources.

The Canadian French *Digest* was launched in 1947; the English, a year after. My pleasantest years were from the middle seventies to middle eighties. I once told editor Charles Magill that the *Digest* was "the best game in town" and at the time believed it.

Over eleven years I wrote fifteen book-length "special features," which ran two or three times normal *Digest* article length, paid much more money and allowed more writing freedom. My special, "The Spy That Fell From the Sky," a space-age detective story on the Russian satellite that crashed in the Northwest Territories in 1978, took me to the Territories, Washington, Ottawa and inside the Cheyenne Mountain fortress at Colorado Springs that was NORAD headquarters. It won the President's Medal, given by the National Magazine Awards program for Canada's best general article of the year. It even provided a smidgen of adventure.

One February morning I buckled myself into the belly of a Canadian Forces Hercules transport that was about to drop supplies on an advance satellite-search base. They'd be flying the lumbering four-engine turbo-prop transport four to five feet off the ground, to eject a heavy load with a rear-end horizontal parachute pull. The all-white landscape made depth perception difficult–and at five feet off the deck an error of inches could be deadly.

The crew warned me, unnecessarily, to sit tight. After travelling countless miles in every kind of aircraft, the laws of probability had made me a white-knuckles flier, equipped with assorted anti-gravity amulets bestowed upon me by understanding daughters. And now–good grief!–the rear doors yawned open at my feet: an enormous picture window framing the frosty landscape.

The thrumming Hercules eased down to just under 150 MPH ground speed and levelled into the drop zone (wheels down, just in case). The ground outside, a white blur with fleeting smudges of bush was . . . *right there.*

"Fifteen seconds." Then . . .

"Deploy the drogue!"

A fifteen-foot parachute snapped out behind, jerking at the Hercules. *Crack!* Three twenty-eight-foot parachutes blossomed behind. Two seconds later–*Whoom*–sixteen tons of load shot out like a cannonball and landed smoothly in a geyser of snow.

For a millisecond the aircraft, relieved of its weight, shuddered and tried to nose down. In that same split second the pilot pulled it into a steep climb with maximum power. A minute later the Hercules made a lazy arc over the drop zone. Far below, the load lay neatly parked a few dozen feet from shore.

Oddly, I felt less terror than on the average commercial flight, perhaps because I had met and trusted this Canadian Forces aircrew. A few years later I heard that a similar drop flight had crashed somewhere in the North. My knuckles turned permanently white.

The next year my feature on the drowning of twelve boys and one teacher in Lake Temiskaming won the runner-up silver award in the President's Medal category. Another book-length piece on Ben Wheeler, a Canadian doctor who became the hero of a

Japanese prison camp during World War II was published in thirty-two *Digest* editions. Most importantly, I was working with people I liked and respected.

Charles Magill had grown from a diffident young Englishman with a small-town newspaper background to an editor with sound judgement and gentle touch. I chatted endlessly with him by mail and he, no matter how busy, always had a thoughtful comment, joke or word of praise. We could discuss anything without embarrassment or restraint–rare in any friendship, rarer still between writer and editor. He appreciated my bent sense of humour, as in my report on the once-popular rural phrase "Real good" (or, in the mouth of a master, "Realgood"):

1) *Describes state of well-being.*
"How you bin keepin' you ole sonabitch?"
"Realgood, jus' realgood."

2) *Expresses pleasure in another's good fortune.*
"Me 'n' the Wife jus' had ourselves one helluva fine holiday down south."
"Realgood!"

3) *Serves as a sign-off in telephone conversation.*
"So awright, the missus 'n' me is comin' over to drink some of yer likker 'bout seven o'clock. So long."
"Realgood." (Both parties hang up.)

Magill chuckled over that and most of my other attempts at wit. A man of exquisite taste.

His second-in-command was Charles Smith, a wild and crazy guy with an errant forelock falling into his eyes. Charles had been a British POW in World War II and afterward worked on the English magazine *John Bull*. He was given to sudden fits of song and dance (he'd once been on stage) and prided himself on his jackets and corduroy suits of fine material but dubious vintage, bought from church rummage sales in Westmount. Superficially, he was the court jester; actually he was perhaps the most intuitive writer and editor in the place.

Erudite Michael Ballantyne, formerly of the *Montreal Star,* was another kindred spirit. Tall, elegantly dressed and scholarly, he loved words and hated mandatory edits as much as I did. Once Michael unearthed a telling passage in the letters of seventeenth-century writer Charles Lamb to William Wordsworth. Lamb was complaining bitterly to Wordsworth about the handling of his latest essay by a certain beastly Baviad Gifford, editor.

> The *language* he has altered throughout. Whatever inadequateness it had to its subject, it was, in point of composition, the prettiest piece of prose I ever writ: and so my sister (to whom alone I read the MS.) said. That charm, if it had any, is all gone: more than a third of the substance is cut away, and that not all from one place, but passim, so as to make utter nonsense . . .

Lamb sounded exactly like a *Digest* writer.

Ballantyne's office was cluttered with books, pictures, memorabilia, touchable stones and other precious junk–just like mine. He read voraciously as part of his job but also in all sorts of non-Digestible publications. His letters, signed in elegant copperplate script, brimmed with references to little- or lesser-known journals or scribes, usually British. My article about Ernestine Gibot–an admirable Alberta Cree woman who in her fifties turned a desperate life around with a lot of help from her friends (including Preston Manning, who has been maligned as racist by political enemies)–mentioned her belief in the Holy Spirit. Michael queried me on it with genuine intellectual curiosity: "Do you mean the Indians' Great Spirit or the Paraclete, the Holy Ghost?"

Ballantyne never wrote "Who He?" nor settled for the normal knee-jerk rejection letter. It was almost worth being turned down just to receive one of his billets-doux. A writer suggested an article on animal abuse. The *Digest* had already published one so Michael politely declined, then verged onto the topic of horses:

> Which reminds me of Dr. Johnson's frank answer to the woman who asked him why, in his Dictionary of the English Language, he defined the word "pastern" as "the knee of a horse" (whereas it is that part between fetlock and hoof). His reply was, "Ignorance, Madame, pure ignorance."

Letters like that, amid a day of "Shape Up Your Sex Life" or "Twenty Ways to Save Your Marriage," made life worth living.

And there was George Ronald, whom I'd known fleetingly at the London *Free Press*. He had gone on to the CBC, then to the *Digest* books' department, then to the magazine. By that time he was a widower with a houseful of children. George raised them well, while serving the *Digest* day and night.

He was a workaholic. When he was still in Books I dropped by to say hello. He looked up wearily and said, "Why don't young writers want to *work* any more?" Some considered him a perfectionist or a tyrant, but all he asked was your very best, within the limits of your capabilities.

George recognized all the *Digest*'s warts (he loved the definition of an editor: "the one who walks down the hill after the battle and shoots the wounded") but never badmouthed the magazine or less talented colleagues. Once David MacDonald, who cares deeply about his writing and who loved George as much as I did, complained bitterly about another staffer's sloppy editing of a MacDonald story.

"The guy didn't even try," he told George.

"You're not being fair," Ronald said. "Sure, it's a lousy job, but the guy did try, and that's the best he can do."

Although some fellow editors couldn't see it, George had a tender heart. He shed tears unashamedly over writing that moved him. A stylish writer himself, he empathized with our professional paranoia. *Maclean's* alumnus Janice Tyrwhitt once turned in a piece with her usual trepidation. It reached George's desk at the end of the day. He took it home, read it and phoned her at 11:00 P.M. to say that, although it still had to go down Murderer's Row, *he* liked it.

For me, those four counterbalanced the *Digest*'s quirks. They made some of my and every other writer's stories better.

They were assisted (although they might not have regarded it in those terms) by Bill C58, introduced in 1975 to help Canadian publications. To that point advertisers could deduct, for income-tax purposes, the cost of ads placed in foreign-controlled *Time* and *Reader's Digest* as with indigenous magazines. It gave those two, with their large circulations, a considerable edge. At one point they raked in more than one-third of the country's magazine advertising revenue.

To qualify for the deduction under C58, a magazine had to be 75 percent Canadian-owned, have no foreign licensing arrangements and have a content largely different from foreign magazines (including the *Digest*'s parent). Later this was set at 80 percent. The Canadian *Digest* mounted a massive lobby (president Paul Zimmerman asked the Americans to stay out of it). In the end, *Time* closed its Canadian edition. The *Digest* stayed, by forming a new Canadian company to embrace its magazines and thanks to a favourable interpretation. It met the 80 percent requirement, partly with original Canadian stories, partly by having much of the material purchased from other sources condensed and edited by Canadians.

This called for a larger Canadian staff and more original Canadian assignments–good for writers. Dave MacDonald was still on staff. Jan Tyrwhitt began writing regularly and eventually became a roving editor. Sid Katz, Fred Bodsworth, my brother Larry, Robert Thomas Allen, Eileen Pettigrew, Loral Dean, Parker Barss Donham and David Lees were among the many other professional contributors.

Since any subject qualified as Canadian content if written by a Canadian, I travelled into many corners of this country and beyond. To Norway to write about Canadian women who married Norwegians during or after World War II. To Holland and Belgium in the late 1980s to take the annual twenty-one-mile march commemorating the liberation of the Lowlands by Canadian troops. To troubled Cyprus, where I rode with Canadian peacekeepers down the barricaded line dividing Nicosia, with trigger-happy Turks and Greeks on either side.

As every business person knows, travel is a mixed blessing. We dribble away whole chunks of our lives in airports, waiting rooms, taxis, hotels with room service and TV for company, hotel rooms with paper-thin walls, where people on the other side are always having more fun than you. I have learned that man's greatest invention is not the wheel or the cathode tube but the foam-rubber ear plug. Once in a Quebec City motel I was kept awake for two hours by a couple making love enthusiastically in the next room. There was not even a vicarious thrill; their wild shouts and terms of endearment were all in French. Unilingual *moi* couldn't understand a damn word. Soon after that I enrolled for a one-month French immersion course in Tours.

There is a flip side: travel is enhanced for writers. We are poised to learn because we must, and so our perceptions and enjoyment become more acute. I remember a vivid moment high on the hundred-foot riverbank where the Northwest Territories village of Arctic Red River slumbers in the August sun. Beside me, in blue jeans, black turtleneck and rubber boots, Father John Colas, the settlement's Catholic priest, gazed down fondly at the Mackenzie River, wriggling like a fat muddy snake toward the distant Arctic shore.

I glanced around his village, population 121, and asked, "What's there to see around here?"

He smiled toward the river. "There is the view," he said, in the lingering accents of his native Paris. "I have seen it for thirty-three years, and I never tire of it."

Doors open to us, even on ordinary assignments. I think of Canterbury Cathedral; millions of tourists see it, but few are invited into the vesturer's office, a medieval hideaway directly under the High Altar; there to peer through a small window into a crypt, just as the vigilant twelfth-century monks did, watching over the tomb of Saint Thomas à Becket to make sure nobody stole the Canterbury pilgrims' offerings.

Yet strangely—although I travelled afar and could have concocted an assignment virtually anywhere on earth—I found myself drawn back, again and again, to the place where I was born.

For a time after I left the farm I had led all my new friends in jokes about rubes and stubble-jumpers. Then, growing older and wiser, I realized that growing up in Saskatchewan's vast space had taught me the difference between loneliness and comfortable aloneness, nurtured my imagination and gave me an abiding link with the natural world—all imperative for a writer. And I recognized that place for what it is: my touchstone.

So, on journeys west for the *Digest* I began finding excuses to detour out to that old abandoned farmstead. I do it still. Its owners are tolerant of my obsession. At the gate I read again the sign proclaiming this a Heritage Homestead, honouring Jack and Floy Collins, and Alfred and Wendy Arnold, original and current owners. Then, in a rush of sweet-sad memory, I plod through the tangle of trees, unrecognizable in their fourth or fifth growth; pick up stones, touch the earth, sniff the scent of green spring or summer heat or autumn wind. I strain for the ghostly jingle of harness, the clomp-clomp of horses' hooves, the call of a woman's voice: "Supper!", the tingling anticipation of stories-before-bed-time.

They are always just beyond reach, but this place, those visits, those memories, are a kind of nourishment. And it took the travelling freedom—I truly *was* a "roving editor"—provided by the otherwise restrictive *Reader's Digest* to lead me to this truth.

12

THE SHRUNKEN WORLD OF READER'S DIGEST

For a time in Montreal, roving editor Adrian Waller–an ebullient Brit who delivered public readings and booming operatic arias in his spare time–churned out *Digest* stories by the gross.

"I have somehow grasped the *Digest,*" he once told a writer for *Saturday Night*. "I catch people in the absolute depths of despair, and show them struggling, resisting, through courage or bravery or sheer persistence, overcoming all obstacles to win. You've got to take the reader up, then down and back up again for that up-beat ending. That's the extra dimension the *Digest* is after."

Although some of us winced at the rhetoric, his analysis of DeWitt Wallace's creation was pretty accurate. Then Adrian went too far.

"I'm working at about half my intellectual capacity," he told the interviewer. This certainly won him no friends around the office; the kindest comment I heard was that "Adrian has blotted his copy book." Yet I knew what he meant. The *Digest* demanded the best of your technical ability but never pushed you to intellectual heights. It was impossible, given the cutting system.

Every magazine edits. Good editors do it judiciously: trimming fat where necessary; keeping the grace and style if any. True editing is highly creative. Its practitioners play it by ear, tuning articles for what they are worth. Some need scarcely be touched. Some are touched so deftly that the writer is hard-pressed to know why it seems to read better.

So when most publications accept your article you sit back

with relief, wait for it to come out and hope for a nod of approval from your mother and your peers. At the *Digest* that's when the script hits the fan. Regardless of merit, it *must* be cut. Significantly, *Digest* editors more often refer to a "cut" than an "edit." The mandatory cut dates back to DeWitt Wallace's original condensations—the distillation of what he felt was the essence of each article into a bite-sized package: something you could read at coffee break or lunch hour or, of course, at the dentist's. Editors from the boonies were sent to Pleasantville to learn, among other things, the Holy Cut. I used to call this going down to have your brains washed.

Over the years the cut acquired a certain mystique. On most magazines an editor receives a manuscript, reads it once and says, "Okay, this is a keeper, given this bit of additional information or that bit of editing." The skillful Magill, Smith, Ronald and Ballantyne operated that way. But other Digesters might say before buying a story, "Let's cut and see how it turns out," lacking the confidence to know at a glance. A *Digest* researcher once told me that ten to twelve factual errors could crop up in a cut through misinterpretation of or inattention to the original. The mistakes were corrected, of course, but it showed where the cutters' attention lay: on getting words out.

Writers were expected and encouraged to write over-long, with the sweet foreknowledge that our 3,000 to 3,500 (or more) words would come down to 2,000 to 2,500. Once, after enduring years of my griping, the editors said, "Okay, write the next one to length." I sent them a tight 2,200 words. They promptly cut it to 1,500. This tempts writers to pad, tossing in material they'd normally edit out themselves, to satisfy the cutters' feeding frenzy.

As a final indignity the castrated article usually had to accommodate a joke or homily. A writer could fight tooth and nail with editors and researchers to save a felicitous phrase, only to see it dropped to accommodate the anecdote or quotable quote that ran at the end of nearly every piece. There was no use fighting it, although I usually did. "Personal Glimpses," "Picturesque Speech," "All In A Day's Work" and others of that ilk nearly always rated higher than most articles on the monthly readership survey. Many readers buy the magazine just for the jokes and anecdotes. Life's Like That at *Reader's Digest*.

Other magazines sometimes cut ineptly. The *Canadian* once lopped the bottom half off an article of mine, which I discovered only when it got into print. Both the *Financial Post* and a prairie newspaper supplement, *Western People,* whacked carefully crafted endings off my stories, on the sloppy old newspaper principle that if it's too long just hack from the bottom up. *Reader's Digest* at least showed its cuts to writers and let them arm-wrestle over restorations. The difference: others do not condense every article as a matter of course.

Some *Digest* editors did the job with great skill, given the perverted nature of their mandate. Others often took the easy route by chopping out anecdotes, nuance and grace notes. This bred conformity of copy. A reader once said, "I didn't know the *Digest* had original writers. It all reads the same."

For a long time many of us *Maclean's* alumni persuaded ourselves that we were writing no differently for the *Digest* than we had for Berton and Allen. That part was true. We wrote our stories, full of creative fervour. There was no explicit "formula" nor preconceived editorial approach. But the final product rarely had the edge or freshness of MacDonald's or Tyrwhitt's or my *Maclean's* writing. The mandatory cuts rendered many an article like a shrunken head: interesting for strangers but not much fun for the owner. Whenever I hear the old Dudley Moore/Peter Cook skit from "Beyond the Fringe," about the one-legged man who applies for a job as Tarzan of the Apes, I think of *Digest* cutting:

> You, sir, are a unidexter. One expects Tarzan to have *two* legs. But if a man with *no* legs should apply, you, sir, will be very high on our list.

Similarly, a cut is better than no story but never as good as a two-legged Tarzan.

Sometimes we broke the rules, sending a copy of our uncut original to a subject whose opinion we valued. I did this with Morley Callaghan and W. O. Mitchell, wanting them to know that their many hours spent with me had not been wasted, and that I was better than I appeared in print.

On the plus side, the two assignments gave me an opportunity to know both those illustrious writers a little better. Many an afternoon I sat entranced in Callaghan's living room, fending off his amorous white dog, while Morley paced and talked animatedly about writing. Afterward he sent me a kind note about my piece but added, "As one writer to another . . . [I loved that gracious aside] . . . I wish they had allowed more of your own perceptions into the article."

As with Callaghan, I pitched Mitchell by mail on the idea of doing a profile, fearing that he, like so many in CanLit, might bridle at being in the "lowbrow" *Digest*. Not so. A couple of weeks later we met at a party. Mitchell marched across the room, white hair halo-ing around his head, and cried in his gravelly voice, "I think you *should* do a story on me. I'm a character!"

He is. It was a dream assignment, the kind of thing English students or readers' clubs would have gladly paid hard cash to attend. In hours and hours of priceless tape–thousands more words than the *Digest* would ever use—Mitchell talked eloquently and entertainingly about writing, life and himself. He never said, "Of course, you can't use this . . ." He was affable and patient. Once in a hotel coffee shop he stood up amidst breakfast and acted out a story, to the delight of everyone in the room, including him.

So finally we were in his favourite Toronto motor hotel opposite the old CBC building: me cleaning up the last tag-ends of questions; Bill getting ready for a dinner with his publisher and the latter's board of directors. By now we were pretty good friends and he insisted I stay, tape recorder rolling, while he got dressed.

We talked about his reputation for never knowing the time or date. Be that as it might, he said, he'd never missed a deadline. "Merna gave me this five years ago," he said, slipping on a wrist watch, "and once I got the hang of it . . ." Without Merna, his wife, manager, social secretary and helpmeet, W.O. might not exist.

Mitchell likes turtleneck sweaters. "I don't suppose I wear a tie five times a year," he said, producing a crisp white shirt ("I only have two white shirts") and handsome cufflinks ("Merna's idea, not mine"). We talked of the gold medal in philosophy he'd won at university, and how his grandchildren call him "W.O." or "Bill" (none of that "Gramps" stuff). He interrupted himself to hold up a necktie. "Goddamn this sonofabitch, how does it go!?"

He worked absent-mindedly on the tie while launching into a fluent discourse on writing: how "the basis of style in writing is the sound of the unique human voice. And of course when you get into fiction it's also the basis of characterization. . . . That sonofabitch [the tie] looks as though I've got it upside down!"

We moved to "authorial intrusion" in fiction and how in his book *Since Daisy Creek* he had avoided the intrusive "he said" and "she said" with long passages of dialogue. This wasn't a borrowed Hemingway style, he added, because he'd never been influenced by Hemingway. But an interviewer ("smart little girl") asked him when the book came out, "How many times did you have to back up in a page and find out whose voice it was, because you'd lost track?"

"Maybe a couple of times," Mitchell had told her.

"A helluva lot more with Hemingway," she grinned. Mitchell liked that.

He went at the tie again. "Shit, it's so long . . . . Shit, I've forgotten how . . ."

"Maybe I can help, Bill," I offered. "But I'd have to do it like I was tying my own. I'd have to stand behind you and reach around . . ."

Mitchell said no thanks. The idea of having my arms around him didn't seem to thrill him. He wrestled the ornery tie, with and without a mirror, like a handicapped Houdini trying to escape from a padlocked trunk. Finally he got it right.

"Great, eh?" It was. "Silk! Homecoming of St. Petersburg Senior High of about five years ago. Just happened to be there when it happened. Merna made me buy this tie and *slacks* and everything. Held in St. Petersburg Yacht Club and I never saw so many fuckin' *old* people with old faces and new teeth. God it was dreadful!"

I drove him to his dinner because Mitchell tends to get lost without Merna (although I suspect that's part of his persona). "One thing Merna won't thank me for mentioning, she phoned me last week and said, 'You didn't even make the finals [for the Governor General's Medal] with *Daisy Creek*.' Then she said, 'That's the way to go, Mitchell! Your record is unflawed.' It's true. I've never made the finalists on a piece of work yet."

I shook my head in disgust.

"Isn't that interesting?" Bill mused. "Doesn't bother me . . ."

Then he vanished into a downtown private club, looking only slightly strangled in the necktie, and wowed the directors with his wit. And I drove into the night wondering, *What's wrong with GG juries? How, over all these years, have they contrived to ignore a genuine Canadian original?*

Of one thing a *Digest* writer could be certain: within its limits the story was accurate. The magazine has perhaps the best and certainly most thorough research staff in Canada. Sources almost invariably ask all writers if they can see the manuscript. The answer should always be a polite but firm "no." At the *Digest* we could always add, "They'll check back the facts with you." The subjects could trust us. The Canadian *Digest* tended to straddle fences but was never guilty of the biased hatchet jobs that have appeared in, say, certain CBC documentaries.

The researchers, mostly female, had dazzling credentials: law degrees, Masters in English, history, sociology and political science. The mercurial senior researcher, Penelope Body, had a Masters in philosophy and French literature and an insatiable thirst for learning. She could eke more information from sources than could most writers. Body also did virtuoso guest lectures at journalism schools, dissecting "factual" stories that the *Digest* had picked up from leading Canadian and American magazines and had double-checked for accuracy. Many, the *Digest* researchers found, were riddled with errors. Invariably, Body left the students gaping at the media's fallibility.

The *Digest* checked every fact and every quote with every source. It saved writers from inevitable mistakes and almost guaranteed we would never be sued (although many would say that a courageous publication should run the risk of court action now and then). It also uncovered cheaters and fakes. One Canadian writer sold the *Digest* a thrilling first-person adventure. The trouble was, Research discovered, he'd made most of it up. When Penelope Body confronted him he was indignant, not repentant. He went on to become the darling of the Toronto magazine clique, but I never believed a word he wrote thereafter. Latterly he found his proper niche: fiction.

The system had its flaws. Sources, upon hearing their own

words read back to them, have an overwhelming urge to shine up their quotes, soften a critical remark or, worse, retract it. Strong researchers resisted such tinkering; others didn't. *Digest* researchers also went to sources the writer had not used, which seemed beyond the call of duty. Any two "experts" will disagree. Once, refusing to accept a statement I'd taken directly from archives–a quote deposited there by a man subsequently deceased–Research went to his surviving friends and relatives and asked if those were the "kind" of things he "might" have said; were they "in character"? That was not "fact" checking.

This zeal reached a ridiculous extreme when I wrote about the wildlife habitat Arnold Zabel created on his ranch south of Swift Current. Arnold had willed the habitat to a wildlife organization, in perpetuity. "And if anybody tries to change it I'll come back and haunt the bugger," he told me.

I suppose "bugger" spooked them. The researcher phoned him. "Did you really say that?"

"Sure did," said Arnold. The researcher was not content. She phoned Arnold's wife, Ruby, who happens to be my cousin. Did her husband really say that? "Sure," said Ruby, wondering what kind of magazine wouldn't accept a man's own word.

Digest fact-checking leaves its mark on a writer's psyche. Once I came home from a stay in hospital and thought, *My garden's turned into a jungle.* Then I heard a voice, definitely a voice, saying:

> Wait a minute. A jungle? Really? With vines and snakes and chattering monkeys in the high dark trees?
>
> *Well no, of course not, it's just a figure of speech . . .*
>
> You hired a couple of native bearers and a guide in a Tilley hat and enough provisions for a week?
>
> *That's stupid, what the hell are you, a research editor from* Reader's Digest?
>
> Yes. Just trying to keep you honest.

There was one other strange and aggravating procedure: issue editing.

Each of four or five editors edited an issue on a rotating basis. During that period–five or six weeks of preparation plus actual issue production–the editor drowned in detail while his writers waited in vain for a response and decision on an unscheduled article.

The *Digest* publishes four or five times more articles than most other magazines, plus a gezillion short items. Once I tried to jolly associate editor Mike McGarry out of the perpetual angst that afflicted him and his colleagues during issue production:

> *Prithee, knave, who is yon pale and ghostly traveller, with furrowed brow and troubled visage?*
>
> Faith, sire, McGarry is his name. He laboreth as scribe for a journal that, though small of size, hath content large of heart-warmingness, redeeming value, uplift and other virtues too numerous to recount; a journal steeped in Drama, in rescues of the wretched from burning vehicles and abandoned wells, in tales of other wretches who, teetering on the verge of death from vile disease, are saved by clever medicine (or, if not saved, who die nobly with a smile).
>
> *Gadzooks, knave, then why doth yon McGarry seem oppressed and laden with gloom, labouring as he does for so estimable a rag?*
>
> Alas, sire, he is an issue editor and these, so say the old men round the fires at night, are sorely tried . . .

I never knew if McGarry laughed. He was too busy to answer.

Most annoying was the remarkable autonomy the system gave to issue editors. Each chose the content of his or her issue and rarely did a higher authority say, "You *must* use this." Successive issues were susceptible to each person's varying attitudes and tastes. Articles could languish in the story bank for months or years, and were sometimes forgotten. This was vexing for writers and their subjects. With each delay even a "timeless" piece becomes dated. People die off.

This worried a Regina woman who sold her first *Digest* short piece in 1988 with coaching and encouragement from her local writer friend Ian Bickle and from me. It was a poignant vignette about a dying man.

The *Digest* bought it; then silence. The author, a senior citizen, began to fear she wouldn't be around to see it in print. When nagging failed I called up my ultimate weapon: verse. No one, to that point, had ever been able to resist my double dactyl.

Poor Edythe Stockton, she
Wrote so heartwarmingly,
Wrote of a man who was down on his luck.
Editors loved it,
Then rapidly shoved it
In storage where now it is, seemingly, stuck.

Poor Edythe Stockton, she
Often says plaintively:
"Two years ago I completed that stint.
"My neighbours, their mothers,
"Their lovers and brothers
"Are eagerly waiting to see me in print."

Poor Edythe Stockton, she
Asks me repeatedly
"When are you printing my story, you guys?
"I'm 80, doggone it,
"Why don't you get on it,
"So I can enjoy it before my demise?"

Nothing happened. No faint echo of laughter from Montreal. Edythe lived to see her story finally appear in 1990, in a "split run" (a version published for a region of the country), but no thanks to my alleged wit.

I'd learned my lesson. Life among the custodians of "Humor in Uniform," "Campus Comedy" and "Laughter, The Best Medicine" is no laughing matter.

13

NOT-SO-PLEASANTVILLE

My *Reader's Digest* letterhead featured Pegasus, the winged horse of mythology, soaring through an embossed oval at the top of the page. In the design, Pegasus's nether regions were missing. That was because, I used to say whenever the parent company got on my nerves, "All the horses' asses are in Pleasantville."

It was a cheap shot and I resolved to someday be a better person. There were many decent talented people on the USRD staff, warmly hospitable whenever we outlanders ventured there. Going to head office, among the wooded hills of northern Westchester County in New York state, was rather like visiting a vice-regal estate. The magazine is located near Chappaqua, not at Pleasantville–the felicitous mailing address it has kept throughout the years–but to everyone in the *Digest* empire, headquarters are "P'ville."

The original office, subsequently enlarged to keep pace with success, looked like an elegant country home. Chimes sounded at midday from a bell tower trimmed with four Pegasuses. A vast acreage of award-winning grounds caressed the eye, as did the priceless fine art adorning senior editorial offices. Other pieces from the $300-million collection begun by Lila Wallace lined the halls: here a Renoir, there a Dufy, everywhere a Chagall. Across the lawn the Guest House, an eighteenth-century restoration, had period antiques and its own hired help. Here, fatted writers and visiting dignitaries were taken to lunch and, sometimes, quizzed so earnestly and attentively by fleets of USRD editors that it was hard to gulp down that last bite of filet mignon medium-rare with lemon butter or final swallow of Mouton-Rothschild '79. I once watched Bruce Hutchison handle this interrogation with aplomb but, years later, bumbled through it myself with severe heartburn.

A visiting writer might also be billeted in the Guest House, if his or her star was in ascendancy. It was a humbling experience to prowl those hallowed halls—after a first-class dinner, a sound sleep amid hushed woodlands, and a breakfast offering every cereal, soup, bread, egg or condiment known to North American kitchens—and ponder the power of the condensed word.

At some levels in P'ville one encountered the same ignorance of Canada that is common across America. A senior secretary at USRD, speaking to her opposite number in Montreal, reported that a conference was scheduled for "B-A-N-F-F"—she spelled it out gingerly, like an acronym gone wrong.

"It's Banff," the Canadian said helpfully.

"Where's that?"

"It's about an hour from Calgary, in Alberta."

"Oh," said the secretary at the world's largest little magazine. "Well, what state is that in?"

USRD editors were much more cognizant of that great white blob to the north and were generally kind, even respectful. The Washington editor relayed to Montreal a rave review from a Pentagon person about my Russian satellite story ("a better report than the one I prepared for the intelligence community"), leading me to wonder if I'd missed my calling in not becoming a spook for the CIA. Sometimes praise took curious word forms, as though the American were straining for an unforgettable thought. One remarked that a story of mine "really roared." Another told his Canadian counterpart that the latter was "fortunate to have steeds like [Janice Tyrwhitt and me] in your stable." The Pegasus syndrome, perhaps?

But all editors have idiosyncrasies, as did even the legendary DeWitt Wallace. His quirk was generosity. Wallace—he liked people to call him Wally—was totally unassuming and famed for his kindness. He might suddenly send a batch of secretaries into New York with pocket money and tickets for a Broadway play. Or dispatch a gaggle of editors and wives for a cruise along the Mississippi. Once he stood up at a party and announced a raise for all the U.S. staff, ranging from 8 percent for the higher-paid to 11 percent for the lesser-paid. He and Lila were famed philanthropists, giving away literally hundreds of millions. When they died, in 1981 and 1984 respectively, there were shuffles, firings and blood on the floor at Pleasantville. The magazine remained prosperous, but the warm fuzzy glow faded.

My own disenchantment with P'ville came earlier. USRD was a rabid foe of everything Red or even shocking pink. For a while I wondered how it would survive without Russia to kick around any more, but there is always China. However its right-wing politics, although annoying even to a non-socialist like me, were not heavily reflected in the Canadian magazine. More importantly, P'ville's attitude toward its satellite editions seemed to me one of plantation owner toward indentured servants: We own you. Do as we say and we'll treat you right. Never did I sense it more acutely than during my stories on nuclear war and acid rain.

In the spring of 1983, at an all-Canadian editorial meeting in Montreal, I suggested we do a piece on nuclear war. You could have heard a pin drop. Then Michael Ballantyne spoke up strongly in support. One by one other editors fell into line with little nods or soft-spoken, tentative approval. Only senior editor Alexander Farrell couldn't understand why we would want to do it, presumably because the subject was so distressing. He turned out to be prescient.

Over the next year I read volumes on the subject, wrote a massive outline, and got approval to proceed. It was agreed that I would insert some personal conviction and passion into an essentially journalistic piece on the general public inertia, the inexorable creep toward such a war, what that war could do to humanity and what we might do to prevent it. It seemed by far the most important article I had ever attempted, so I kept a diary of events.

Hoping to parlay it into a special feature, I turned in six thousand words. *Eight* editors read it and attached comments—a career high for me at the *Digest* or anyplace else. The eight differed considerably and in some cases were contradictory. Overall, editor

Charles Magill and executive editor Charles Smith, with their long experience and innate good judgement, seemed to have the right handle on it.

My initial piece included a graphic scenario on exactly what could happen to a city hit by a nuclear bomb, as deduced from books and scientific papers. Magill and others balked at the ugly detail, so I trimmed that portion back to 750 words. I also wrote a detailed description of the then-new nuclear winter theory. Some editors thought this too was pretty gloomy, but I argued that the average reader knew nothing about nuclear winter. If they didn't know that a nuclear war could end the human race, how could we hope to stir them to support bilateral nuclear disarmament?

The resultant rewrite of five thousand words was still a strong plea for peace but covered all the options, tried and untried. It didn't take sides with the Russians. It did not dump on the Americans. Although sorely tempted, I did not say that President Reagan—who used to doze off during cabinet meetings—might someday fall face first on the Doomsday button. But I pointed out that his policies to that point had been disastrous.

I described the hopeful signs of a thaw in U.S.-Soviet relations. On the personal side, I mentioned how my daughter Lesley, like so many of her generation who grew up in the shadow of the Bomb, feared the world would not survive.

Finally everyone in the Montreal office seemed pleased. We commissioned a cross-country opinion poll, which dramatically bore out my thesis: Canadians cared about the threat but felt confused and impotent. As always, Pleasantville would view the manuscript, but Charles Magill, master diplomat, by now had forged an excellent working relationship with the Yanks and had earned a comfortable degree of autonomy.

A few days later Charles phoned unhappily. Pleasantville's editor-in-chief was outraged. My article was, he told Magill, too long, too personal, too scary and "totally unacceptable." Magill explained to him how carefully it had been discussed, rediscussed, written, rewritten and edited. He mentioned the poll that reinforced my theme. He noted that Canadians are different from Americans (a fact you have to keep reminding Americans). He stressed that the writer was a westerner and small-c conservative (to ward off suspicions that I was some kind of limp-wristed pinko Commie-loving bastard).

Threats were levied from the other side. We Canadians were acutely conscious that it *was* P'ville's magazine. The conversation was put on hold, to let tempers cool. It resumed a day or so later. Canadian president Ralph Hancox got in on it. My humble attempt to help save the human race was turning into an international incident. Finally Magill suggested a compromise: the Canadian edition would run a companion piece by an American writer of USRD's choosing on the other point of view (which had to be militaristic, since I'd covered the middle ground). That's what we did.

Before that, Magill flew to Toronto. We had a good lunch and amiable talk. Sucking in my gut, I agreed to completely drop my macabre descriptions of what could happen to people in a city hit by the Bomb. Nearly everyone in Montreal now found it too repellent and Magill, having gone to the mat for me, deserved my support. But we retained full detail on the nuclear winter, and this cautionary paragraph:

> You must therefore understand that you would be part of a nuclear war, for whatever brief time you survived. Think of everything that is precious to you: family, friends, flowers, trees, bird song, the smell of grass, the changing seasons, all the wonderful life, intelligence and civilization so painfully achieved since we crawled from the muck—and imagine all of it vanishing in seconds or in agonizing weeks.

When the articles appeared (only in Canada; pity), mine did moderately well in the readership survey—well behind "Laughter, The Best Medicine," "Life's Like That," "Campus Comedy" and "It Pays to Enrich Your Word Power," but ahead of "Cartoons in Clay" and "The Beauty of Yoga." I received two letters. One chided me for not urging *Digest* readers to pray which, the writer said, was the sole solution to mankind's dilemma. The other warned that unless my daughter and I shaped up we'd better not celebrate Christmas anymore; we obviously weren't Christians [because we feared Armageddon].

If the Americans had insisted on killing the story I, and perhaps Magill, would have resigned. I came away with even greater respect for Charles. Fair as always, he understood the parent company's stance on the arms' race: negotiate from strength. He empathized with the American editor's consternation at my radical departure from a normal USRD position. The very fact that USRD let my story run with viewpoint and essentials more or less intact was, Charles told me, "a considerable concession, a true first for the *Digest* and something that would not have happened with any other edition."

He was right. But there was an overriding issue. "My disappointment remains rather deep," I wrote Magill. "Not because [the Americans] exerted their authority, which is their prerogative, but because the editor of one of this world's great international magazines proved to be so parochial over a subject of such profound importance to the human race."

In 1980 I wrote separate stories for the Canadian and U.S. editions on acid rain, with no more than the usual problems. The Canadian article brought no reader mail, but many thoughtful Americans wrote to me about the USRD version. Americans take their *Reader's Digest* seriously.

When Alexander Farrell became Canadian editor in 1985 he asked me to update the piece. I did, with my customary voluminous research and much new information. What wasn't new was America's foot-dragging over reducing acid rain, as I accurately reported:

> The Reagan administration—pressured by powerful coal and utility lobbies—has been loath to act. Indeed, for years it refused to admit there *was* a problem.

I should have known better. The story went smoothly through Montreal but in Pleasantville hell hath no fury like a Republican president scorned. I thought I had been polite to Mr. Reagan, not saying, as did many journalists on both sides of the border, that the ancient actor was rowing with only one oar in the water. Or that this was the same Reagan who once stated that trees cause pollution.

But Farrell was told in vigorous terms that my story was unfair to America's acid rain policies (ignoring the fact that Ohio Valley pollution was killing our lakes) and, anyway, was old information (ignoring the stiff new Canadian legislation enacted since the earlier story).

To his credit, Farrell did not kill the story, as recommended. He pulled it from the lineup and asked Penelope Body, our ace researcher, to go over it all again. I amassed piles of supplementary evidence. Body found nothing inaccurate or unfair to the Reagan administration. In the end, we published a story substantially the same as the original. The Reagan reference, gently brushed and curried, appeared as:

> The Reagan administration, pressured by coal and utility lobbies, has been loath to act. Indeed, for years it maintained that the existence of the problem had not been adequately demonstrated.

I could understand the arch-Republican USRD taking umbrage, and was pleased that, presented with unassailable facts, it let the story run in Canada. But it demonstrated Pleasantville's myopia, like that of Americans generally, toward the Canadian condition.

In 1989 I took early retirement from the staff job, but stayed on as "contributing editor" (freelancer on retainer) at Farrell's request. For one thing, Alex was scrupulously fair with me. For another, although I'd prepared successfully for retirement, I still had family obligations and liked the *Digest*'s financial cushion.

Mainly I stayed, despite the years of griping, because I still began each assignment with youthful hope and curiosity. Each time, I put aside the latest squabble with cutters or researchers, and misgivings about P'ville, and set out with the dumb unquenchable excitement of finding something new, getting the great quote, the great anecdote, maybe a story better than anyone had written before.

And there was in nearly every assignment those aforementioned pleasures and fringe benefits–reflections, fleeting encounters that remained fixed in my memory. Two examples.

There were strange new sights and sounds on our press tour among Canada's military peacekeepers in Egypt. A dead camel floating down the Nile. Calls to the Koran booming over loudspeakers in the steamy dawn. Foul public latrines where toilet paper was unknown. So there was something pleasantly homey about the sidewalk chess game we discovered one evening in downtown Ismailia.

A boy of maybe fifteen was playing an older man, surrounded by a male crowd. We were in a genial mood, having hoisted a few in the officers' mess. We spoke no Arabic, but the smiling Egyptians asked in halting English if we'd like to match our designated hitter against their boy. Bob Riddell, TV cameraman and most sweet-natured of humans, agreed to play for Canada.

The bright-eyed boy sat down across the board. His fellow Egyptians were beside themselves with grins, nudges and knowing glances. In a rare flash of insight, I muttered to Winnipeg broadcaster Jim Coghill, "This kid is probably the Egyptian Bobby Fischer."

The boy *was* good but Riddell, although operating under a three-gin handicap, was better. "He was toast," Bob told me recently from his home in Edmonton. "I had him. I knew it, he knew it, they all knew it."

Then the clever lad picked up a pawn, kissed it for good luck—and put it on a different square. Suddenly Riddell was in trouble. He couldn't believe it. Then he spotted the cheat.

"You moved your pawn!" he cried. The kid looked pained, baffled, a picture of innocence. His cheering section clucked their disapproval. There were fifty more of them than us. So Ismailia's Bobby Fischer won, to passionate cheers. Riddell, although miffed, kept smiling. The Egyptians waved farewell with warm shouts, limpid eyes and dazzling white teeth.

In the postmortem we concluded that Riddell had unwittingly done more to cement Canadian-Egyptian relations than any twelve ambassadorial missions. There's still time to put him up for the Order of Canada.

That frivolous vignette didn't belong in the story, of course. Nor did my poignant encounter with the old veterans in England appear in my article on Major Ben Wheeler, a relatively unsung hero of World War II. Wheeler, an Alberta doctor attached to the British forces, was captured at Singapore and spent more than three years in Japanese prison camps. For sheer barbarism and misery, Japanese POW camps were by far the worst of the war.

Wheeler not only survived but kept others alive with the crudest of instruments, smatterings of medical supplies, extraordinary skill and his own exemplary courage. And through all those years he kept a secret diary hidden from his captors.

Wheeler returned to Alberta and lived until 1963. After the war, three of his former mates wrote a letter to a Canadian newspaper, dubbing him "a man sent from God." Years later his daughter Anne, now a prominent Canadian filmmaker, produced a sensitive eighty-two-minute docudrama on Ben's ordeal for the National Film Board.

I took the story a step farther: a ten-thousand-word special feature for the *Digest*. I pored over Ben Wheeler's diaries, interviewed Anne and her mother in Edmonton and went to England to talk to some of his surviving prison mates. I met three of them in a Yarmouth hotel lounge one busy Friday night. They spoke of Ben with awe and reverence.

After I shut off my recorder they produced an amateur's tape of two songs composed by POWs during their stay in Kinkaseki, the worst of the horrific camps. One was "Down the Mine," about the death-trap where they worked. Another was "Laughing Boy," their nickname for one of the sadistic guards. Would I play it for them?

Neither tune nor lyrics amounted to much, but suddenly the three elderly men were singing softly along with the tape. It caused a small stir in the lounge. People stopped and stared. The white-haired men ignored them. For a few minutes they were transported back to the worst time of their lives. Nothing would ever hurt or mark them as much as the years in Kinkaseki. Yet it was a time, one of their number had said, that shaped men like pieces of wood battered by the sea: their soft parts washed away, their solid cores intact.

The incident was peripheral to Wheeler's story; just one of those fleeting moments in a writer's job—sometimes more important than the words or deeds of the famous and powerful—when humanity at its finest shines through.

Increasingly, my pleasure in such stories was tempered by a changing mood at the Canadian *Digest*. The sense of fun so essential to every editorial job was missing. The staff seemed trapped on a treadmill of labour. I said as much when invited to give them a pre-retirement speech; some of the younger editors privately agreed.

Smith had retired. Magill was now director of publishing. George Ronald had taken early retirement. When Alexander Farrell was made editor in 1985, a job many of us thought George should have had (and I suspect secretly wanted), he remained totally loyal. But two years later he confided to me: "It's no fun anymore." By then he had remarried, to fellow *Digest* employee Pat McCormack. They were ecstatically happy. It seemed as though his best years were still to come.

Then George contracted cancer. He fought it hard, the way he did everything else and for a while seemed to have it licked. "You can beat it, George," I wrote him once, wanting to believe it, and he pinned the words on his bulletin board at home.

But by autumn 1990 it was racing through his body. Charles Magill and I went to his Montreal hospital room one grey November afternoon. He was thin and stoic. At first we talked trivia, skirting the obvious. Finally I said, "Are you hurting today?" Then we talked about it, as George wanted; he was never one for dodging reality. He hadn't expected it to come with such sudden ferocity, he said; now it was a matter of making his remaining time quality time.

I idly mentioned a story I was about to begin. George's eyes sharpened.

"Better check the file," he said. "I think Fred McGuinness tried that one on us years ago. What he sent in wasn't quite right, but you might want to let him know you've taken it on." So McGuinness won't think we stole his idea, was what he meant. George's bottomless memory was accurate as usual. And as usual he was thinking of the writer's feelings, even on his deathbed.

I shook his hand for the last time, went back to the Manoir Le Moyne, sat alone with a glass of wine and blurry eyes, and wrote some thoughts about George. He died two days later.

Sometimes I re-read this Sanskrit passage he sent to me on his retirement day:

Look well to this day,
For it is life,
The very life of life.
In its brief course lie all
The realities and verities of existence,
The bliss of growth,
The splendour of action,
The glory of power.

For yesterday is but a dream,
And tomorrow is only a vision,
But today, well lived,
Makes every yesterday a dream of happiness
And every tomorrow a vision of hope.

Look well, therefore, to this day.

Copyeditors and researchers were being promoted into editing positions in the Canadian office. They were sent to Pleasantville for training, of course, and came back glowing with discovery. One young editor—according to my informant, Dry Throat—began referring to editorial material as "a product" to be "shaped." Others demanded, "Why do our writers always complain? They're getting the best editing in the world!" They were confusing quantity—as many as five editors laying hands on a story—with quality.

In autumn 1991 things took a dramatic turn. The admirable Charles Magill was abruptly removed from his job as vice-president and director of publishing and made a roving editor. The notice of his demotion was co-signed by the Canadian acting publisher and the liaison editor at USRD, but it bore the heavy hoof prints of Pleasantville. It had been my hunch for a long time that P'ville wanted to regain its firm grip on the Canadian edition, which seemed to have slackened with Bill C58. (There is no longer a CRD director of publishing, and I should not be surprised to see Pleasantville kill off the Canadian edition, sooner rather than later.)

Four months later five Canadian senior editors and two researchers were let go on three days' notice. The mass firings, we were assured, were the sole decision of the Canadian office. I found that impossible to believe, given the heavy traffic between Pleasantville and Montreal before the event, as described by another of my informants, Deep Slough.

When I learned that one of the victims was the scholarly Michael Ballantyne (whom I'd insisted be my "sponsoring" editor when George retired), I quit. Withdrawing a finished article I had just sent in, I told Montreal I could never write for *Reader's Digest* again. After 117 articles, including 15 book-length "specials," and twenty-six years of association, my trust and respect for the organization were gone.

Still, I have few regrets. I was sometimes very proud of my work at CRD. I won ten national awards for *Digest* articles. Recently, after a dozen years, I re-read "The Spy That Fell From the Sky" and it stands up with any other piece of writing, anywhere. And thanks to the *Digest* and my books, I was financially secure for the first time in my life.

The paternalism of DeWitt Wallace and the camaraderie of Magill, Smith, Ronald, Ballantyne, How, MacDonald, Tyrwhitt and the rest are gone, but the magazine will endure. The passing of writers and editors means little. There are no stars at the *Digest*. The *system* is the thing and it works admirably as prescribed.

The ultimate summation of *Reader's Digest*—put more honestly and lucidly than any official utterance I ever saw or heard—came from George Ronald in response to one of my diatribes:

> We believe, and I suspect some writers and others sometimes miss this point, that it's the reader, specifically the *Digest* reader, whom we seek to satisfy. We manage, despite all the agony, to give the *Digest* reader what he wants and has come to expect from the *Digest*. He goes elsewhere when he wants stories on other subjects, stories treated differently, longer stories, less tightly written stories, less well-researched stories, more heavily illustrated stories, more repetitive stories, stories that some argue are more substantial or that "flow better."
>
> In the *Digest*, however, we present him with stories as he expects them to be in the *Digest*. So it's with the reader—the *Digest* reader—in mind that the cutting and condensation are

done. *Digest* requirements about space and the *Digest*'s editing is in the interests not of us editors but of our readers. And readers tell us, through their response and through the measurement of the time they spend in the magazine, that they like the *Digest* the way it is—and considerably better than they like magazines in which writers, in effect, do as they wish when it comes to length, clarity, research and so on.

Always with a willingness to consider something new, to review an editing decision, to experiment, and never with a closed mind, our job is to select, condense, edit with the *Digest* reader in mind.

That, indeed, is its raison d'être. Because of that—beloved by its readers, immune to detractors—the *Digest* will go on and on.

14

WAS SIR WILLIAM REALLY INTREPID?

My file marked "Intrepid" is a jumble of clippings, notes, Telexes from Bermuda, a tape recording of an old man's husky voice and a condensed *Digest* article. These, plus some vivid and hitherto unpublished memories, are the legacies of my brief encounter with Sir William Stephenson, the Canadian-born "man called Intrepid."

Some stories never let go, especially if you are cursed with chronic fretfulness: *Did I get it all and get it right?* Stephenson is a classic case.

My article on him appeared in 1984. He was a man of considerable wit and charm, with the knack of quickly winning your loyalty. You sensed that if you played fair with him, he would back you to the hilt. But even then there were hints of discrepancies in his record. I tried to check them all. Research for an article or book can be a bottomless pit. How much is enough, or too much? A good writer goes by hunch and instinct and, when in doubt, *over*-researches. Increasingly over the years, notably with *Reader's Digest*, I gathered far more material than ever appeared in print. Inevitably, good stuff was always left on the cutting-room floor, but at least I knew no fact had been overlooked.

I thought that was true of my Intrepid story. But after his death in 1989 a swarm of critics in Canada and England–most of whom were remarkably restrained during his lifetime–burst out of the woodwork to challenge his achievements. They said he did not do many of the things attributed to him; that his mind was muddled; that maybe he was a fraud.

None of this would have surprised Stephenson. He once told his friend Tomasina Fountain, a Bermuda journalist, "Just wait until I die, Tommie, and those afraid to assault me while I still live will be brave enough to come out with their guns blazing."

My instinct was to believe him. But had I been too accepting or too lazy in 1984? Suddenly the Stephenson case had me by the throat again. In preparing this book, I spent months rechecking the story, tracking down new sources, seeking the truth anew. It was a matter of professional pride.

For me it had begun in 1983 when the University of Regina jubilantly announced it had acquired Sir William's private papers. His wartime exploits had been lauded in books and film. He was awarded some of the western world's most prestigious honours. He counted kings, prime ministers, presidents, heroes and rogues among his friends. Surely his papers were a treasure trove. Would *Reader's Digest* do a story on them? It sounded like a thin idea, but I never turn down a chance to visit Saskatchewan.

In Regina the university turned me loose one morning with six cartons of uncatalogued material. Years of research give you the knack of quickly sorting wheat from chaff. By early afternoon I knew that the acquisition was a disappointment. Five boxes were little more than the papers (including some old expense accounts) of author William Stevenson, whose 1979 best-seller, *A Man Called Intrepid,* catapulted author and subject into international celebrity.

The sixth container was mildly interesting: wads of Telexes from Stephenson to Stevenson (no relation), addressed to "STEVERITE" and signed "INTREPID." One Telex, in code, purported to be a tip-off from Sir William to the author about the Israeli raid on Entebbe (Stevenson wrote a book on that event). There were scribbled notes on backs of envelopes and numerous letters to Stephenson from such notables as one-time heavyweight boxing champion Gene Tunney, novelist Roald Dahl and others who worked for Sir William during World War II.

I found no state secrets, but the trip was not a total loss. Lloyd Barber, U of R president, and Ron Robbins, head of the journalism school, were just back from Bermuda brimming with tales of Sir William's remarkable grasp of world affairs, his searching questions about the fairly new Devine government in Saskatchewan, his speed at getting from private sources the results of a Canadian Tory convention before Barber or Robbins found them by radio.

Maybe the old boy would consent to an interview. I phoned author Stevenson in Washington. He volunteered to sound out Intrepid. The latter didn't want to be interviewed. Now, although I'd been cool to the original idea, perversity took over. This was a challenge. I'd get him! I sent Sir William a wildly persuasive letter, suggesting a visit in the spring. Back came a Telex:

> WHO COULD RESIST THE BLANDISHMENTS IN YOUR LETTER OF AUGUST 3RD 1983
> OF COURSE WOULD BE PLEASED TO SEE YOU NEXT MARCH
> BILL [STEVENSON] CAN FILL YOU IN
> IN THE MEANTIME GREETINGS AND ALL GOOD WISHES

In other words, he'd grant an audience even though I was sucking up.

As became my habit over the years, I first scrawled a brief outline of the subcategories of information I'd be digging for—a kind of phantom framework for the unborn article. Naturally it would change as hard research came in, but for now it provided some direction and kept me from flailing blindly in a sea of facts. As always, I read clipping files (for leads only; all experienced writers know that newspaper stories can't be trusted for accuracy) and biographies: *The Man Called Intrepid* and British author H. Montgomery Hyde's less sensational *The Quiet Canadian.*

Winnipeg-born Stephenson had served in World War I, first as infantryman, then with the Royal Flying Corps. After the war he stayed in England and invented a way of sending pictures by radio which, wrote Hyde, revolutionized pictorial journalism and paid him an average $500,000 a year in royalties for eighteen years. Stephenson moved in high circles and controlled a score of manufacturing companies. In the 1930s, Hyde related, Stephenson travelled often in Germany and fed Winston Churchill facts and figures that bolstered the latter's fear of Germany rearming. When war broke out, Stephenson went to Washington at Churchill's bidding to set up British Security Coordination, an all-embracing operation dedicated to wooing isolationist America into the fray. He would bear the code name "Intrepid."

A Man Called Intrepid had him as a key figure in Enigma (the machine and procedures by which Britain cracked the Nazi wartime codes). It credited him with being Britain's top espionage man in the U.S., responsible for the training, at a "Camp X" east of Toronto, of spies and saboteurs for missions in occupied Europe.

Some critics were claiming the "spy master" designation was a myth. His biographers said he'd shot down twenty or twenty-six German planes in World War I; his critics said it was only six (later I discovered they were all wrong). His biographers made much of his close relationship with and special mandate from Winston Churchill, but I found no mention of Stephenson in Churchill's memoirs. All this had to be sorted out.

One April morning in 1984 I arrived at Stephenson's one-storey house among verdant gardens and stone walls, high on a Bermuda hill. A maid ushered me into his living room-cum-study: books lining cedar-panelled walls, furled Union Jack in the corner, a sweeping view of the distant Atlantic. A Telex chattered in a distant room. Intrepid limped in slowly on the arm of his adopted daughter, Elizabeth. He was a small man with thinning grey hair, natty in sand-coloured slacks, ascot, blue corduroy jacket. Years before he had been partially crippled by a stroke. His voice was rasping and sometimes difficult to understand, but the hooded eyes could skewer you with a glance.

He took a big leather chair in the corner, surrounded by telephone, stereo-recorder and TV/VCR, and waved me to another. Elizabeth brought glasses of chilled white wine. Intrepid was just getting over the 'flu. "A bad bout?" I asked rhetorically.

"Don't know," he said with a flicker of amusement. "I never had 'flu at eighty-eight before." He told of having influenza in the war until the day his Sopwith Camel biplane went into a terrifying spin. "When I pulled out of it, the 'flu was gone," he concluded, "but I'd not recommend that cure for everyone." We smiled at his wit. Things seemed to be going well.

Then he said, "Well, I really have nothing to tell you." While I stared, speechless and disbelieving, he said he'd play an audio of a recent appearance in New York where he'd received a medal, a video of a CTV interview following the award, and an audio of a Lloyd Barber speech about the University of Regina papers. The rest, he said amiably, I could get from books.

There is more than one way to skin a cat, or an interviewee. Blustering or pleading wouldn't work with this man. I turned on my recorder and patiently listened to the speeches (all standard, useless stuff). Listening is one of the simplest and most neglected arts of interviewing (TV interviewers, I notice, tend to listen to themselves more often than to their subjects).

Then I tossed a few friendly questions; anything to keep this non-interview alive. One of them struck pay dirt: odd, wasn't it, that the happenstance of World War II had plunged businessman Stephenson into security work? Sir William perked up.

"Yes and that's where they go completely awry about this thing," he said. "They all love this word 'spy,' but that wasn't my job at all." Now we were getting somewhere. He seemed to be refuting the image established in *A Man Called Intrepid*. Yet he had let the book appear.

"Do you dislike that term 'spy master'?"

"Yes, because that wasn't the job."

His job with BSC, he said, was to get materials of war from America into the fray. (To that end he succeeded, as revealed in late 1989 with publication of the definitive document on his wartime work: "British Security Coordination: An Account of Secret Activities in the Western Hemisphere, 1940–45." At that time a British MP told the Bermuda *Royal Gazette,* "This document represents the authentic version of what really happened during World War II without any of the ridiculous embroidery. You just don't need any of that because Sir William's career speaks for itself.")

William Stevenson's second book, *Intrepid's Last Case,* had recently come out. In part it dealt with the case of Soviet defector to Canada, Igor Gouzenko, in which Intrepid had a role; in part it was about the late Col. Charles Ellis, a Stephenson friend posthumously accused of being a double agent. It had been heavily panned by some critics. What about it?

"I agreed to Bill going ahead with that book on two counts," Sir William told me. "That it would bring active Reds and pseudo-Reds from the woodwork to attack me in every possible way. And that it would clear Ellis. He [Stevenson] failed in that completely."

He went on to berate Canada as "the only so-called advanced country in the world that hasn't got a secret intelligence agency." The Canadian Security Intelligence Service was then in the making. "As a matter of fact, I've been grooming the right man for that job for over two years." He wouldn't name him, then. He went on to express his loathing of then-Prime Minister Pierre Trudeau, who he felt was soft on Russia. I kept listening, questioning and beginning to genuinely enjoy this sharp-eyed old man.

Stephenson was becoming animated. Suddenly he said, "I'm going to place myself in your hands." Then and later he told a few things that he said might give comfort to his enemies if published: "You have to know that my knowledge of these affairs has to come from behind the Curtain." I knew he was up and prowling most days by 4:00 A.M., hanging over the Telex; and that a stream of important people still made their way to his Bermuda home.

"You don't know me. Why are you telling me these things?"

"Because if you let me down, I could make things very unpleasant for you," Stephenson said with a wicked little grin. I laughed out loud at his moxy. Maybe he could. More to the point, if there was even a remote chance of a careless word sending some luckless person into an eastern European prison camp, as Stephenson implied . . .

I honoured the arrangement. Maybe an "investigative" journalist would say I was suckered. But if I had taken the textbook hard-nosed stance—"Don't tell me anything I can't print"—I'd have been on the next plane home. Was I being manipulated? Maybe, but I had a gut feeling that much of what he was saying was true.

The next day he and Elizabeth took me to lunch at the Royal Bermuda Yacht Club. Elizabeth, a capable, pleasant woman of forty-six with a young son by a broken marriage, had come to Sir William as nurse, secretary and all-around helper after his wife's death. Having no children of his own, he'd adopted her in 1983.

He insisted I call him "Bill." I told him my mother, were she still alive, would have been mortified at such instant familiarity. He told how one night during World War I, he and Canadian ace Billy Bishop flew their planes across the Channel to London, "danced until dawn," then flew back to the war. Then a Hemingway tale: how the macho Ernest liked to spar with Stephenson (a boxer in his youth) until one day, tiring of the game, Stephenson brought along his friend ex-heavyweight champion Gene Tunney and called Hemingway's bluff.

I remarked that the University of Regina acquisitions were not really his papers. He promptly agreed. (Recently a U of R archivist confirmed that conclusion.) What about the discrepancy in numbers of German aircraft he had shot down in World War I? I asked. "Who can remember?" Stephenson said. "The Hyde book will have it right." The records were a mess, he said, and Hyde had trouble pinning it down.

Back home I talked to people who had known and/or worked with Stephenson. They all worshipped him. During the war some had nicknamed him "God." I asked the British *Digest* to check his World War I record. BRD produced a breakdown from two sources that I regard as definitive: the Royal Air Force Museum at Hendon and the combat report of No. 73 Squadron Royal Flying Corps for 1918. Stephenson had *nine* confirmed kills and *two* probables. The Hendon source added that World War I pilots also shot down many observation balloons, which, although never recorded, were regarded as important targets. He suggested this might account for the discrepancies in Stephenson's record.

These and other unanswered questions in his "official" record bothered all of us at the *Digest,* particularly George Ronald. "Should we postpone the story?" I asked. In the end we decided to go ahead, but I kept checking. All summer, Telexes flew between Toronto and Bermuda: my questions, Sir William's amiable replies. Critics were now saying he had never received the Legion d'Honneur. Stephenson, who *wore* the medal, sent me a lengthy account of the aerial action leading up to the award, adding, "I well remember the presentation ceremony because Marshal Foch [French general and supreme commander of Allied forces in Word War I], presiding, kissed me on both cheeks and I was fearful of being blinded by his huge moustache."

After some prodding by Telex, Stephenson gave me the name of his CSIS "protégé": former RCMP superintendent Archie Barr. I phoned him in Ottawa. Barr, with thirty years' police experience behind him, said he had needed no "grooming" by Stephenson. But he'd travelled frequently to Bermuda to confer with Sir William; understood the latter's eagerness to be part of this new venture; remained a great admirer and did not consider him unsound of mind.

A year after my working visit, I went to Bermuda on holiday with daughter Lesley. She–a tall sunny, gentle woman who befriends children, old people and street waifs, and smiles even when she is scared inside–was apprehensive now. "Sir William, the Man Called Intrepid" sounded formidable.

Stephenson, Elizabeth and young Rhys met us at the airport. It was a stifling 88°F and Sir William looked painfully frail. He didn't have to be there but was, in linen jacket, white trousers and ascot. He instantly warmed to Lesley's transparent honesty. She, in turn, was captivated when he kissed her hand in courtly old-world manner.

The next day he was eager to discuss world affairs. He played me a taped speech by a dropped-out KGB officer; said George Bush had a greater grasp of foreign affairs than Reagan; asked what I thought of Brian Mulroney. Knowing Stephenson had hosted the Mulroneys I said diplomatically, "He's a good politician." Sir William liked that, and said Mila was smarter and more natural than Brian. I couldn't argue with that. Stephenson's contempt for Trudeau remained unabated. "He'll never be secretary of the UN, I'll see to that," Intrepid cried. I doubted that Stephenson had such clout, but kept my peace. The whole morning demonstrated Sir William's acuity and his burning desire to be au courant, remarkable in a man of nearly ninety.

By now Lesley regarded him as a rather dear older gentleman. She prowled around his study, not embarrassed to ask ingenuous questions. That's how we learned over a photo of Lorne Green that the Canadian-born actor was dying of cancer and, over a photo of Lord Louis Mountbatten's ship, that Mountbatten and Stephenson used to chat regularly by Telex before the former was assassinated by Irish terrorists. Stephenson's face saddened at the thought of another friend gone.

We dined out together a few times. Stephenson picked slowly at light meals (but did not exist on wine and ice cream as implied by *Saturday Night* magazine). Lesley exuded good cheer. Elizabeth was relaxed. The mannerly Rhys, with dark brown intelligent eyes, was a curious mixture of child (he spilled chocolate ice cream all over his clean white shirt) and grown-up. "He's not a little boy," Lesley said afterward. "He's a short adult."

I have two lingering memories of the visit. Stephenson labouring valiantly up a long flight of stairs en route to some restaurant, in great pain but refusing to quit. And Stephenson, a game but shrunken figure, waving his last good-bye when he and Elizabeth dropped us at the airport for the flight home.

What have I learned? In the shadowy world of espionage, is there ever absolute truth?

Was Sir William really Intrepid?

David Stafford, English-born historian, academic and director of the Canadian Institute of International Affairs, has stated that "Intrepid was never his code name." But Stephenson had already told me, "Only Winston referred to me as 'Intrepid.' My symbol to SIS was '48000' and for SOE it was 'G.' "

Did Winston Churchill know Stephenson?

The late Sir John Colville, wartime secretary to Churchill, claimed the latter never met Stephenson. Yet Canadian author Maj. Gen. Richard Rohmer tells me that Colville was away from No. 10 Downing Street for extended periods during the war (he and Rohmer were once in the same air force training unit). Conclusion: Colville didn't necessarily know everything about Churchill.

Another former secretary alleged that Winston "never heard of Stephenson, nor did anyone else at No. 10." This is impossible. Stephenson was knighted in 1945 and his nomination, like every other, *had* to pass directly through the prime minister's hands. Further, if the Stephenson/Churchill connection was untrue, why did Winston, alive and relatively healthy in 1962, not refute the Montgomery Hyde biography when it appeared?

In 1991 Tomasina Fountain, now back in her native England,

showed me a copy of a report Stephenson sent to American president Harry Truman, via a senior executive of the U.S. Office of Strategic Services at war's end. It described Stephenson's dinner at the home of Lord Beaverbrook on the day in May 1940 when Churchill became prime minister:

> The dinner party was a serious affair. Other guests included 'Boom' Renchard of the RAF and Scotland Yard fame, General Weygand of France and Billy Hughes, Prime Minister of Australia, who as usual had his hearing aid with him. It consisted of a small black box containing an amplifier which was controlled by a knob which controlled the rheostat inside it to adjust the volume.
>
> When the port and cigars appeared Winston rose from his seat and beckoned to me. We walked over to the heavily draped dining room window where Winston said quietly to me, "Bill, you know what you must do at once. We have discussed it most fully, and there is a complete fusion of minds. So off you go; you will have full support of every resource at my command, and God will guide your efforts as He will ours. . . ."

Could Stephenson have invented such detail? asks Fountain. Maybe, I say, but why would he bother, in a private report long before his biographies were dreamed of? She also remembers a conversation with the late Ernest Cuneo, lawyer and a wartime advisor to President Franklin Roosevelt. Cuneo told Fountain that his greatest wartime ambition had been to meet Churchill. He said Stephenson made that dream come true, by personally taking him to No. 10 Downing Street very early one morning.

Anthony Cave Brown, author of several works on World War II intelligence activities, in 1987 published *"C," The Secret Life of Sir Stewart Graham Menzies, Spymaster to Winston Churchill.* Menzies and Stephenson were associates but apparently not friends. Brown interviewed Menzies at length for his exhaustive work. From it comes persuasive testimony that Sir William's relationship with Churchill was much as his biographers state.

Brown refers to Stephenson as "a member of Churchill's circle of prewar days." He writes that Menzies proposed an alternate candidate for the head of BSC in America but "Churchill pressed

Stephenson's name upon 'C.' " Menzies accepted on condition that he be Stephenson's boss; Stephenson wanted "independent command with the right at all times of direct access to Churchill.

"Only Churchill could resolve such an impasse and that was settled when Stephenson, as he claimed, dined with Churchill on May 10. . . . Stephenson discussed 'C's demands with Churchill privately after dinner and, as Stephenson also claimed, Churchill declared that it was Stephenson's duty to accept the post, but that, though he would have to accept 'C's directions, he would also have direct access to Churchill . . ."

Later in the war, writes Brown, Menzies tried to oust Stephenson, but "Churchill and Stephenson remained close friends" and it appeared that "Churchill had intervened in favour of Stephenson," who kept his post to war's end.

Brown's research and the Cuneo story seem irrefutable evidence that Churchill knew Stephenson. Yet why was Stephenson not mentioned in Sir Winston's memoirs? In 1992 I put this to Sir William Deakin, who worked for Stephenson at BSC, and was one of a small team that subsequently selected documentation and drafted briefs for the Churchill history. Deakin, now in France, had no answer. The extent of the Churchill-Stephenson connection may never be satisfactorily established, now that the principals are gone.

Was Stephenson living in a fantasy world?

After Stephenson's death, David Stafford wrote in *Saturday Night* of a visit he paid the former in 1985. He described Stephenson showing a video of the TV movie *A Man Called Intrepid* and identifying actor Michael York as "my young man" (meaning a real-life Camp X agent from wartime). Implication: the poor old gent was bonkers.

Stafford added that "William Stephenson . . . was a genuine hero of the First World War who also did sterling work in the Second," but for "at least the last twenty-five years of his life . . . inhabited a dream world. . . ." He quoted some damning remarks from Sir Edwin Leather, former governor of Bermuda, and cited Leather as one of Stephenson's "closest friends and neighbours for the last fifteen years of his life." Tomasina Fountain, who saw Stephenson regularly, responds, "Edwin most certainly was *not!*"

Stafford concluded with a little homily on the perils of

hero-worship and how the North American public had been taken in by the Intrepid "myth."

His portrayal of Stephenson is so unlike the man most of us remember that we wonder if he was pulling Stafford's leg. "Bill pulled my leg on that video too," says Fountain. "When David Niven first appeared on screen he whispered in a 'put-on' English accent, 'I'll bet you never thought I would agree to play the part of myself in the movie!' " Former Ontario Lieutenant Governor Pauline McGibbon, a long-time friend, visited Stephenson not long before his death. She found him weak of body but acute of mind.

Myths *did* surround Stephenson. Stafford's scholarly 1986 book, *Camp X,* reveals that much that was claimed for the camp was untrue. Stafford added, "Stephenson's mandate never extended beyond the Western Hemisphere; he had no operational role in European activities."

Stephenson had told me as much two years before. Yet he didn't bother to dispel the myth until questioned–just as he had lived with the "spy master" and ambiguous "Intrepid" labels until I asked. Perhaps–as he ferociously clung to life in a world that was passing him by, a world that was rapidly forgetting its World War II heroes–he felt he deserved any recognition he could get. On my second visit he pressed upon me scrapbooks of his postwar exploits, not because I would write anything more but because he was proud of them. He brought up again his World War I kills, saying he didn't care how many he was credited with. But he *did* care, about that and everything else from the old days.

So what have I learned? That some truths may elude us forever. What do I think? That Stephenson, whatever the glitches in his record and contrary to posthumous character-assassination, deserves our respect. I once remarked to Archie Barr of the CSIS that Sir William, while clearly of sound mind, liked to revel in past glories, as do we all. Barr agreed.

"I think we should be a civilization capable of letting him live on those glories," he said, "because he has a storehouse of them that most of us would envy."

That is one of the wiser observations about Intrepid. It may not be the last word on his controversial career, but should be.

15

DEATH OF A YOUNG MAN: A CASE HISTORY

Near midnight on July 20, 1981, nineteen-year-old Jeffrey Collum finished his evening job at a restaurant north of Toronto and drove south toward home on Highway 400. About four minutes later he entered a shallow depression on the six-lane road with its fenced median, a mere dip but enough to mask, until the final terrible split-second, the last sight he would ever see: headlights approaching rapidly *in his lane*.

He had no time to react. The two cars crashed head-on. Jeffrey Collum died instantly.

The story ran briefly on an inner page of the Toronto *Star* the next day. In the *Globe and Mail* it rated page nine, melded with another traffic fatality, in the classified section. Traffic deaths, even when caused by a drunk driver as this one was, are relatively commonplace in the big city.

I knew nothing of the tragedy until, three years later, a call came from Heather McCallum, my friend from *Canadian Homes & Gardens* days. She had an article idea for me. Helen Collum, Jeff's mother and Heather's university classmate, had become an outspoken advocate against drunken driving.

I was intrigued. Heather was no fan of *Reader's Digest*. This story must be special. After meeting Howard and Helen Collum I knew it was. It would become the most engrossing, difficult story of my career.

The Collums were opposites. Helen, dark and dynamic, was an

elementary school teacher. Howard, sixty-one when I met them, was a lean, gentle retired architect and town planner. Helen had emerged from her grief to become fighting mad, an articulate spokeswoman for P.R.I.D.E. (Parents to Reduce Impaired Driving Everywhere). Howard, holding more within himself, was still moved to tears by memories, especially on the anniversary of Jeffrey's death.

Helen wondered if I would write about P.R.I.D.E. But the real story, I knew, was not just the accident and the virtues of sober motoring, but the befores and afters: how the death of one young man, like a pebble in a pool, sent widening ripples of pain, touching, marking or changing irrevocably the lives of family, friends and total strangers. After several meetings with the Collums and an exhaustive story outline to the *Digest* editors we were agreed. As well as being a spectacular drama it could make an eloquent statement about drunken driving. Maybe it would save some other young person's life.

The Collums, having decided I was a sensitive writer (I think Helen read *Butter Down the Well,* memoir of my rural childhood), promised to be candid. I would interview everyone who had touched Jeffrey's life including, if possible, the man who killed him. Fair enough, the Collums said, but hoped I wouldn't pose that man as a victim.

I began assembling this enormous jigsaw puzzle. Through one winter I spent many evenings with Howard and Helen over miles of tape as they patiently, painfully, told of Jeffrey and themselves, the intimate details of that dreadful night, and the aftermath. I grew acquainted with a boy I'd never known: slight of build, brown haired, quick to smile, even tempered, in the bloom of life when it was taken from him. He'd been a good student, musician, poet, photographer. He handled his father's sailboat with aplomb, got along amiably with both parents and had met the girl he wanted to marry.

In the last weekend of his life, alone at the family cottage, he wrote an extraordinary poem, "Shores of Eternity," almost a premonition of what would follow. Howard and Helen showed me photos of his room as he had left it. On his desk was a list of things to do and a copy of *The Girl in a Swing,* Richard Adams's haunting story of love and the supernatural. It was open at page

367. I re-read the book, looking for omens in that page. There were none.

Robert Benmergui, twenty-six, whose car killed Jeffrey, had been driving with three times the blood-alcohol limit and had been sentenced to a year less a day. He served sixty-six days in prison and ninety-two more in a halfway house. In short, he'd done only 43 percent of his time, in any form, and only 20 percent in actual prison. Helen said she felt about him "the way some people feel about cockroaches." Howard admitted to "an animal feeling of wanting revenge."

The coroner's report, proceedings of the preliminary hearing and Benmergui's sentencing proceedings gave me a multitude of leads and details: who said what in court; how Benmergui behaved and looked; how he had celebrated on Grand Marnier that day, after getting a promotion at work; who else was at the accident. A St. Catharines' couple who witnessed the crash gave me vivid accounts, which became the story's lead. Brad Dunbar, the first Ontario Provincial Police constable on the scene, seemed glad to talk. He dug out his notebook with its meticulous police details, and remembered how after that night he worried whenever his own kid brother drove down Highway 400.

The Crown attorney explained why he didn't go for a harsher sentence: Benmergui had no past record and was rated an "excellent" employee by his boss. A year less a day would keep him out of penitentiary. The Crown felt sure a judge would go for that. (Sentences have since become stiffer.) Judges at the time tended to be lenient, the Crown told me; perhaps thinking, *There but for the grace of God go I.* I could relate to that: although always a careful driver, I changed my driving/drinking habits drastically after writing "Death of a Young Man."

Benmergui's lawyer refused to be interviewed, saying he had discarded the file (which surprised me). I was now ready for Benmergui himself, but he was not listed in the phone book or city directory. At the halfway house where he'd finished his sentence, psychologist Ramsay Kane told me more than I ever wanted to know about halfway houses plus a good account of Benmergui's behaviour there. At times the latter had been deeply remorseful; at other times he claimed he was a victim of society. "Our counsellors never told us anything about this in high school," he told Kane. "All you ever got was the coach laughing because everybody was going out for a beer after the game!" Which was undoubtedly true, but Kane did not allow drinking drivers to take refuge in excuses.

Would Benmergui meet with me? Kane volunteered to find out. Meanwhile the halfway house sold me a videotape of Benmergui and other inmates being interviewed by university students as a class project. If all else failed I would at least have "seen" and heard him.

Through the middleman, Benmergui said he would talk if he could be anonymous. I refused: his name had already appeared in the video and in news items; I'd be doing the story, regardless; this was a chance to express his side of it. He then dropped the "no name" stipulation and agreed to meet me in Ramsay Kane's presence.

I casually mentioned it to the Collums. A day later they phoned back in distress. They had launched a civil suit against Benmergui; their lawyer feared that my talking to him might jeopardize their case.

It seemed most unlikely. A *Reader's Digest* lawyer in Montreal confirmed that, legally, I was under no obligation to postpone the interview. But if I went ahead and somehow affected the civil suit, the Collums would never forgive me, or cooperate again. They'd been unstinting in their help. A dozen important interviews were still outstanding—people who would shut me out if I thwarted the Collums. So I opted to postpone the Benmergui interview. It was a gamble but I had a gut feeling he would still talk to me when the time was right.

Nevertheless I was acutely aware of a journalistic hazard: getting too close to one's sources. Howard and Helen had become friends. We were of a similar age. We talked easily about everything. As a parent I deeply empathized with their loss. Our friendship was inevitably part of my decision to delay that crucial interview.

But when they invited me to their Georgian Bay cottage, two summers in a row, I declined. Although they weren't trying to co-opt me, socializing at that stage seemed unwise, if not unethical.

A year passed. I wrote other stories. Benmergui and the

Collums settled out of court. It was now mid-1987. The *Digest* editors asked if I wanted to drop the assignment. Definitely not; I'd invested almost a year in it. Could I revive my enthusiasm for it again? Absolutely, if Benmergui would be interviewed.

He had left Toronto. I tracked him by phone to a northern Ontario city. He was brusque and cool; he wanted to forget it all. I understood, I said, and kept talking. Finally Benmergui remarked, "You sound like an honest reporter. I'll think about it."

I sent a letter, spelling out my proposed approach: I could not condone what he did but would tell what happened and how he felt, without editorial comment. Maybe it would do some good. Maybe it would make some other drinker think twice before driving. He could not read the manuscript, I cautioned, but researchers would double-check with him every word of his we used. I phoned again.

Benmergui, while still backing away, began to tell details that had never come out in court—such as the long ride home he had given a woman friend on that fateful night. I phoned her; she talked freely. Now I knew better than anyone (including Benmergui) exactly where he'd been and what happened on the night of the accident.

I drove and timed Benmergui's route: from the hotel where he'd hoisted his final celebratory drinks to the young woman's home many miles north, then back toward Toronto. Suddenly I understood why he had driven blindly onto an exit ramp and into the wrong lanes of Highway 400. In his fuddled state he thought he had turned onto Highway 401, which runs at right angles to 400. He thought he was driving east toward home; instead he was heading north toward disaster.

From that point I twice drove Benmergui's last northbound miles and poor Jeff Collum's southbound route three times, timing each to the second. Each time I came to the spot described in general terms by Brad Dunbar and the eyewitnesses. Now I knew, *This is where it all happened; where Jeff Collum, happily driving home in his little blue Toyota, minding his own business, saw those onrushing headlights rising over that blip in the road. This is where the young man died.*

Every journalist has his or her own way of handling other people's grief. Mine is simply to be as gentle and sympathetic as I would expect some intrusive stranger to be with me. It does not, nor should not, ever become easy.

In the late 1970s when I wrote a *Digest* special feature about the drowning of twelve boys and one master during a school canoeing outing on Lake Temiskaming, I spoke to nearly all the bereaved parents. Most seemed grateful to talk. It was five or six weeks after the tragedy; their sons were buried; their friends and relatives had heard all the details many times over. Now here was a new listener to help shoulder some of their pain.

After those interviews, mostly at night when the parents were together, I drove home, flopped on my bed fully clothed and stared at the ceiling–numb and drained from other peoples' anguish.

Now, the same.

A teacher told me how Jeff Collum once impulsively brought her a bouquet of wild flowers (never worrying that it was not the macho thing for a teenage boy). His closest male friend, who would have roomed with him at university that autumn, told how he went to college alone–but soon dropped out, tortured by memories of Jeff. Another friend refused to apply for her driver's license for five years afterward, and then only because her job depended on it. Other friends no longer allowed guests to leave their homes by car if they'd had a drink. Jeff's sister, Melanie, who'd been at home alone when the awful news came, told how–in the curious way we sometimes fend off grief and shock–she began cleaning the house in the middle of the night. Jeff's brother remembered the last day the two spent together.

Jeff's girl friend, gentle and poised, was working as a probation officer. As we sat in her office one night she generously told of his letters, funny cards and loving ways. She had been unable to relate to another man for years after. "More than anything," she told me, "I miss him as a friend. Sometimes I think, 'Ah, Jeff would really understand this problem!' He was just so sweet, so giving." And she added softly, "It seems such a long time since I've seen him. He would be twenty-six now. . . ."

I knew that would be my story's ending.

I kept phoning Robert Benmergui. Finally he said quizzically, "You really want this story, don't you?" I did. At last he agreed to an interview. I started north very early one morning and arrived at 10:00 A.M. for a noon appointment. I checked my tape recorder three times, and carried a backup just in case. There would be no second chance.

We met in a restaurant at the edge of town where no one would know him. Benmergui was on time, a big dark man, now in his early thirties, unsmiling, nervous. The restaurant was crowded, noisy and with open tables–the worst possible place for an intimate interview. We found a table in the rear against a wall. I asked permission to tape. Benmergui nodded.

He didn't touch his food. He broke down again and again. He had been sick for two days at the thought of the interview, he said, but wanted to try to explain his feelings: "I'd like to do something. My problem is to figure out how to do something positive. It's not like giving back. I can't give back. You can't pay for it. You know how many people I've hurt, don't you?"

We talked of how in the winter before his sentencing he had asked the people at his temple to pray for Jeff Collum. How he discussed the case almost daily with his father and sometimes said, "Dad, I've already paid" (but, of course, he had not). How in the halfway house he had worked with children with cerebral palsy, on day passes. "It made me feel like I was worth something. It gave me a little self respect." How his father later died of a heart attack, perhaps related to the strain of the tragedy. "He was a good father and he'd been proud of me," Benmergui said brokenly. "I really disappointed him. . . ."

He was married now with three small children and had re-established himself in business. He buried himself in work, twelve hours a day.

"Do you still drink?"

Surprisingly he said, "Yes," but if he had more than two he took a cab home. I admired his honesty if not his judgement.

"I *will* do something, I definitely will do something," he began again. "I wasn't a bad guy, you know. I didn't mean for it to happen. I'd really like to touch the Collums and tell them that, you know, to really touch them. . . . I would speak to them if they would want to talk to me. . . ."

Suddenly he rose abruptly, tears welling up. "Nobody could understand, nobody will ever understand, what's in my mind, how I agonize. It gets worse, it doesn't get better . . ."

He had to leave, he said. I pointed to a secluded way out the back. That was the last I saw of Robert Benmergui.

I went to my car and put the tape in the cassette player. It was all there, through the din of other voices and clatter of tableware as I slowly turned toward home. I felt no great elation. Just anticlimactic weariness, and sadness for everyone in the senseless tragedy. I passed the turnoff to the Collum's summer cottage where Jeff had spent his last weekend, and kept going.

Five drafts later a story of ten thousand words emerged from a hundred thousand words of research. I wrote in my journal: "The CRD people accepted the Collum story diffidently. No sounds of approval." It ran in September of 1988. Later a man from the *Digest* business department asked me, "Couldn't you have just said the driver got drunk on 'liquor' instead of 'Grand Marnier'?" He was afraid he might lose an advertiser.

"Death of a Young Man" topped the *Reader's Digest* readership poll, even ahead of "Life's Like That." It drew for me more letters than any other *Digest* article, mostly from parents who had lost children to drunken drivers. They said my story helped. The next year it won the top award for general articles, given out by the Foundation for the Advancement of Canadian Letters.

I never heard from Benmergui again. He and the Collums never met or spoke. Jeffrey's girl friend finally married. Howard and Helen are now separated.

16

"I JUST WANT TO TELL YOU HOW MUCH I HATED YOUR FILTHY BOOK"

Whenever my head grows too big for my hat, I recall the March day in 1982 when a publisher's representative sat me down at a table in Eaton's in a Regina mall. At my back was Ladies' Lingerie. Before me a gratifying queue of fans waited to get autographs on *Butter Down the Well* and, I modestly assumed, to touch the hem of my garment. It was not going to be one of those humiliating signings where nobody shows up.

The book, published eighteen months before, had sold fourteen thousand copies and was still going strong. The reviews had been fabulous; the mail, awesome. Now all these erudite and perceptive Saskatchewan folk began telling me how *Butter Down the Well* had struck a chord in them, or their parents, or grandparents. I was stroked, cosseted, adored. My ego unfolded like a giant sunflower.

Then a hefty woman with wind-reddened face stepped forward. Her husband in plaid windbreaker and tractor-driver cap stood two paces to the rear, smiling relentlessly with bright new dentures. From my haven among the bikini briefs and see-through bras, I radiated goodwill and reached for my felt-tip pen.

She said, "I just want to tell you how much I hated your filthy book."

There was more. Boys never held other boys up against girls in *her* school district: "WHAT KIND OF PEOPLE *WERE* YOU?" (*Butter* had described a teasing sexless game that big kids inflicted on little kids in my rural school.) Nobody in her district ever used "those words" (my gentle book once mentioned "penis" and "cow shit"). My mother must be ashamed of me, my tormentor said (my mother, a leading character in *Butter Down the Well,* was by then quite enjoying her celebrity).

When the woman stopped for breath, I pulled myself together and growled that her version of reality certainly differed from mine. Riposte has never been my long suit. She stalked away, husband following at the requisite two paces, still grinning like a robot with a broken fuse.

I turned to the publisher's rep: "What'd you think of that?"

"I'm looking for the dirty bits," she chuckled, thumbing hastily through the book, "but I can't find them!"

Moments like that are devised by the gods of publishing to keep authors humble–should we be so lucky as to find a publisher, have a manuscript accepted and actually sell a few copies. Hubris is not encouraged in our profession.

Every year about five thousand new books pour out of Canadian publishing houses and from self-published authors' basements. The chance of winning a lottery is considerably better than of having a best-seller. For one thing, best-seller lists are suspect. Nancy Colbert, who with husband Stanley heads up HarperCollins Publishers in Canada, knows of authors who appeared briefly on best-seller lists yet never sold more than a couple of thousand. For a long time five thousand sales was considered a best-seller; now it might be ten thousand. An author who sells more than twenty thousand copies in Canada, says Colbert, is rare.

Yet in the face of these daunting odds, nearly every writer wants to do a book. It is the pinnacle of our craft. It allows us to spread our wings into a level of writing that other media do not permit. A book also has your picture on the flap and a glowing biography listing all the quaint, demeaning things you did before hitting big-time authorship. If you are really lucky, it might even get into a bookstore.

Publication lifts you, fleetingly, from years of solitude and obscurity into the sunlight of radio and TV shows where, on rare occasions, the interviewer has actually *read* your book. Hard covers are permanent or, anyway, more permanent than yesterday's newspaper story, which is today's toilet trainer for the cat. It is our fruitless bid for immortality.

Like many other Canadian writers of my time, I owe my start in books to Jack McClelland. In the mid-1950s he invited me to parlay one of my *Maclean's* articles into a history of the Wawanesa Mutual Insurance Company, a firm with comical origins, doing big business from a tiny Manitoba town. The idea was exciting and flattering. Ever since Edward A. McCourt, author and English professor at the University of Saskatchewan, spoke kindly of my fumbling attempts at short stories, I'd vaguely thought of writing A Book.

That one was stillborn; the Wawanesa wanted no part of it. After leaving *Maclean's* I proposed to McClelland another non-fiction book, mostly profiles of people I'd met in western Canada. That didn't work either, but Jack remembered me when, in the early sixties, he launched his Secret Circle Mystery series for young readers. I joined Arthur Hammond, Max Braithewaite, Scott Young and a couple of others in my first crack at fiction.

The Legend of the Devil's Lode, based on an old Alberta gold-mine saga, was written on evenings and weekends while I edited Imperial Oil *Review*. It earned me less than one thousand dollars but, published in conjunction with Little Brown, sold 7,500 copies–best-sellerdom, then–and drew some nice letters from kids. I contracted to write another; it appeared alone (the second series didn't get off the ground) and failed miserably, although years later Seal Books gave it brief new life as a paperback.

McClelland was back again in the late sixties with a new series: Canada's Illustrated Heritage, on this country's significant decades. For an entire winter I happily immersed myself in the people and events of the 1870s, resulting in *The Age of Innocence*. Again, I was in distinguished company: Jack Batten, Max Braithwaite, June Callwood, Alan Edmonds, Leslie Hannon, Harold Horwood, Alan Phillips and Alexander Ross were among the contributors. Pierre Berton was editorial director. McClelland paid us a flat ten thousand dollars per book, good money at the time (even today many writers don't earn that much from a book).

So, although McClelland is no longer a publisher and

although I once had a rousing good quarrel with him over royalties, I owe my book-writing career to him. Once during a Writers' Union party at Pierre Berton's Kleinberg spread, I was standing on a hillock watching the parade of egos when a woman beside me wagged her head toward a prominent author: "Look, she's slurping Jack McClelland with her eyes!" She was, too. Most Canadian authors have slurped McClelland at one time or another, figuratively speaking. He is our literary godfather.

I'm not about to suggest that celebrity is better than money, but there's no denying the pure enchantment of seeing one's name on a book cover, during those ephemeral days or weeks before it comes off the shelves and into the dumpster. We treasure bylines. Which is why I was shocked and appalled to discover that a writer in Ottawa has stolen my name.

I say this without fear of legal action because, although we haven't met, he is two years younger than me (I looked him up in *Who's Who*). Therefore I can only assume that when Robert G. Collins was still a nameless infant, his parents sent gypsies to steal my two-year-old name, guessing that someday it would be priceless.

All of this came to my attention when the other Robert Collins published a novel, *Tolerable Levels of Violence*. It was favourably reviewed. Nancy Colbert–former agent, now a publisher–phoned to say (without much disappointment, I regretfully add), "You said you'd show *me* your first novel." True, but this phantom Collins, I explained, wasn't me. His middle initial is "G," not "J." I had not yet written my novel, I assured her, so she was spared for a while the unpleasantness of having to reject it.

I thought of asking Robert G. Collins to change his byline to R. George Collins, since I *am* the older. But he appears to be a distinguished bloke: PhD, English prof, a contributor to literary magazines. What the heck; let him be. As long as he keeps getting good reviews and giving me a good name.

In the late 1960s, the now-defunct Ryerson Press asked me to write a social history of the automobile in Canada. Since I was a freelance and they paid no advance against royalties, Ryerson urged me to apply for a Canada Council handout. I did, uneasily; my free-enterprise father would have been mortified. Fortunately for both of us, I was turned down; the project was deemed "not of sufficient historical interest."

Bemused but not discouraged, I wrote *A Great Way to Go* regardless, sandwiched between twelve magazine articles and assorted other kinds of paid writing. The book received excellent reviews and sold a healthy 7,519 copies.

Part of my income while doing the book came from news features for, of all things, The Hudson's Bay Company's employee newspaper and such forgettable pieces as "Can Your Wife Afford to Be a Widow?" for *Reader's Digest*. Years later, at a Saskatchewan awards night, I was accosted by a bright young poet in mutton-chop whiskers.

"So you're with the *Digest*?" he said curiously. "How does that work out?"

"It's my Canada Council grant," I said. Instantly he understood.

My point is: a writer *can* publish without grants. It is more difficult. That writer may have to take other, perhaps mundane or distasteful work to support his/her literary habit—but such are the trade-offs in our hazardous ill-paid business. I never again applied for a grant and never will.

I appreciate the difficulty of sustaining a distinct Canadian culture in the shadow of America. Many a small press has, I know, been able to launch future writing stars only with government support. I can see a one-time grant to help a future Alice Munro or Michael Ondaatje get a toehold. But why should the bedevilled taxpayer subsidize established writers returning to the trough again and again?

Robertson Davies says it more eloquently than I in his McClelland & Stewart book *The Enthusiasms of Robertson Davies*:

> I think of an author as somebody who goes into the marketplace and puts down his rug and says, "I will tell you a story," and then he passes the hat. And when he's taken up his collection he tells his story, and just before the denouement he passes the hat again. If it's worth anything, fine. If not, he ceases to be an author. He does not apply for a Canada Council grant.

It is impossible to remain simon-pure if an author writes for a publisher that receives government support, goes on a book promotion tour partially subsidized by the Council or participates in the Public Lending Right program (wherein writers are paid a small fee for holdings of their books in selected public libraries). But those, it seems to me, are somewhat or wholly earned. Beyond that, I'm content to put down my rug in the marketplace, tell my story and pass the hat.

Books are uneconomic for most of us, but there are other compensations. My seventh, *The Medes and the Persians,* a social history commissioned by McGraw Hill, sold 8,400 copies, mostly in the United States, but my contract was so abysmal that royalties barely covered expenses.

Still, I learned something (apart from watching out for the next insulting contract). My technical consultant, Dr. T. Cuyler Young Jr. of the Royal Ontario Museum, introduced me to the archaeological detective work that helps us understand ancient times and peoples. That was how I heard the muted voice of a frustrated Greek artist, reaching across twenty-four centuries. . . .

. . . Around 520–500 B.C., Greeks by the hundreds were dragged unwillingly into what is now Iran to help King Darius decorate Persepolis, his colossal palace. (Its ruins have since been partly excavated and restored.) The Persians, with no talent for art and no real understanding of the Greeks' abilities, imposed their own wooden style on the captives.

My nameless artist must have hated being forced by Persian overseers to carve flat, stiff likenesses of kings and courtiers on walls and stairways. There was no depth, no extra fold in the tunics that fell across the hips; no emotion or warmth in the stone-wall people marching in orderly ranks. The Greek must have longed to draw a human finger on a human hand, the way a hand and finger really look.

So once, when no one was looking, he swiftly sketched some heads of bearded men, vivid and lifelike, on the massive foot of a huge carved Persian figure. Then, with an overseer breathing down his neck, he hastily covered them with red paint.

Twenty-four hundred years later an archaeologist found the sketches at Persepolis, their red camouflage weathered away by the ages. The drawings were almost identical to those found on Grecian vases of 510–500 B.C. From this, the archaeological Hercule Poirots deduced our little story.

Did that artist ever go home again? At least, for a few moments of exile and forced labour, he must have felt truly alive. Is there an artist among us—painter, musician, sculptor, writer—who does not empathize with him?

The most tantalizing prospect in publishing is the sleeper: a book that succeeds against all reason and expectations. My book number eight, although no blockbuster, was a sleeper of sorts. It began against all the dictates of common sense. I wrote it without a publishing commitment because I wasn't sure what if anything was growing under my hands and, anyway, couldn't find a publisher to believe in it.

It sprang from two prairie nostalgia pieces I'd written for *Reader's Digest,* and from the encouragement of editors Ralph Hancox and Charles Magill. In 1974 I wrote Magill about it, still tortured with uncertainty:

> A labour of love but I hope publishable eventually. It isn't yet another piece on the Depression era although that comes into it. It is primarily a very affectionate (and sometimes sad, sometimes humorous) look back at a certain time, place and some people—my home and environs in the West, circa late 1920s-early 1940s. The focal point is the farmhouse (in which I was literally born and which I saw inhabited for the last time on the morning I went away to join the air force). The cast of characters is led, I suppose, by my parents, who were as different as night and day but loved and supported one another all their lives. It is about a way of life that is gone forever, and I guess it is a salute to that way of life. . . .

It turned out to be an uncannily accurate summary of *Butter Down the Well,* published in 1980 after six years of writing, rewriting and doubt. During that same period I held a full-time job and wrote one other book. *Butter* was rejected by six eastern publishers. By then I believed in it so deeply that I was prepared to self-publish if all else failed.

As a last resort my friend Ian Bickle, with Saskatchewan Wheat Pool, routed it to the Pool's Western Producer Prairie Books. Publisher Rob Sanders liked it and took it, against the advice of others in his company. He brought me the news one April morning in 1979. That night I won the President's Medal for magazine writing. It was one of those days I was glad I'd got out of bed.

Butter Down the Well was an immediate hit. The first print run sold out in eight weeks (it is now around the fifty-thousand mark, still selling by word of mouth after thirteen years). It had a long run with Book-of-the-Month Club and received enthusiastic reviews that fill a scrapbook. *Reader's Digest* Books condensed it. One reviewer compared me favourably to Wallace Stegner and W. O. Mitchell. An Edmonton broadcaster was reminded of country singer Tom T. Hall (who, I later learned, tells homespun stories in song). At least five couples have made pilgrimages to my former Saskatchewan homestead because of the book.

The wife of a leading Canadian bank president gave it to her husband for Christmas. He, a prairie expatriate, later came out of his study with tears in his eyes. (The only other time I made a banker cry was when I asked for a loan.) A woman in Rockglen, Saskatchewan, listening to a radio show about the future of the family, phoned in to say if they wanted a good example of parenthood they should read *Butter Down the Well.*

A friend, Barbara Mercer, professional artist and occasional musician, composed for me an original piece of piano music, based on the moods she detected in the book's chapter on the elements and change of seasons. A Saskatchewan man, angered by my family's loathing of the Liberal prime minister McKenzie King, wrote that "you must be one of those NDP assholes." He was wrong, of course. I was never NDP.

When *Butter Down the Well* came out I wrapped a copy for my mother with this note:

> Here at last is what I think to be the best and most important book I have ever written. . . . More than anything else I hope you will like it and not regard it as an intrusion upon times that were precious to us all. You will not like every word

in it. You will no doubt disagree with some of the comments in it. You may find my memory faulty in places.

But I had to write it in my own way, from my own point of view and as seemed appropriate for readers of 1980. Whatever else it may be, I hope you will see it for what it is: my great and loving tribute to Dad and you, and a happy recollection of just about the best time of my life.

Then I fled town on the promotion trip. The note scared the hell out of my mother. She knew what I'd been doing but hadn't taken it too seriously. For two days she couldn't bring herself to read the book. Then she went through it twice. "Penis" and "cow shit" were anathema to her, but she allowed that they perhaps reflected contemporary mores. She gently chastised me for omitting such memorable moments as the day the skunk got under the verandah. But in the end–especially after her minister praised it, Kingston Road United Church library bought a copy and friends in the women's auxiliary began lionizing her–she was pleased. To the end, though, she insisted that the book was about my father, not her.

Book writing is not all butter, cakes and ale. My daughter Catherine once commissioned an article about the business of being an author for her *Financial Post Magazine* and wrote her own column on it. An excerpt:

> . . . [A book writer will] learn to handle criticism from strangers but you're defenceless when your own relatives set you up as
>
> *Live bait.* We had been visiting our Great-Aunt Nell, who lived in Michigan and was slightly senile. As we rose to leave for the long drive home to Toronto, Aunt Nell swept the collected works of Robert Collins off her shelf and thrust them into his arms. "Here," she said, "take your worms." Whether she meant "words" we'll never know, but the thought of Dad's art reduced to the level of lower invertebrates had my sister and me convulsed with laughter for miles. With family like that, you'll wonder
>
> *Who Needs Enemies?* And there'll be plenty of them in this competitive business, all waiting to batter your ego and flatten

> your sales. To survive in this jungle, you'll need guerrilla tactics. My father has ambushed several bookstores in his time, stealthily repositioning his books in front of his literary rivals'. This year *The Holy War of Sally Ann* is being fought on top of Peter Gzowski. This aggression won't earn you points or money, but remember, you're not in it for the pay. If you are, you can
>
> *Advance to Go Broke.* On my father's bulletin board is a piece of paper that sums up the whole humbling story of book writing: a 59-cent royalty cheque.

It was all true. The aforementioned Salvation Army book underscores Cathy's final point. Artistically, *The Holy War of Sally Ann* was one of my best. Financially, it was disaster. It was not a sponsored or official book and I am not a Salvationist, just a longtime admirer of the Army. I spent five thousand dollars of my own money (my choice, my gamble) travelling into every province, examining the Army's people, paradoxes and everlasting war on sin and despair. The publisher urged me to apply for a Canada Council grant but I couldn't.

We hoped that maybe ten thousand of the multiple thousands of Canadian Salvationists would buy it. They didn't. Sales inched to 4,500 before the publisher finally let it go out of print. I earned expenses.

Yet I'm glad I did it. I saw places I shall never forget and people who reinforced my faith in humanity. Such as the night on Vancouver's Skid Row with a ministering angel named Captain Christine MacMillan. And the two weeks in Newfoundland, the Army's Canadian heartland, culminating in a Sunday night service at a jam-packed school gymnasium in the outport of Dildo. The band thundered out old hymns in rollicking double-time that brought the place to its feet. The drums crashed, the brass shrilled out to Heaven, the tambourines were a swirling blur of ribbons. And a torrent of penitents flowed to the mercy seat to kneel, pray, accept their Saviour, and rise again tear-stained from the catharsis of decision or relief from a burden lifted.

Yet again there was an evening service among the Gitksan people of Glen Vowell, British Columbia—an eighty-year-old church with ornate towers, walls lined with glowing cedar, wooden pews built by the locals, a chandelier of light bulbs set in coal oil lamps, a stained glass window behind the altar. The Gitksan (meaning "people of the Skeena") are religious, industrious and handsome with strong dark faces. The service was long and heartfelt with vigorous hand clapping, songs and prayers in both English and Gitksan, and fervent testimony around the mercy seat. Afterward I drove home by full moon, feeling at peace and a little closer to God.

Let us draw a veil of silence, as they used to say in Victorian novels, over the agonizing process of writing a book, and jump to the fun part. The book comes out. The author wavers between giddy exaltation and acute depression. This roller coaster begins with the reviews, which often degenerate into a showcase for the reviewers' sarcasm and alleged wit. I'm not sure that good or bad reviews make much difference to sales. Rave reviews didn't save my Salvation Army book. Conversely, author Arthur Hailey does rather well despite heavy flak from reviewers, who do not regard his heavily researched thrillers as an art form.

But reviewers' darts stay quivering in our flesh forever. A bad newspaper review hurts all the more when we realize that the reviewer has ten or twenty times the readership we'll ever have. A decade ago Douglas Gibson, a publisher with a marvellous wry sense of humour, wrote a "Guide for Authors." It is wildly funny and bitterly true.

"Do not, ever, expect to read a review of your book that will strike you as constructive and helpful to you in perfecting your craft as a writer," wrote Gibson. Actually, the most constructive review for my taste is the kind that suggests I am already close to perfection. Such as: "His poignant and sensitive account is a rare chronicle of history. . . . Collins has joined the ranks of Canada's major current writers" (Halifax *Chronicle Herald*)—much better for my self-esteem than: "The book is really an extended magazine article" (Toronto *Globe and Mail*) or "A disappointing read" (Regina *Leader-Post*).

Nowadays, more and more writers refuse to lie still and let reviewers kick sand in their faces. My all-time favourite is the rapier thrust delivered by author John Ralston Saul to one of his tormentors in the *Globe and Mail*. His opening paragraph gives you the gist:

> There is something embarrassing about a minor academic who takes to reviewing books he himself has failed to write. The result, in place of a critique, is supercilious one-liners which misrepresent the chapters the reviewer seems to have dipped into. This sort of article has more to do with his own sense of rage and failure than with examining the book he has been assigned.

Still, none of us can afford to alienate reviewers. So I offer them my new CAN-LITTER computer program. Reviewers need only fit the name of author and book into designated spaces among any or all of these key phrases that I have gleaned from actual reviews:

> "reach exceeds her grasp";
> "what is most frustrating, though, is a nagging sense of underlying substance to the book";
> "a suspiciously fuzzy and sentimental snapshot";
> "unfortunately, it is also preachy and didactic, with minimal characterization and attempts at humour that fall quite flat";
> "marred by inappropriate vocabulary, an unfocused plot, and a weak resolution."

If the review still suffers from excessive clarity and insufficient abuse, the user can call up this passage (also taken from real life) as the coup de grace: "Yet when colloquialisms fall outside the range of a character's consciousness, they simply become authorial quirks, the sort of careless indulgence that distracts from the narrative, dissipating vitality in the bathos of a tired rhetorical device."

I certainly hope I get some thanks for this.

If book and author survive the reviews, they may be treated to a promotion tour. Each autumn hundreds of our species hit the road: lemmings marching blindly off the cliff of ego into the sea of publicity, soon to be lost and forgotten. Each autumn, too, you can count on some author writing a piece for some newspaper about what a tiresome bore is the tour: "Gawd it's hard work"; "Aaaiiieeee, what a hangover I had the morning I went on 'Canada AM'!"; "Wurra wurra, not one interviewer had read my book." Behind all this bombast lies the naked truth: authors love the tour. It is their one chance to be stroked.

One November dawn, at the end of a book tour I looked out, tired but content, from my hotel window in St. John's and contemplated the fortnight just past. I had sniffed Pacific salt, traversed a stubbled prairie bedding down for winter, paused in Fat City, where even government cannot tarnish the magnificence of Parliament Hill. Here at the Atlantic's edge, the soft morning lights of Newfoundland fell like pools of butter on an inner lagoon. The media had been remarkably attentive and kind, given that they are deluged in autumn books. I had viewed the whole of Canada all in the line of duty. I felt incredibly lucky.

True, a coast-to-coast tour is strenuous. I remember boarding an Air Canada cattle-car flight in, I think, Regina on a certain November night. I had just shoe-horned myself between two fat men when columnist, author and playwright Rick Salutin dragged himself aboard. I felt tired just looking at him. We've never been introduced, but as he plodded wearily down the aisle our eyes met with a flicker of mutual sympathy. He recognized in me only a face he'd seen at a Regina TV station that morning. I knew his name because he was interviewed ahead of me. We'd done the rounds all day and now we were bound for Winnipeg and more of the same.

Authors usually begin promotion tours by cramming up on their book (months-old in memory by that time), the better to lead floundering interviewers. In Toronto I once rendezvoused outside a CBC studio with a broadcaster I'd known for years. It was five minutes to air time. "So what's the name of your book and what's it about?" he said cheerily. I swallowed my terror, gave him a four-minute crash course on *The Long and The Short and The Tall* and we got through with whole skins.

Our guides, organizers and one-day friends on these adventures are publishers' representatives, mostly women, who do their jobs surpassingly well, plagued though they are by erratic media and eccentric writers. One rep told me of a famous author who expected her to pimp for him. Another remembered a prominent writer and media personality who stepped off the plane into an Alberta winter wearing a knitted stole and spiked heels (they found her a parka and boots before the poor ninny turned into an icicle). Another writer went flat broke mid-tour and had to borrow two hundred dollars from a publisher (not her own). Still another panicked when she couldn't charge expenses en route to her publisher, whose credit rating at the time was zero. It amazes publicists that authors who have successfully navigated life thus far, suddenly on tour can't find their way out of an airport.

A good rep is more precious than rubies. One of the best, Lorna Tergesen of Winnipeg, once warned as we approached a TV station that the host, although stunning to look at, would not have read my book and was incapable of winging an interview.

"Let's make up a list of questions," Lorna said. I composed it while we waited to go on air. The host followed it slavishly. Her questions were wonderfully perceptive and insightful. She was touchingly grateful. Me too.

On tour for *The Long and The Short and The Tall* in 1986, my Vancouver publicist was Frances Eger. She was tall, dark, jolly, irrepressible; the consummate press agent. She burst onto media telephones with a cheery. "Hey, hey it's Frances Eger . . . EGER. As in Beaver . . ." She charmed interviewers into finding time slots they didn't think they had.

Our three days, including one on Vancouver Island, were rewarding but hair-raising. Frances lived on the edge. She was always losing her car keys. We travelled a whole day in heavy rain with one windshield wiper which, fortunately, was on her side. She drove with verve and parked outrageously in loading zones and other prohibited areas. Once we arrived with seconds to spare, as usual, for a radio interview in Victoria's Empress Hotel. Frances charged into the hotel lot, abandoned her car in front of a door and walked away waving at the screaming attendant. She had three hundred dollars outstanding in tickets; there was a warrant out on her.

We met again the following spring when I was in Vancouver on business. I learned that a few years earlier she'd entered the Pulp Press annual three-day novel-writing marathon, working from a desk on the sidewalk outside an east Vancouver bookstore. She didn't win the contest, but won a job as Pulp Press's publicity director. I met her lively teenage daughter and son, Vija and Acron, whom she adored. Frances drove me to Vija's school, where I gave a talk we hadn't delivered in the previous autumn's madcap tour. And that was the last I ever saw of Frances Eger.

In December 1988 she, her children and two friends went on a Caribbean holiday. One morning they left St. Vincent in a chartered boat. They were sighted once that afternoon, then never seen again. There were winds of fifty knots that day, and heavy seas building up to sixteen-foot waves. Weeks of search turned up no trace. The storm or–some locals feared–pirates who roam the Caribbean had taken the bright spirits that were Frances Eger and her family.

Sometimes autographing sessions crop up along the tour. These are invigorating or degrading, depending on whether anyone shows. Douglas Gibson said it all: "As you sit there flanked by towers of unsold copies of your book and backed by a blown-up photograph of yourself taken fifteen years ago, [the bookstore manager] and her staff will look at their watches a lot and mention, by name, several of the customers who had expressed eagerness to come in and meet you, but who obviously have been prevented from doing so because it is so cold/hot/icy/wet/good for gardening after that wet/windy/cold spell . . ."

During a 1984 stint in Saskatoon I had sessions where (a) nobody came (the publisher's booth was at the local Exhibition; a number of stockmen passed by, examined my stance, conformation and pedigree, and found me wanting); and (b) one man turned out. He stood grinning for five minutes. I grinned back in nervous reflex action.

"You don't remember me, do you?" he said happily. Someone from my past.

"The face is familiar," I lied, "but you have the advantage of me . . ."

He played who-am-I? for another ten minutes, then uttered a single word: "Marvin."

Marvin?

"Marvin!" I said enthusiastically, playing for time. Then something clicked in the old part of my brain . . . Grade 6! Marvin had been a classmate at Standon School in southern Saskatchewan. He didn't buy a book or want an autograph but helped fill the empty hour.

If your book makes a tiny splash in the literary pond you may be invited to give public readings. Douglas Gibson again: "Beware of giving public readings in tandem with authors who are practised public performers, old troupers who know how to milk a laugh." Wise advice. After a reading tour of the Wheatland Regional Library system in central Saskatchewan one autumn, my companion and driver Francis Young—who'd escorted W. O. Mitchell the year before—said, "We should get you and W. O. on the same program." Not a chance! That wily old actor would eat me alive. I can humiliate myself without help.

Overall the Wheatland tour—fifteen appearances in five days—was a success. At a school in Eston or Kenaston the enthusiastic students and staff said they'd never heard a writer before—an admission so touching that I would go back there anytime. In Biggar one woman laughed so hard at my reading that I feared for her life, but not enough to ask her to stop.

But, alas, there was the reading in Eatonia's public library before an assembled high school class. I read my heart out. They sat motionless, expressionless, like aliens from a distant planet. At the end they rose in unison, and silently filed out. Only one stayed behind to ask intelligent questions. I could have kissed her, but that would have added a sexual harassment charge to an already lousy day.

There comes a time in life when we recognize our limitations. I wish that I were better than I am, keep trying to *be* better, but accept that I will never be a superstar. Has it been worth the doing?

Although writers rarely talk about it, we want most of all to touch people, make them laugh or cry, make a difference in their lives or in the conduct of life on this earth. When I receive letters that say: "Every middle-aged man is entitled to write one fan letter in his life. Let this be mine . . ." or "There are no words to describe how I felt as I tore through your book . . ." or "I laughed and cried all the way through these nostalgic pages . . ." or "Your book is a little masterpiece in its genre . . ." I am glad not only for the praise but for having made a human connection. An Australian writes that my World War II memoir, *The Long and The Short and The Tall,* mirrors his own service in the

R.A.A.F. Amazing. I have touched someone on the other side of the world.

In a speech to industrial editors I mention *One Thing for Tomorrow,* my book with and about Saskatonian Joyce Brack and her valiant lifelong fight against multiple sclerosis. Afterward a young woman, who appears to be the picture of health, comes forward to tell me she has MS, feels totally alone, wants to talk to someone who shares her illness. I put her in touch with my coauthor. That day, Joyce and I made a difference.

One of my finest students at Ryerson Journalism School writes me a note that brings tears to my eyes: "It is so rare to get an instructor who really puts time in and does a careful, thinking job of editing our stuff. . . . It has made a difference to us that you take this class seriously. . . . Everything I am exposed to in this course strengthens my resolve to take writing seriously as a career." That made a year's work worthwhile.

There is as well, for every book writer, one more purely sensual pleasure: that moment when the first newly published volume arrives. You tear open the parcel of advance copies, full of hope and trepidation. You pull out the first book, crisp, unsullied, with its heady scent of fresh paper and ink. All the years of labour and doubt melt away. All you have done, the best you can do, is between those covers.

Ahead, unknown: the kind or cruel reviews, good or bad sales, fan letters or no letters. For now though, at this glorious moment, the writing life is the best life on earth.

EPILOGUE

The much-loved Margaret Laurence, whose integrity shone out from her books and from her honest face, liked to fondly refer to fellow-writers as the "tribe." It was the only thing she ever said that made me squirm. If she meant we are linked by bonds of occupation, obsession and the struggle to survive, fair enough. But "tribe" signifies to me more cuddly consensus than I feel for others of my kind.

We are alike, true enough, in our neuroses. Years ago, I was flattered but astonished when Morley Callaghan–a genuine Canadian superstar who never quite achieved the acclaim he deserved in his own country–asked me to read and comment on the galleys of his just-completed book. We'd struck up some rapport during my magazine article on him, but I was ill-equipped to critique fiction, especially the work of this man I revered. Finally I did, when it dawned on me that Callaghan simply wanted a reaction from a fairly intelligent average reader, somebody he'd come to trust, before laying himself open to the savage professional critics. For all of his accomplishment, he suffered from self-doubt like the rest of us.

Beyond that, writers–including those bearing the amorphous label "journalists"–are as mixed a bag as the population at large: introverts, grandstanders, raging rednecks, screaming socialists; the kilt-flipping Farley Mowat, the unavoidable Atwood, the indefatigable Berton and the late shy Ernest Buckler, who wrote exquisitely from his chosen seclusion in the Annapolis Valley. We do not necessarily like each other nor want each other to succeed. *Schadenfreude*—pleasure in the misery of others—is a common emotion among us.

I empathize with an increasingly cynical public, which rates the media fraternity somewhere around used-car salesmen on the believability scale. Who, really, can we trust? Integrity (the quality Margaret Laurence had in abundance), or lack of it, is the operative word.

Sometimes integrity gets lost or obscured in the blinding light of the media circus. I think of Eli Mandel. Those of us who floundered in his wake in University of Saskatchewan English classes some forty-five years ago were not surprised when he went on to become an acclaimed teacher, critic and poet. His book of poems *An Idiot Joy* won a Governor General's Award. What is more important, Eli left his imprint, his honourable legacy, on hundreds of grateful students of English.

In September 1992, he died. The newspapers gave him a respectable obituary, but he was not a "personality"—those creatures revered in journalism whether they are exhibitionist authors, soap-serial stars, Juno-award winners or famous TV faces. I compared Eli's modest send-off with the days of written and oral outpouring that followed the death a few months earlier of CBC's Barbara Frum.

Let's accept that Frum was a fine human and a principled broadcaster. In one fleeting encounter with her, I was struck by her way of giving me her total attention when other celebrities would have been looking over my left shoulder for someone important. Yet the wash of words—particularly on the CBC—that followed her untimely death was so excessive and overpowering that you wondered: are there any adjectives left to cover the death of Mother Teresa?

It was a disservice to Barbara Frum. Given the person she was, I suspect she would have been embarrassed by it.

The most astonishing eulogy came from William Thorsell, editor of the Toronto *Globe and Mail*. He wrote that when he was associate editor of the Edmonton *Journal,* Frum taught him "to think like a reporter." She prodded him into realizing, the repentant Thorsell confessed, that in an appraisal of Peter Lougheed he had "not gone behind the obvious, or applied any real analytical or insightful thought to what Mr. Lougheed was up to. I had not sought the views of insiders, his allies and opponents. I wasn't adding anything of value to what everyone else already knew. I wasn't practising journalism."

Obviously not. But how in heaven's name had the man survived so many years in the business, including editorship, before this epiphany? Thorsell didn't need Barbara Frum; he needed Journalism 101.

Far more alarming than media wretched-excess is the apparent decline in journalistic ethics. Television "docudramas" tinker with truth for the sake of entertainment. "Faction," a confusing mixture of fact and fiction, is now an accepted authorial genre. Nonfiction writers are redefining their craft. (A review of Farley Mowat's *Rescue the Earth* has the author describing his approach as "subjective nonfiction" and saying he "will never let facts interfere with truth." Another, of *The Danger Tree,* says approvingly of its author: "Where research trickled out, [David] Macfarlane invented, and those vivid stories resound with truth.")

Naturally it is impossible to ever arrive at whole truth. But what are readers to believe? Surely we nonfiction writers owe them this much: not to deliberately invent when facts run dry, not to deliberately muddle fact and fiction, but to tell the story the way it is–entertainingly if possible, but as *honestly* as we can. It's a quaint old-fashioned idea, but it just might catch on.

Then there's Allan Fotheringham. For a time I thought Dr. Foth, as his pals affectionately call him, was the funniest writer in Canada. His columns were wickedly clever. He became an equally celebrated mouth. When he, another author and I gave readings for The Different Drummer bookstore in Burlington, Ontario, Fotheringham slew the crowd with hilarious one-liners.

Then rumours went around that The Foth was dipping into other people's work. Writer Moira Farr, close friend of my daughter Catherine, caught him red-handed. In December 1990 Moira wrote a masterful piece for *Toronto Life* on the demise of Fenton's, a popular Toronto restaurant. Later that month, she discovered a Fotheringham column in *Maclean's* (on how recession was hitting the beautiful people) with several verbatim quotes and phrases from her article.

Farr wrote an aggrieved letter to *Maclean's.* Fotheringham

invited her to lunch. She declined. ("I didn't want to schmooze with him," she told me later.) There'd have been no problem if he had had the courtesy to credit Farr or even just *Toronto Life* as his source. But according to Sean O'Malley, who wrote about The Foth for the *Ryerson Review of Journalism,* the famous columnist reasoned, "Nobody knows her name in Moose Jaw, Saskatchewan, or Dildo, Newfoundland. I didn't think I had to mention her by name."

So Allan Fotheringham isn't the funniest man in Canada. Not to me, anyway.

There's no question about Robert Fulford's ethics; he even teaches the subject to student journalists. A prolific and gifted writer, he deserves the many accolades he receives. Fulford and I are not intimates; he's one of those writers I admire from afar. On rare occasions we meet, greet one another warmly, then instantly run out of conversation as I shrink back from his superior grey cells. But I am concerned for his health. The media are running the legs off him. What a chore it must be just *being* Bob Fulford, CanLit's most-quoted man.

Consider a typical day in Toronto, navel of Canada's media world. A reporter needing a fast, thoughtful quote on something, anything, dips into a Fulford column or Fulford essay or calls up Fulford himself. An artist dies: the agreeable Fulford pronounces him "a very important figure" in the Alberta literary community. Somebody writes a feature on comedienne Nancy White; Fulford is ready: "She may be the funniest Canadian; certainly she is the best singer writing and the best writer singing." An estimable opinion magazine, *The Idler,* is struggling for survival: Fulford proclaims it "one of the great inventions of modern Canadian journalism." A newspaper is in the financial doldrums; Fulford comes up swinging: any newspaper that does not listen to its readers is on its way to "either irrelevance or bankruptcy."

You can see why reporters depend on him: the accommodating Fulford is always ready and coherent. But surely there are mornings when he thinks, *Oh hell, why don't they call Berton or Callwood or Richler today?* Fortunately, Peter Desbarats, currently dean of the University of Western Ontario Graduate School of Journalism, is taking up some slack. A dean who can view with sagacity or alarm is almost as good as a Fulford. Desbarats is up to it and I'm relieved. It means that Bob Fulford can now finish his cereal and toast most mornings, and that neither he nor the toast will burn out before their time.

Some of my closer writer-friendships have been by mail. It is a safe, sure and gentle way to let acquaintance mature. I think of two whose integrity shone for me.

One year novelist Jane Rule and I were on the Writers' Union membership committee, she on B.C.'s Galiano Island, I in Toronto. As we corresponded every couple of weeks on committee business, helping decide who should or shouldn't get into the Union, our mutual love of letter-writing emerged. Gradually we began revealing our private quirks, amusements, senses of humour in the remote yet strangely intimate way of the private letter. Once I voiced my wistful hope of writing fiction, and my qualms about my ability. She kindly responded that fiction seemed easy compared to factual articles and books.

Over a year and a half I acquired a thick packet of Jane's whimsical thoughts, which I shall always keep. Some snippets:

> "We're snowed in, having just survived a sixteen-hour power failure which took out the pool pump (anybody for ice skating?) . . . Even the padlock on the mail box is frozen shut, but a neighbour breathed on it for me, and it opened! I asked him in for a beer. But I thought it too demanding to suggest he breathe on the pool."
>
> "How would you feel about the author of a book of recipes on cooking various people's geese?"
>
> "I walked into a Canada Council jury and within a few moments realized that the other jurors were nervous of me, not, I must say, because I'm a fiction writer, but because I'm a six-foot-tall feminist. It was a great temptation to have them on for a few minutes, vetoing all grants to men on principle, but my better nature did prevail."
>
> "The daffodils are blooming here, and the juncos are going through five pounds of bird seed a week. The purple finches are beating hell out of the pigeons at the feeder. The eagles are mating and I met a peacock widower yesterday so pressed by

spring that he's courting a turkey. There's a lesson in there somewhere . . ."

When I wrote for her permission to quote from these private letters, she informed me she'd retired: "Twelve books are surely my generous allotment of trees." I hope she reconsiders. That fertile mind deserves another tree.

Another pen pal, the late Robert Thomas Allen, lived his latter years in Sun City, California, but pined for writer gossip from home. Allen's letters, like his magazine articles and the man himself, were warm, funny, self-deprecating, chatty; full of xx'ed-out words and indifferent punctuation. He wrote in April 1990:

> . . . No, I don't have a word processor and have a strong feeling I'll die at my Smith Corona manual portable. (If I'm not mistaken that's how Ian Sclanders went—working at his typewriter at a motel in the Maritimes, I mean; and I can't think of a nicer way to make the passage, or of a better guy who made it.) This is a new second-hand Smith Corona—and as you can see it skips—but it has the advantage of being exactly the same model as the one I bought in Santa Ana around 1955 and used up until six, seven years ago. The last time I took it in to have something fixed, the guy wouldn't fix it—it was just too un-American for him to try to preserve anything that old. He probably thought I was one of them god damned communists. He said he'd never seen a typewriter worn like it and that it was just like a Volkswagen with 300,000 miles on it. I found a nice young guy at a shop downtown, by the way, who fixed it for seven, eight dollars, and I used it for another four years.

A few weeks later Bob Allen died. He wasn't sitting at his typewriter, but he'd been working almost to the end, the way he wanted.

Knowing him, Jane Rule, W. O. Mitchell, Morley Callaghan—and a host of similarly honest writers, who, believe me, still outnumber the other kind—has been a privilege. They have made the journey worth the taking.

INDEX